**EIGHTEENTH-CENTURY EVANGELICALS
AS SPIRITUAL MENTORS**

| THE CHRISTIAN MENTOR | Volume 3

"Love is unfurled"

EIGHTEENTH-CENTURY EVANGELICALS
AS SPIRITUAL MENTORS

Michael A.G. Haykin

www.joshuapress.com

Published by
Joshua Press, Kitchener, Ontario, Canada
Distributed by
Sola Scriptura Ministries International
www.sola-scriptura.ca

First published 2018
© 2018 Michael A.G. Haykin. All rights reserved. This book may not be reproduced, in whole or in part, without written permission from the publishers.

Cover and book design by Janice Van Eck

The publication of this book was made possible by the generous support of The Ross-Shire Foundation.

Library and Archives Canada Cataloguing in Publication

Haykin, Michael A.G., author
    Eighteenth-century evangelicals as spiritual mentors : "love is unfurled" / Michael A.G. Haykin.

(The Christian mentor ; volume 3)
Includes bibliographical references and index.
Issued in print and electronic formats.
ISBN 978-1-894400-93-0 (softcover).— ISBN 978-1-894400-94-7 (HTML).— ISBN 978-1-894400-95-4 (PDF)

    1. Evangelists—Biography. 2. Evangelical Revival. 3. Great Britain—Church history—18th century. 4. United States—Church history—18th century. I. Title. II. Series: Christian mentor (Kitchener, Ont.) ; volume 3

BR758.H394 2018   274.107   C2018-904538-8
    C2018-904539-6

George Whitefield
(1714–1770)

here in the following summer that he first met John Wesley and his younger brother Charles, who were regularly meeting with a group of men known to history as "the Holy Club." This was a company of ten or so men who were ardently trying to live religious lives in an extremely dissolute age.

Whitefield, like-minded and longing for spiritual companionship ever since coming up to Oxford, joined them. He engaged in numerous religious exercises such as fasting, praying regularly, attending public worship and seeking to abstain from what were deemed worldly pleasures. Systematic reading of Puritan and Pietist devotional literature also occupied much of Whitefield's time.[13] Despite the evident zeal he brought to these religious activities he had no sense of peace with God or that God was satisfied with what he was doing. He was, though he did not know it at the time, treading a pathway similar to the one that Martin Luther (1483–1546) had taken over 200 years earlier. And just as Luther's conversion was the spark that lit the fires of the Reformation, so Whitefield's conversion would be central to kindling the blaze of the eighteenth-century evangelical revival.

Conversion came in the spring of 1735 after Charles Wesley had given him a copy of *The Life of God in the Soul of Man* (1677) by Henry Scougal (1650–1678), a former professor of divinity at Aberdeen.[14] This book was a frontal challenge to Whitefield's ardent endeavour to create a righteous life that would merit God's favour. As Whitefield recalled it many years later in a sermon that he preached in 1769:

> I must bear testimony to my old friend Mr. Charles Wesley, he put a book into my hands, called, *The Life of God in the Soul of Man*, whereby God shewed me, that I must be born again, or be

---

13 On the role that reading played in his conversion and his subsequent growth as a Christian, see Lambert, "Pedlar in Divinity," 17–21. It is interesting that it was Christian literature, not the spoken word, that played the vital role in the conversion of Whitefield, although he is best remembered as a preacher (Lambert, *"Pedlar in Divinity,"* 18). On Whitefield's later reading, see the helpful article by John Lewis Gilmore, "Preparation: the Power of Whitefield's Ministry," *Christianity Today*, 24, no. 5 (March 7, 1980): 22–24.

14 For a modern edition of this work, see Henry Scougal, *The Life of God in the Soul of Man* (Fearn: Christian Focus Publications, 1996).

damned. I know the place: it may be superstitious, perhaps, but whenever I go to Oxford, I cannot help running to that place where Jesus Christ first revealed himself to me, and gave me the new birth. As a good writer [i.e. Scougal] says, a man may go to church, say his prayers, receive the Sacrament, and yet, my brethren, not be a Christian. How did my heart rise, how did my heart shudder, like a poor man that is afraid to look into his account-books, lest he should find himself a bankrupt: yet shall I burn that book, shall I throw it down, shall I put it by, or shall I search into it? I did [search it], and, holding the book in my hand, thus addressed the God of heaven and earth: Lord, if I am not a Christian, if I am not a real one, for Jesus Christ's sake, shew me what Christianity is, that I may not be damned at last. I read a little further, and the cheat was discovered; O, says the author, they that know any thing of religion know it is a vital union with the Son of God, Christ formed in the heart; O what a ray of divine life did then break in upon my poor soul....[15]

Awakened by this book to his need for the new birth, Whitefield passionately struggled to find salvation along the pathway of extreme asceticism but to no avail. Finally, when he had come to an end of his resources as a human being, God enabled him, in his words, "to lay hold on His dear Son by a living faith, and, by giving me the Spirit of adoption, to seal me, as I humbly hope, even to the day of everlasting redemption." And, he went on, "oh! with what joy—joy unspeakable—even joy that was full of, and big with glory, was my soul filled...."[16]

"THE OPEN BRACING AIR": THE LIFE OF A PREACHER

Always the avid reader, it was Whitefield's prayerful perusal of the Puritan biblical commentaries of William Burkitt (1650–1703) and Matthew Henry (1662–1714) a few months after his conversion that led to his becoming convinced of "free grace and the necessity of being justified in His [i.e. God's] sight by faith only."[17] Following his ordination

---

15 "All Men's Place," in his *Sermons on Important Subjects* (London: Thomas Tegg, 1833), 755.
16 *Journals* (London: Banner of Truth Trust, 1960), 58.
17 *Journals*, 62. On his reading of Matthew Henry, see David Crump, "The Preaching

as deacon in the Church of England the following year these Reformation doctrines came to occupy a central place in his preaching arsenal.[18] There is, for instance, a recently published account of Whitefield's preaching drawn up by an unknown French contemporary. Dated August 1739, this observer states that Whitefield preaches "continually about inner regeneration, the new birth in Jesus Christ, the movement of the Spirit, justification by faith through grace [*justification par la foy de grace*], the life of the Spirit."[19]

The following year Joseph Smith, a Congregationalist minister from Charleston, South Carolina, defended Whitefield against various attacks in his *The Character, Preaching, etc. of the Rev. George Whitefield*.[20] In the section dealing with the doctrinal content of Whitefield's sermons, Smith lists four "primitive, protestant, puritanic" doctrines that Whitefield regularly heralded in his preaching in America—original sin, "justification by faith alone," the new birth and "inward feelings of the Spirit."[21] Smith recalled the way in which Whitefield

> earnestly contended for our justification as the free gift of God, by faith alone in the blood of Christ, an article of faith delivered to the saints of old...telling us plainly, and with the clearest distinction, that a man was justified these three ways; meritoriously by Christ, instrumentally by faith alone, declaratively by good works.[22]

Whitefield's preaching on the new birth, though, was not at all well received by the Anglican clergy in England, and churches began to be

---

of George Whitefield and His Use of Matthew Henry's Commentary," *Crux*, 25, no. 3 (September 1989): 19–28; and Barry C. Davis, "George Whitefield's Doctrine of Scripture in light of 18th century Biblical Criticism," *Methodist History*, 36, no. 1 (October 1997): 20.

18 Dallimore, *George Whitefield*, 1:124–128.

19 Jeremy Black, "The Origins of Methodism: an unpublished early French account," *Enlightenment and Dissent*, 6 (1987): 116.

20 For this tract, originally a sermon, see *Sermons on Important Subjects*, 791–799. For its historical context, see Dallimore, *George Whitefield*, 1:511–514.

21 *Sermons on Important Subjects*, 792–795.

22 *Sermons on Important Subjects*, 793.

barred to him. Whitefield, however, was not to be deterred. On Saturday, February 17, 1739, he made the decision to take to the open air and preach to a group of colliers in Kingswood, a coal-mining district on the outskirts of Bristol. These men with their families lived in squalor and utter degradation, squandering their lives in drink, violence and sex. With no church nearby, they were quite ignorant of Christianity and its leading tenets. It was a key turning-point in not only his life but also in the history of evangelicalism.[23] The concern that has gripped evangelicals in the last 200 years to bring the gospel message directly to ordinary people has some of its most significant roots here in Whitefield's venturing out to preach in the open air.

From this point on Whitefield would relish and delight in his calling as an open-air preacher. He would preach in fields and foundries, in ships, cemeteries and pubs, atop horses and even coffins, from stone walls and balconies, staircases and windmills.[24] For instance, referring to this calling in a letter dated December 14, 1768, he wrote, "I love the open bracing air." And the following year he could state: "It is good to go into the high-ways and hedges. Field-preaching, field-preaching for ever!"[25]

---

23 For much of the nineteenth and twentieth centuries, Whitefield's innovative role in this regard was forgotten. The publication of Dallimore's two-volume George Whitefield has certainly gone far in redressing this amnesia. Yet, even today, good historians can forget this fact and see John Wesley as the real innovator. See, for example, Mark Noll, *Turning Points: Decisive Moments in the History of Christianity* (Grand Rapids: Baker Books, 1997), 221–244, where Noll mentions Whitefield as an innovator in open-air preaching (*Turning Points*, 223, 238–239), but then emphasizes that it was Wesley's decision to preach in the fields two months after Whitefield that was the critical turning-point in the history of evangelicalism. Gordon Wakefield, though, in his essay "John and Charles Wesley: A Tale of Two Brothers" has it right when he says that it was Whitefield "and not the Wesleys who may be said to have begun the Evangelical Revival in 1737" (in Geoffrey Rowell, ed., *The English Religious Tradition and the Genius of Anglicanism* [Nashville: Abingdon Press, 1992], 172).

24 In light of his own itinerant ministry, it is interesting to read the following remarks on Jesus' ministry. Christ, he wrote in 1756, "taught all that were willing to hear, on a mount, in a ship, or by the sea-side" (Letter MCXVII to the Bishop of B—, February 2, 1756, [*Works*, 3:157]).

25 *Works*, 3:379, 387. It is noteworthy that Whitefield never lost elements of his West-country accent. He would pronounce "Christ" as "Chroist," for example (Packer,

It should also be noted that Whitefield never confined his witnessing about Christ to preaching occasions. He took every opportunity to share his faith. "God forbid," he once remarked, "I should travel with anybody a quarter of an hour without speaking of Christ to them."[26] On another occasion, during his sixth preaching tour of America, he happened to stay with a wealthy, though worldly, family in Southold on Long Island. The family discovered after the evangelist had left their home that he had written with a diamond on one of the windowpanes in the bedroom where he had slept, "One thing is needful"![27]

At that first open-air service in February 1739, there were 200 or so. Within six weeks or so, Whitefield was preaching numerous times a week to crowds sometimes numbering in the thousands![28] Whitefield's description of his ministry at this time is a classic one. To visualize the scene at the Kingswood collieries, we need to picture the green countryside, the piles of coal, the squalid huts, and the deep semi-circle of unwashed faces as we read his words:

> Having no righteousness of their own to renounce, they were glad to hear of a Jesus who was a friend of publicans, and came not to call the righteous, but sinners to repentance. The first discovery of their being affected was to see the white gutters made by their tears which plentifully fell down their black cheeks, as they came out of their coal pits. Hundreds and hundreds of them were soon brought under deep convictions, which, as the event proved, happily ended in a sound and thorough conversion. The change was visible to all, though numbers chose to impute it to anything, rather than the finger of God.[29]

"The Spirit with the Word," 170). And his fellow evangelical John Wesley could mention Whitefield's "little improprieties…of…language" (Packer, "The Spirit with the Word," 171, n. 20).

26 *Jacob's Ladder* (*Sermons on Important Subjects*, 774).

27 Iain H. Murray, "Introduction" to *George Whitefield's Journals* (London: The Banner of Truth Trust, 1960), 13.

28 George Whitefield, Letter to Daniel Abbot, February 24, 1739 (Graham C.G. Thomas, "George Whitefield and Friends: The Correspondence of Some Early Methodists," *The National Library of Wales Journal*, 27 [1991]: 83).

29 Cited Dallimore, *George Whitefield*, 1:263–264.

Here is another description from this same period of time, when others besides the miners of Bristol were flocking to hear Whitefield preach:

> As...I had just begun to be an extempore preacher, it often occasioned many inward conflicts. Sometimes, when twenty thousand people were before me, I had not, in my own apprehension, a word to say either to God or them. But I never was totally deserted, and frequently...so assisted, that I knew by happy experience what our Lord meant by saying, "Out of his belly shall flow rivers of living water" (John 7:38). The open firmament above me, the prospect of the adjacent fields, with the sight of thousands and thousands, some in coaches, some on horseback, and some in the trees, and at times all affected and drenched in tears together, to which sometimes was added the solemnity of the approaching evening, was almost too much for, and quite overcame me.[30]

Revival had come to England! And to that revival, and its confluent streams in Wales, Scotland and British North America, no man contributed more than Whitefield. Over the thirty-four years between his conversion and death in 1770 in Newburyport, Massachusetts, it is calculated that he preached around 18,000 sermons.[31] Actually, if one includes all of the talks that he gave, he probably spoke about a thousand times a year during his ministry.[32] Moreover, many of his sermons were delivered to massive congregations that numbered 10,000 or so, some to audiences possibly as large as 15,000.[33]

In addition to his preaching throughout the length and breadth of England, he regularly itinerated throughout Wales, visited Ireland twice, and journeyed fourteen times to Scotland. He crossed the Atlantic thirteen times, stopping once in Bermuda for eleven weeks, and preached in virtually every major town on the Atlantic seaboard.[34]

---

30 Cited Dallimore, *George Whitefield*, 1:268.
31 Augustus Montague Toplady, "Anecdotes, Incidents and Historic Passages," in his *Works*, 495.
32 Dallimore, *George Whitefield*, 2:522.
33 For the numbers, see Dallimore, *George Whitefield*, 1:263, 267, 295–296; 2:522–523.
34 He was in America during 1738, 1739–1741, 1744–1748, 1751–1752, 1754–1755, 1763–1765 and 1769–1770.

What is so remarkable about all of this is Whitefield lived at a time when travel to a town but twenty miles away was a significant undertaking.

In journeying to Scotland and to America he was going to what many perceived as the fringes of transatlantic British society and culture. And yet some of God's richest blessing on his ministry was in these very regions.[35] For example, Harry Stout, commenting on Whitefield's impact on America, writes:

> So pervasive was Whitefield's impact in America that he can justly be styled America's first cultural hero. Before Whitefield, there was no unifying intercolonial person or event. Indeed, before Whitefield, it is doubtful any name other than royalty was known equally from Boston to Charleston. But by 1750 virtually every American loved and admired Whitefield and saw him as their champion.[36]

Whitefield's ministry—insisting, as it did, on the vital necessity of conversion and the work of the Holy Spirit in the heart—was not without its critics, many of whom castigated him for what they regarded as fanaticism. And it needs to be admitted that in his early ministry Whitefield did make some unguarded statements and adopted certain attitudes that helped fuel this opposition. On his second preaching tour of America, for instance, Whitefield appears to have maintained that assurance belonged to the essence of saving faith and that a mature Christian could discern the marks of conversion in another individual. To his credit, Whitefield would later admit his injudiciousness and that he had been far "too rash and hasty" in his speech and published writings. "Wild-fire has been mixed with it," he wrote in 1748, "and I find that I frequently wrote and spoke in my own spirit, when I thought I was writing and speaking by the assistance of the Spirit of God."[37] Despite these faults—basically overcome by his early

---

35 Whitefield had a great admiration for many American ministers. As he said in his final sermon in England, "no place under heaven produces greater divines than New England" ("The Good Shepherd," in *Sermons on Important Subjects*, 782).

36 Harry Stout, "Heavenly Comet," *Christian History* 38 (1993): 13–14.

37 Letter DCXL to the Rev. Mr. S—, June 24, 1748 (*Works*, 2:144).

thirties—multitudes of Whitefield's hearers found his preaching "moving, earnest, winning, melting" and rooted in a doctrinal framework that was "plainly that of the Reformers."[38]

"AN INSATIABLE THIRST FOR TRAVELLING": TAKING THE WORD OVER LAND AND SEA

In the early years of the revival Whitefield's itinerant, open-air preaching was also often paraded as evidence of his "enthusiasm," or fanaticism. Part of Whitefield's response to this criticism was to go back to the example of the apostle Paul as found in the Book of Acts. "Was he not filled," he asked his opponents, "with a holy restless Impatience and insatiable Thirst of travelling, and undertaking dangerous Voyages for the Conversion of Infidels?"[39] Here Whitefield reveals the spiritual passion that spurred his own incessant travelling over land and sea: the longing to see sinners embrace Christ as Lord and Saviour and find their deepest spiritual thirst and hunger satisfied in Christ alone.

Criticism of the wide-ranging nature of his ministry also came from such ardent evangelicals as Ebenezer Erskine (1680–1754) and his younger brother Ralph (1685–1752), founders of the Secession Church in Scotland.[40] This body of churches had seceded from the national church in the 1730s over the issue of whether or not the people of a congregation had the right to refuse a minister chosen for them by the Presbytery or heritors (i.e. landowners who possessed hereditary rights to property within a parish). The Erskines had invited Whitefield to preach solely in their churches. But Whitefield refused to be pinned down to a few locales and insisted on preaching wherever he

---

38 These are the words of Thomas Prince (1687–1758), a New England pastor and historian (cited John Gillies, *Historical Collections of the Accounts of Revival* [1845 ed.; repr. Edinburgh: The Banner of Truth Trust, 1981], 350, 351).

39 *Some Remarks on a Pamphlet, entitled, The Enthusiasm of Methodists and Papists compar'd* (London, 1749), 26.

40 On the Erskines, see Alan P.F. Sell, "The Message of the Erskines for Today," *The Evangelical Quarterly*, 60 (1988): 299–316; Joel R. Beeke, "The Ministry of the Erskines" (Two papers presented at the 21st Annual Banner of Truth Ministers' Conference, Grantham, Pennsylvania, May 26–27, 1999). For another perspective on Whitefield's relationship with the Erskines, see also Kenneth B.E. Roxburgh, *Thomas Gillespie and the Origins of the Relief Church in 18th Century Scotland* (Bern: Peter Lang, 1999), 31–39.

was given a pulpit in Scotland.[41] He told the Erskines that he was "more and more determined to go out into the highways and hedges; and that if the Pope himself would lend me his pulpit, I would gladly proclaim the righteousness of Jesus Christ therein."[42]

That Whitefield failed to understand the concern of the Erskines for the reformation of the church is evident in the sad disagreement between them. Yet, his reply well reveals his passion for the salvation of the lost wherever they might be. As he told the Scottish Lord Rae a few days after this discussion with the Erskines, the "full desire" of his soul was to "see the kingdom of God come with power." He was, he went on, "determined to seek after and know nothing else. For besides this, all other things are but dung and dross."[43] Still in Scotland two months later, the same spiritual desire still deeply gripped him. "I want a thousand tongues to set off the Redeemer's praise," he told the Earl of Leven and Melville.[44]

Five years later, while the surrounding scenery is different—he is on his third preaching tour of America—this passion burned as bright as ever. "Oh that I was a flame of pure & holy fire, & had [a] thousand lives to Spend in the dear Redeemer's service," he told Joshua Gee (1698–1748), for the "sight of so many perishing Souls every day affects me much, & makes me long to go if possible from Pole to Pole, to proclaim redeeming love."[45] "Had I a thousand souls and bodies," he noted on another occasion, "they should be all itinerants for Jesus Christ."[46]

Nothing gave Whitefield greater joy than to report to his friends that God was blessing his preaching. "The word runs and is glorified," a line from Paul's second letter to the Thessalonians (2 Thessalonians 3:1), and Jesus' statement to his disciples that the fields were "white already to harvest" (John 4:35) were frequent refrains in his correspon-

---

41 Letter 33 to John Willison, August 17, 1742 (*Letters of George Whitefield for the period 1734–1742* [Edinburgh: The Banner of Truth Trust, 1976], 514–515).

42 Letter CCCXXXIX to Thomas Noble, August 8, 1741 (*Works*, 1:308).

43 Letter CCCXLIII, August 11, 1741 (*Works*, 1:311).

44 Letter CCCLVI, October 2, 1741 (*Works*, 1:323).

45 Letter to Revd. Mr. Gee, June 21, 1746, in John W. Christie, "Newly Discovered Letters of George Whitefield, 1745–46, III," *Journal of The Presbyterian Historical Society*, 32 (1954): 261.

46 Letter [DCCCCLXXXV] to Mr. G—, July 21, 1753 (*Works*, 3:24).

dence. Writing from Pennsylvania in May 1746, Whitefield informed a correspondent in Gloucestershire, England, that Christ "gives me full employ on this side the water, & causes his word to run & be glorified. ...Everywhere the fields are white ready unto harvest. I am just now going to tell lost sinners that there is yet room for them in the side of Jesus."[47] Upon hearing of the marriage of one of his nephews in 1756, Whitefield observed, "Alas, what a changing world do we live in! Blessed be God for an unchangeable Christ! Amidst all, this is my comfort, his word runs and is glorified."[48] Christ "vouchsafes daily (O amazing love) to own my feeble labours," he told a friend in 1757. Then he added: "The word runs and is glorified."[49] Or writing to a fellow minister in Scotland only a couple of years before his death: "In London the word runs and is glorified, and in Edinburgh, I trust, the prospect is promising. The fields are white ready unto harvest."[50]

THE NEW BIRTH

Prominent in Whitefield's thinking about the Christian life was the new birth. His thoughts on this subject are well seen in a letter to Louise Sophie von der Schulenburg (1692–1773), the Countess of Delitz. The countess was the illegitimate daughter of George I by one of his mistresses, Melusina von der Schulenburg (1667–1743), the Countess of Kendal. The Countess of Delitz was also a friend of Selina Hastings (1707–1791), the Countess of Huntingdon, and she appears to have been converted through Whitefield's ministry at either Selina's London apartment or Chelsea residence. Writing to the Countess of Delitz from Plymouth in February 1749, Whitefield rejoices in her conversion.

> Blessed be the God and Father of our Lord Jesus Christ, who, I trust, hath imparted a saving knowledge of his eternal Son to your Ladyship's heart. Your letter bespeaks the language of a soul which hath tasted that the Lord is gracious, and hath been initi-

---

47 Letter to Mr. Adams, May 15, 1746 (Christie, "Newly Discovered Letters II": 163).
48 Letter MCXLII to Mrs. C—, June 21, 1756 (*Works*, 3:185).
49 Letter MCLXIV to the Reverend Mr. B—, March 10, 1757 (*Works*, 3:202).
50 Letter MCCCLXXXIX to the Reverend Mr. T—, July 4, 1768 (*Works*, 3:371).

ated into the divine life. Welcome, thrice welcome, honoured Madam, into the world of new creatures! O what a scene of happiness lies before you! Your frames, my Lady, like the moon, will wax and wane; but the Lord Jesus, on whose righteousness you solely depend, will, notwithstanding, remain your faithful friend in heaven. Your Ladyship seems to have the right point in view, to get a constant abiding witness and indwelling of the blessed Spirit of God in your heart. This the Redeemer has purchased for you. Of this he has given your Ladyship a taste; this, I am persuaded, he will yet impart so plentifully to your heart, that out of it shall flow rivers of living waters. This Jesus spake of the Spirit, which they that believe on him should receive. As you have, therefore, honoured Madam, received the Lord Jesus, so walk in him even by faith. Lean on your beloved, and you shall go on comfortably through this howling wilderness, till you arrive at those blissful regions,

> *Where pain, and sin, and sorrow cease,*
> *And all is calm, and joy, and peace.*[51]

The new birth entails a "saving knowledge" of the Lord Jesus Christ that is far more than simple factual knowledge. It marries belief in him as the "eternal Son" of God to trust in him as one's Redeemer from sin and its punishment. It means that one's trust for acceptance by God is no longer focused on one's own moral achievements but upon what God has done through Christ's spotless life, propitiatory death and resurrection. As Whitefield wrote on another occasion to a different correspondent:

> I hope you take particular care to beat down self-righteousness, and exalt the Lord Jesus alone in your hearts. I find, the only happiness is to lie down as a poor sinner at the feet of the once crucified, but now exalted Lamb of God, who died for our sins and rose again for our justification.[52]

---

51 Letter to Louise Sophie von der Schulenburg, February 22, 1749 (*Works*, 2:236–237).
52 Letter to Serjeant B—, July 25, 1741 (*Works*, 1:284).

Moreover, the new birth is intimately bound up with the gift of the Spirit. Those who experience the new birth are "initiated into the divine life" as the Spirit comes to dwell in their hearts. This new birth ultimately comes from God. Only he can graciously enable a person to look to Christ alone for salvation. Finally, it is the new birth alone that sets a person on the road to heaven. In a sermon that he preached eleven months later on Ephesians 4:24, Whitefield put this final point more bluntly: "unless you are new creatures, you are in a state of damnation…I tell thee, O man; I tell thee, O woman, whoever thou art, thou art a dead man, thou art a dead woman, nay a damned man, a damned woman, without a new heart."[53]

Understandably Whitefield was critical of the doctrine of baptismal regeneration, prevalent in many quarters of the Church of England and which he referred to more than once as "that Diana of the present age."[54] His earliest printed sermon, *The Nature and Necessity of our Regeneration or New Birth in Christ Jesus* (1737), was ardent and plain in its rejection of this doctrine. It is "beyond all contradiction," he argued, "that comparatively but few of those that are 'born of water,' are 'born of the Spirit' likewise; to use another spiritual way of speaking, many are baptized with water, which were never baptized with the Holy Ghost."[55] Regeneration is not automatically dispensed when water baptism takes place. Rather, a person must experience "an inward change and purity of heart, and cohabitation of his [i.e. Christ's] Holy Spirit."[56] A genuine Christian is one "whose baptism is that of the heart, in the Spirit, and not merely in the water, whose praise is not of man but of God."[57]

---

53 Cited L. Tyerman, *The Life of the Rev. George Whitefield* (New York: Anson D.F. Randolph & Co., 1877), II, 242.

54 See, for example, *Some Remarks on a Pamphlet, entitled, The Enthusiasm of Methodists and Papists compar'd* (London: W. Strahan, 1749), 30. The allusion is to the riot in Ephesus over the threat that Christianity posed to the worship of the goddess Artemis or Diana (Acts 19:21–40).

55 *Sermons on Important Subjects*, 544. In this particular volume this sermon has the title *On Regeneration*. When it was first published, it had the title given in the text.

56 *Sermons on Important Subjects*, 544.

57 *Sermons on Important Subjects*, 545.

It is noteworthy that Whitefield was not afraid of turning the substance of this criticism against the Baptist emphasis on believer's baptism. Writing in the summer of 1741 to a Baptist correspondent in Georgia, he urged him:

> I hope you will not think all is done, because you have been baptized and received into full communion. I know too many that "make a Christ of their adult baptism," and rest in that, instead of the righteousness of the blessed Jesus. God forbid that you should so learn Christ. O my dear friend, seek after a settlement in our dear Lord, so that you may experience that life which is hid with Christ in God.[58]

JUSTIFICATION BY FAITH ALONE
Turning to the doctrine of justification, there is probably no better place to view Whitefield's thinking on this subject than his sermon on 1 Corinthians 1:30, *Christ, the Believer's Wisdom, Righteousness, Sanctification and Redemption*.[59] It was written out early in 1741 while Whitefield was on board ship on his way home to England from Georgia. It appears, though, that he had preached it various times in the preceding months on what was his second visit to America. It was eventually published in Edinburgh in 1742, and subsequently came out in further editions in other cities in England and America.

After emphasizing that the blessing of justification is rooted in God's everlasting love, Whitefield deals with the first thing that is attributed to Christ, "wisdom." True wisdom, he argues, is not "indulging the lust of the flesh," a reference to the open immorality and godlessness of his day. Nor is it found in the acquisitive "adding house to house." Neither is it merely intellectual knowledge, for "learned men are not always wise."[60]

What then is genuine wisdom? Well, first, Whitefield says and here he quotes an ancient Greek maxim, it is to "know thyself." What do the children of God need to know about themselves? Well, that before

---

58 Letter CCCVIII to Mr. I—F—, July 24, 1741 (*Works*, 1:281).
59 The full sermon can be found in *Sermons on Important Subjects*, 500–511.
60 *Sermons on Important Subjects*, 500–502.

their conversion they were darkness, and now, they are light in the Lord (see Ephesians 5:8). They know something of their lost estate. They see that "all their righteousnesses are but as filthy rags; that there is no health in their souls; that they are poor and miserable, blind and naked." And knowing themselves they know their need of a Saviour. This knowledge is basic and foundational to any biblical spirituality.

The type of self-knowledge that Whitefield is advocating also logically leads to the realization of the need for Christ as one's righteousness. Whitefield develops this thought in terms of Christ's active and passive obedience. By the former Christ fulfills the entirety of the law's righteous demands. This righteousness is imputed to the believer so that he or she now legally possesses the righteousness of Christ. "Does sin condemn? Christ's righteousness delivers believers from the guilt of it." By the latter, Christ passively bears the punishment for the elect's sins—he takes legal responsibility for them, so that God the Father blots out the transgressions of believers, "the flaming sword of God's wrath…is now removed."[61] The spiritual importance of this truth Whitefield later laid out in a letter he wrote to a friend in 1746: "Blessed be his [i.e. Christ's] name if He lets you see more & more that in Him and in Him only you have Righteousness & strength. The more you are led to this foundation, the more solid will be your Superstructure of Gospel holiness."[62]

And the means of receiving these precious benefits of Christ's death? Faith alone—believers, Whitefield affirms in his sermon on 1 Corinthians 1:30, are "enabled [by the Father] to lay hold on Christ by faith." Whitefield clearly indicates that faith itself does not save the sinner—only Christ saves. Faith unites the sinner to the Saviour. Thus, faith, though a necessary means to salvation, is not itself the cause or ground of salvation. As Whitefield says, "Christ is *their* Saviour."[63]

---

61 *Sermons on Important Subjects*, 502.
62 Letter to Jonathan Thompson, May 11, 1746 (Christie, "Newly Discovered Letters, II": 161). See also his *Jacob's Ladder* (*Sermons on Important Subjects*, 772–773): "You need not be afraid of our destroying inward holiness, by preaching the doctrine of the imputation of Christ's righteousness, that one is the foundation, the other, the superstructure; to talk of my having the righteousness of Christ imputed to my soul, without my having the holiness of Christ imparted to it, and bringing forth the fruits of the Spirit as an evidence of it, is only deceiving ourselves."
63 *Sermons on Important Subjects*, 502. Italics added.

Little wonder then that Whitefield, employing the text of Romans 8, goes on to underline the fact that such genuine self-knowledge not only provides the foundation for a truly biblical spirituality but also gives that spirituality a tone of triumphant joy: "O believers!...rejoice in the Lord always."[64] Whitefield knew that when the biblical truth of justification is grasped and appropriated, a deep sense of joy and freedom from the burden of sin floods the heart and one's relationship with God is firmly anchored.

Whitefield has a number of ways of describing this reliance on Christ. In one letter he talks of Christ as the believer's "asylum." Christ's "Wounds and precious Blood is a Sure Asylum & Place of Refuge in every Time of Trouble," he told a friend.[65] In yet a third example, he speaks of Christ alone being able to fill the deepest caverns of the human heart: "Happy they who have fled to Jesus Christ for refuge: they have a peace that the world cannot give. O that the pleasure-taking, trifling flatterer knew what it was! He would no longer feel such an empty void, such a dreadful chasm in the heart which nothing but the presence of God can fill."[66]

In another letter, he calls Christ "the believer's *hollow square.*" This metaphor is drawn from the European battlefields of the eighteenth century, where armies would regularly form massed squares of infantry three or four rows deep for protection and consolidated strength. If a soldier were wounded his comrades would place him in the centre of the square, where he would be a lot safer than if he were behind a skirmishing line.[67] "If we keep close" in the square that is Christ, Whitefield continues with the thought of the metaphor, "we are impregnable. Here only I find refuge. Garrisoned in this, I can bid defiance to men and devils."[68]

---

64 *Sermons on Important Subjects*, 502–503.
65 Letter to John Sims, November 30, 1745 (Christie, "Newly Discovered Letters, I": 73). See also his Letter to Mr. Straham, June 16, 1746 (Christie, "Newly Discovered Letters, III": 257): Christ is "the Believer's Asylum. He is the Believer's all in all. I find Him to be so dayly [sic]. Having nothing, in Him I possess all things."
66 Letter to Lady G—H—, December 15, 1757 (*Works*, 3:225).
67 John Keegan, *The Face of Battle* (London: Jonathan Cape, 1976), 183–184.
68 Letter to Colonel Gumley, February 8, 1750 (*Works*, 2:324–326).

THE PRIORITY OF GOSPEL HOLINESS

The new birth and justification by faith alone were hallmarks of Whitefield's spirituality, but so also was a concern for personal and social holiness.[69] While Whitefield never flagged in emphasizing that our acceptance with God can never be based on our sanctification, for the believer's sanctification is always incomplete in this life in a practical sense. Sin, to some degree, still indwells him. "Our most holy thoughts," Whitefield wrote to a correspondent in 1741, "are tinctured with sin, and want the atonement of the Mediator."[70] But although faith alone saves, saving faith is never alone. It always issues in good works.

In the sermon *Christ, the Believer's Wisdom, Righteousness, Sanctification and Redemption*, Whitefield thus explicitly rejects the error of those practical Antinomians who "talk of Christ without, but know nothing of a work of sanctification wrought within." As Whitefield stresses, "it is not going back to a covenant of works, to look into our hearts, and, seeing that they are changed and renewed, from thence form a comfortable and well grounded assurance" of salvation. If "we are not holy in heart and life, if we are not sanctified and renewed by the Spirit in our minds, we are self-deceivers, we are only formal hypocrites: for we must not put asunder what God has joined together."[71] In other words, believers cannot be in union with half a Christ. Or as he puts it pithily in the sermon *The Lord Our Righteousness*: "if you are justified by the Blood, you are also sanctified by the Spirit of the Lord."[72]

Whitefield was also unsparing in his criticism of doctrinal Antinomianism, which on one occasion he succinctly defined as believers looking for "all…Holiness without," that is, outside of themselves.[73] Its error, in Whitefield's mind, was so overemphasizing freedom from the condemnation of the law that the passionate pursuit of godliness

---

69 Timothy L. Smith, "George Whitefield and Wesleyan Perfectionism," *The Wesleyan Theological Journal*, 19, no. 1 (Spring 1984): 74–75.

70 Letter to Titus Knight, February 20, 1741 (*Works*, 1:251–252).

71 *Christ, the Believer's Wisdom, Righteousness, Sanctification and Redemption* (*Sermons on Important Subjects*, 505).

72 *Sermons on Important Subjects*, 193.

73 Letter to Herbert Jenkins, May 12, 1746 (Christie, "Newly Discovered Letters, II": 162–163).

in everyday life was downplayed.[74] He could thus describe it as a "great Evil," "a rank weed" sown by Satan.[75] When doctrinal Antinomianism actually began to appear among Whitefield's English colleagues and supporters, in particular through the teaching of William Cudworth (c.1717–1763), Whitefield fervently prayed that Jesus might "crush [this] Cockatrice in its bud."[76]

Following the lead of the New Testament Whitefield never implied that Christians must possess inherent holiness to be reckoned saints. However, he rightly assumed that those who have been made saints by faith alone will indeed lead holy lives. "Live near to Christ," he writes to an American correspondent, and "keep up a holy walk with God. ...Hunger and thirst daily after the righteousness of Christ. Be content with no degree of sanctification."[77] Writing to the Countess of Huntingdon on the last day of 1755, he told her: "Every day and every hour must we be passing from death to life. Mortification and vivification make up the whole of the divine work in the new-born soul."[78] Or as he put it to a friend in Philadelphia:

> I trust you will never rest till you are possessed of the whole mind which was in Christ Jesus. He is our pattern; and if we have true grace in our hearts, we shall be continually labouring to copy after our great exemplar. O the life of Jesus! How little of it is to

---

74 Letter to Gabriel Harris, May 2, 1746 (Christie, "Newly Discovered Letters, I": 87).

75 Letter to Howel Harris, May 2, 1746 (Christie, "Newly Discovered Letters, I": 88); Letter to Mr. Kennedy, May 2, 1746 (Christie, "Newly Discovered Letters, I": 89); Letter to Herbert Jenkins, May 12, 1746 (Christie, "Newly Discovered Letters, II": 162–163).

76 Letter to Elizabeth Longden, May 2, 1746 (Christie, "Newly Discovered Letters, I": 86). Elizabeth Longden was Whitefield's mother, who, six years after the death of her first husband, married Capel Longden in 1722. It was not a happy marriage. See Arnold Dallimore, *George Whitefield: The Life and Times of the Great Evangelist of the Eighteenth-Century Revival* (1970 ed.; repr. Westchester: Cornerstone Books, 1979), I, 52–55. On William Cudworth and his views, see Peter L. Lineham, "Cudworth, William" in Donald M. Lewis, ed., *The Blackwell Dictionary of Evangelical Biography 1730–1860* (Oxford: Blackwell Publishers, 1995), I, 278–279.

77 Letter CCLXII to Mrs. S—, February 17, 1741 (*Works*, 1:245).

78 Letter MCXII to Lady Huntingdon, December 31, 1755 (*Works*, 3:153).

be seen in those that call themselves his followers. Humility, meekness, love, peace, joy, goodness, faith, and the other blessed fruits of the Spirit, whither are they fled? I fear most take up with the shadow, instead of the substance. God forbid that I, or dear Mr. B—, should be of that unhappy number. Dear Sir, there is an unspeakable fulness, unsearchable riches in Christ. Out of him we are to receive grace for grace. Every grace that was in the Redeemer, is to be transcribed and copied into our hearts. This is Christianity; and without this, though we could dispute with the utmost clearness, and talk like angels, of the doctrines of grace, it would profit us nothing.[79]

Whitefield wisely, and in New Testament fashion, sought to keep the medium between two extremes. On the one hand, he did not insist so much upon Christ's imputed righteousness as to exclude the vital importance of the believer having godliness to evidence that he or she belongs to Christ. But nor did he give such priority to the believer's inherent righteousness as to diminish his or her resting in the righteousness of Jesus Christ alone for salvation.

Whitefield's perspective on the issue of holiness, though it captures well New Testament thinking on the subject, brought considerable grief to the evangelist. For he found himself forced to defend it against two of his closest friends, namely, John and Charles Wesley.[80] An honest evaluation of the eighteenth-century evangelical revival cannot belittle the central role played in it by John Wesley. One thinks, for instance, of his fearless and indefatigable preaching of Christ crucified

---

79 Letter CCCXCV to Mr. B—, February 5, 1742 (*Works*, 1:366–367).

80 For different perspectives on this controversy between Whitefield and the Wesleys, see Iain H. Murray, "Prefatory Note" to George Whitefield, *A Letter to the Rev. Mr. John Wesley in Answer to His Sermon Entitled "Free Grace"* (Iain H. Murray, "Introduction" to *George Whitefield's Journals* [London: The Banner of Truth Trust, 1960], 564–568); Frank Baker, "Whitefield's Break with the Wesleys," *The Church Quarterly*, 3, no. 2 (October 1970): 103–113; Arnold Dallimore, *George Whitefield: The Life and Times of the Great Evangelist of the Eighteenth-Century Revival* (1979 ed.; repr. Westchester: Cornerstone Books, 1980), II, *passim*; Timothy L. Smith, "George Whitefield and Wesleyan Perfectionism," *The Wesleyan Theological Journal*, 19, no. 1 (Spring 1984): 63–85; J.D. Walsh, "Wesley vs. Whitefield," *Christian History*, 38 (1993): 34–37.

for sinners year in and year out throughout the length and breadth of Great Britain after his conversion in 1738. Or there is the genius he displayed in preserving the fruit of the revival in small fellowship groups called "classes." Again, one calls to mind his promotion of the matchless hymnody of his brother Charles, whom J.I. Packer has rightly named "the supreme poet of love in a revival context."[81] Yet, for all the good that John Wesley did, he was a lightning-rod for controversy. His propagation of evangelical Arminianism, for example, did much to antagonize Whitefield and other key evangelical leaders.[82]

Equally serious an error was Wesley's commitment to the doctrine of Christian perfection. In the year before his death, he plainly indicated his conviction that God had raised up the Wesleyan Methodists primarily for the propagation of this doctrine.[83] Yet, no other doctrine involved Wesley in more controversy than this one. It was a key factor in creating a rift between him and Whitefield, it alienated him from many of the younger leaders in the revival, and eventually it even caused a slight division between him and his brother Charles.[84]

Convinced that Scripture taught this doctrine, though, John Wesley was determined to publish it to the world. Yet, unlike his clear presentation of the heart of the gospel, his teaching about perfection is somewhat murky and at times difficult to pin down. He always contended that he was not advocating "sinless perfection."[85] Yet he could

---

81 "Steps to the Renewal of the Christian People" in his *Serving the People of God* (*The Collected Shorter Writings of J. I. Packer*, vol. 2; Carlisle: Paternoster Press, 1998), 74.

82 On one occasion Howel Harris told Wesley: "You grieve God's people by your opposition to electing love" (cited George E. Clarkson, *George Whitefield and Welsh Calvinistic Methodism* [Lewiston: Edwin Mellen Press, 1996], 78).

83 Letter to Robert Carr Brackenbury, September 15, 1790, in *The Letters of the Rev. John Welsey, A.M.*, ed. John Telford (1931 ed.; repr. London: The Epworth Press, 1960), VIII, 238.

84 W.E. Sangster, *The Path to Perfection. An Examination and Restatement of John Wesley's Doctrine of Christian Perfection* (London: Hodder and Stoughton, 1943), 25; John R. Tyson, *Charles Wesley on Sanctification. A Biographical and Theological Study* (Grand Rapids: Francis Asbury Press, 1986), 227–301. Further examination of this aspect of Wesley's thought may be found in Harald Lindström, *Wesley and Sanctification: A Study in the Doctrine of Salvation* (Stockholm: Nya Bokförlags Aktiebolaget, 1946).

85 *A Plain Account of Christian Perfection* (1777), in *The Works of the Rev. John Wesley, A.M.* (London: John Mason, 1830), XI, 396.

talk about the one who experienced this blessing as having "sin... separated from his soul" and having a "full deliverance from sin."[86] Such perfection freed the person from evil thoughts and evil tempers. As he wrote to the Baptist authoress Anne Dutton, this blessing brings freedom from "all faintness, coldness, and unevenness of love, both towards God and our neighbour. And hence from wanderings of heart in duty, and from every motion and affection that is contrary to the law of love." All this sounds very much like sinless perfection despite Wesley's protest, "we do not say that we have no sin *in us*, but that we do not *commit sin*."[87]

It is curious that Wesley himself never claimed to have experienced Christian perfection, or what he sometimes called "the second blessing."[88] But as he preached it, others did, which to his mind was further confirmation of the scriptural truth of the doctrine. George Whitefield mentions in a letter that he wrote a friend in 1741 that he had met one of Wesley's followers who claimed he had not "sinned in thought, word, or deed" for three months. This man affirmed that he was "not only free from the power, but the very in-being of sin" and asserted that it was "impossible for him to sin." In the same letter Whitefield mentions another, a woman, who claimed she had been perfect for an entire year during which time she "did not commit any sin." When he asked her if she had any pride, she brazenly answered, "No"![89] As Gordon Wakefield wisely sums up Wesley's teaching on Christian perfection: It was "confused, divisive, provoked scandals, errors, mania and the very evils of pride, malice and all uncharitableness it was intended to obliterate forever, and rested on an inadequate concept of sin."[90]

---

86 *Plain Account of Christian Perfection* (*Works of John Wesley*, XI, 402); Wesley, Letter to Sarah Rutter, December 5, 1789 (*Letters*, VIII, 190).

87 Letter to Mrs. Ann Dutton (June 25, 1740?), in *The Works of John Wesley*, ed. Frank Baker (Oxford: Clarendon Press, 1982), 26:15. See also the remarks on Wesley's inconsistency at this point by Jeffrey, "Introduction," 32–33.

88 John A. Newton, "Perfection and Spirituality in the Methodist Tradition," *The Church Quarterly*, 3, no. 2 (October 1970): 102.

89 Letter to a Friend in London, April 25, 1741, in *Letters of George Whitefield For the Period 1734–1742* (Edinburgh: The Banner of Truth Trust, 1976). This book is a reprint of the first volume of the *Works* along with 34 additional letters.

90 "John and Charles Wesley: A Tale of Two Brothers," in Geoffrey Rowell, ed., *The*

It was from Whitefield that significant opposition to this teaching first came. Despite his friendship with John and almost deferential respect for him, Whitefield was not afraid to challenge his erroneous thinking on Christian discipleship. Between 1740 and 1742 he wrote letters to Wesley and preached a number of sermons which opposed his views about Christian perfection with frankness, but also with evident love. Writing on March 26, 1740, from Savannah, Georgia, for instance, he told Wesley that to the best of his knowledge "no sin has dominion" over him, but he went on, "I feel the strugglings of indwelling sin day by day."[91] Yet, despite his evident conflict with Wesley, he did not relish the prospect of disagreeing with him. Will not their disagreement, he said, "in the end destroy brotherly love, and insensibly take from us that cordial union and sweetness of soul, which I pray God may always subsist between us?"[92] In September 1740, Whitefield wrote to a Mr. Accourt of London: "Sinless perfection...is unattainable in this life. Shew me a man that could ever justly say, 'I am perfect.' It is enough if we can say so, when we bow down our heads and give up the ghost. Indwelling sin remains till death, even in the regenerate."[93] Scriptural support for this position was found by Whitefield in texts like 1 Kings 8:46 ("there is no man that liveth and sinneth not") and James 3:2 ("In many things we all offend"), as well as examples drawn from the lives of King David and the apostles Peter and Paul.[94] Two months later, Whitefield told Wesley: "I am yet persuaded you greatly err. You have set a mark you will never arrive at, till you come to glory." The following month found Whitefield wintering at Bethesda in Georgia. From there he published an open letter against Wesley in which he once again dealt plainly with his brother in Christ. On the subject of perfection he confessed that since his conversion he has "not doubted a quarter of an hour of having a saving

---

English Religious Tradition and the Genius of Anglicanism (Nashville: Abingdon Press, 1992), 191.

91 In 1753 he could similarly declare: "I can truly say, that for these many years last past, no sin hath had dominion over me" (Letter DCCCCLXXV to Mr. S—, May 27, 1753 [*Works*, 3:14]).

92 Letter CLXIX to the Rev. John Wesley, March 26, 1740 (*Works*, 1:155–156).

93 Letter CCXIX to Mr. Accourt, September 23, 1740 (*Works*, 1:209).

94 Letter CCXXI to the Rev. John Wesley, September 25, 1740 (*Works*, 1:210–212).

interest in Jesus Christ." But, he also had to acknowledge "with grief and humble shame...I have fallen into sin often." Such a confession, though, was not unique to him: it was the "universal experience and acknowledgment...among the godly in every age."[95] Whitefield's perspective rests squarely on the testimony of Scripture, an adequate theological analysis of indwelling sin, and the testimony of God's people in the history of the church.

CODA

Wesley's teaching carried enormous weight in the century after his death in 1791. It formed the heart and substance of the transatlantic holiness movement of the nineteenth century. And taking the nomenclature that John Fletcher (1729–1785), Wesley's godly lieutenant, used for Christian perfection, namely his description of it as "the baptism of the Holy Spirit," Wesleyan perfectionism prepared the soil for the emergence of Pentecostalism in the twentieth century. What would the later history of evangelicalism have been like if Wesley had listened to Whitefield? We have no way of knowing, of course, for God's sovereignty deemed otherwise. But it strikes this writer that his brother Charles eventually came to a much more balanced and clearer perspective on this matter than John, a perspective that was essentially the position of Whitefield. Writing to the great Yorkshire evangelist William Grimshaw in March 1760, the younger Wesley stated:

> My perfection is to see my own imperfection; my comfort, to feel that I have the world, flesh, and devil to overthrow through the Spirit and merits of my dear Saviour; and my desire and hope is, to love God with all my heart, mind, soul, and strength, to the last gasp of my life. This is my perfection. I know no other, expecting to lay down my life and my sword together.[96]

---

95 See Dallimore, *George Whitefield*, II, 563.
96 Cited Tyson, *Charles Wesley on Sanctification*, 301.

3

"Sacramental glory"

The Lord's Supper and the power of the Holy Spirit in the hymnody of Charles Wesley[1]

> Jesu, dear, redeeming Lord,
>   Magnify thy dying Word,
>   In thine Ordinance appear,
>   Come, and meet thy Followers here.
> —CHARLES WESLEY[2]

---

1 This chapter first appeared as " "Sacramental glory": The Lord's Supper and the power of the Holy Spirit in the Hymnody of Charles Wesley" in Rob Clements and Dennis Ngien, eds., *Between the Lectern and the Pulpit: Essays in Honour of Victor A. Shepherd* (Vancouver: Regent College Publishing, 2014), 3–15. Used by permission.

2 Hymn XXXIII, stanza 1, John Wesley and Charles Wesley, *Hymns on the Lord's Supper* (Bristol, 1745), 24–25. This hymnal is henceforth cited simply as *Hymns on the Lord's Supper*.

In 1678 a Puritan preacher by the name of John Howe (1630–1705) preached a series of sermons in London based on Ezekiel 39:29 in which he dealt with the subject of the outpouring of the Holy Spirit. In one of these sermons he told his audience:

> When the Spirit shall be poured forth plentifully I believe you will hear much other kind of sermons, or they will, who shall live to such a time, than you are wont to do now-a-days.... It is plain, too sadly plain, there is a great retraction of the Spirit of God even from us; we not know how to speak living sense [i.e. felt reality] unto souls, how to get within you; our words die in our mouths, or drop and die between you and us. We even faint, when we speak; long experienced unsuccessfulness makes us despond; we speak not as persons that hope to prevail.... When such an effusion of the Spirit shall be as is here signified...[ministers] shall know how to speak to better purpose, with more compassion and sense, with more seriousness, with more authority and allurement, than we now find we can.[3]

The effusion of the Spirit for which Howe, and others of his generation longed, did occur, but not in their lifetime. As we have noted, it was not until the 1730s and 1740s that remarkable scenes accompanied the preaching of the gospel throughout the length and breadth of the British Isles, and preachers were enabled to preach, to quote Howe, "with more compassion and sense, with more seriousness, with more authority and allurement" than preachers in general had known for many a year.

Among these preachers was Charles Wesley, the somewhat overlooked younger brother of John Wesley.[4] One gets a vivid sense of the

---

3 *The Prosperous State of the Christian Interest Before the End of Time, By a Plentiful Effusion of the Holy Spirit: Sermon IV*, in *The Works of the Rev. John Howe, M.A.* (New York: John P. Haven, 1838), I, 575. For the explanation of "living sense" as "felt reality," I am indebted to J.I. Packer, *God In Our Midst. Seeking and Receiving Ongoing Revival* (Ann Arbor: Servant Books, 1987), 33.

4 For the life and ministry of Charles Wesley, see especially Gareth Lloyd, *Charles Wesley and the Struggle for Methodist Identity* (Oxford: Oxford University Press, 2007) and John R. Tyson, *Assist Me to Proclaim: The Life and Hymns of Charles Wesley* (Grand Rapids: Eerdmans, 2007).

Charles Wesley
(1707–1788)

spiritual power that often attended his preaching in this eyewitness account by Joseph Williams, Dissenter and merchant from Kidderminster, who happened to be on hand when Wesley preached in a Bristol brickyard in early October 1739. Not familiar with the area of Bristol where Wesley was preaching, Williams got a guide to take him to the brickyard. There Williams found Wesley "surrounded by...more than a thousand People." After praying for about fifteen minutes, the Methodist preacher spoke, Williams related, for

> about an Hour in such a manner as I have scarce ever heard any man preach: i.e. though I had heard many a finer Sermon, according to the common Taste, or Acceptation, of Sermons, yet, I think, I never heard any man discover such evident Signs of a vehement Desire, or labour so earnestly, to convince his Hearers that they were all by Nature in a sinfull, lost, undone, damnable State; that, notwithstanding, there was a possibility of their Salvation, thro' Faith in Christ; that for this End our Sins were imputed to him, or he was made Sin for us, tho he knew no Sin, i.e. had no Sin of his own, & this in order that his Righteousness might be imputed, as it certainly will, to as many as believe on him; and that none are excepted, but such as refuse to come to him as lost, perishing, yea as damned Sinners, & trust in him alone, i.e. in his meritorious Righteousness, & atoning Sacrifice, for Pardon, & Salvation; that this is the method Infinite Wisdom hath chosen for reconciling the World unto himself, & that whosoever believeth in him shall certainly receive Remission of Sins, & an Inheritance among them that are sanctified. All this he backed with many Texts of Scripture, which he explained & illustrated, & then by a Variety of the most forcible Motives, Arguments and Expostulations, did he invite, allure, quicken & labour, if it were possible, to compel all, and every of his Hearers, to believe in Christ for Salvation.[5]

Now, reading an account like this or other similar narratives it would be easy to believe that the "place" where the Spirit's power was

---

5 "Charles Wesley in 1739 by Joseph Williams of Kidderminster," introd. Geoffrey F. Nuttall, *Proceedings of the Wesley Historical Society*, 42 (1979-1980): 183–184.

most readily expected during this era was in the preaching of the Word. And this certainly would be in line with the Puritan and Reformation roots of the revival. But Wesley himself would also point us to another place, namely, in the celebration of the Lord's Supper. As he rebuked some who denied that the Supper was a place where the Spirit was especially active:

> Ah tell us no more
> The Spirit and Power
> Of Jesus our God
> Is not to be found in this Life-giving Food![6]

But how exactly does Wesley consider the bread and the wine—this "Food"—to be "Life-giving"? Or to ask this question from a pneumatological angle: What exactly is the Spirit doing in the Lord's Supper?

THREE PATTERNS OF EUCHARISTIC PIETY

Broadly speaking, there were three traditions of Protestant eucharistic piety that preceded Wesley's answers to these questions, all of which had emerged at the time of Reformation, and Wesley's answers to these questions should be considered apart from this background of thought about the Lord's Supper. All of the Reformers clearly rejected the Roman Catholic answer to these questions, namely, transubstantiation, but they were unable to find a common answer to these questions that satisfied them all. For Martin Luther, after the prayer for the Holy Spirit to consecrate the elements of bread and wine, Christ's body and blood are present "in, with and under" the bread and the wine. Contrary to the Roman dogma of transubstantiation, the bread remains bread and the wine remains wine. Yet, through the Spirit's power, they also actually contain Christ's body after the prayer of consecration.

The Swiss German-speaking Reformer Huldrych Zwingli (1484–1531), on the other hand, regarded the bread and the wine as mainly signs of what God has accomplished through the death of Christ, and the Supper, therefore, as chiefly a *memorial*. The Spirit used the ele-

---

6 Hymn XCII, stanza 1, *Hymns on the Lord's Supper*, 78.

ments to enable the participant at the Table to remember with gratitude, devotion and affection what Christ had done for him or her in his death. In discussions of Zwingli's perspective on the Lord's Supper it is often maintained that Zwingli was not really a Zwinglian, that is, he saw more in the Lord's Supper than simply a memorial.[7] Be this as it may, a tradition did take its start from those aspects of his thought that stressed primarily the memorial nature of the Lord's Supper.

Finally, there was the view of John Calvin (1509–1564), which sought to find a mediating position between the Lutheran and Zwinglian perspectives on the presence of Christ at the Table and the work of the Holy Spirit in that regard.[8] In Calvin's perspective on the nature of the Lord's Supper, the bread and wine are signs and guarantees of a present reality. To the one who eats the bread and drinks the wine with faith there is conveyed what they symbolize, namely Christ. The channel, as it were, through which Christ is conveyed to the believer is none other than the Holy Spirit. The Spirit acts as a kind of link or bridge between believers and the ascended Christ. Christ is received by believers in the Supper, "not because Christ inheres the elements, but because the Holy Spirit binds believers" to him. But without faith, only the bare elements are received.[9]

Where then does Charles Wesley stand with regard to these various traditions? More specifically, how does he conceive of the Spirit's activity at the Table and the presence of Christ during the celebration of the Lord's Supper? In answering these questions, my primary resource will

---

7 See Derek R. Moore-Crispin, " 'The Real Absence': Ulrich Zwingli's View of the Lord's Supper" in *Union and Communion, 1529–1979* (London: The Westminster Conference, 1979), 22–34.

8 Cf. William Henry Brackney, *The Baptists* (New York: Greenwood Press, 1988), 62–63.

9 Victor A. Shepherd, *The Nature and Function of Faith in the Theology of John Calvin* (Macon: Mercer University Press, 1983), 220. Other helpful studies on Calvin's theology of the Lord's Supper include B.A. Gerrish, "The Lord's Supper in the Reformed Confessions," *Theology Today* 13 (1966–1967): 224–243; John D. Nicholls, "'Union with Christ': John Calvin on the Lord's Supper," in *Union and Communion*, 35–54; John Yates, "Role of the Holy Spirit in the Lord's Supper," *Churchman* 105 (1991): 355–356; B.A. Gerrish *Grace and Gratitude: The Eucharistic Theology of John Calvin* (Minneapolis: Fortress Press, 1993).

be John and Charles Wesley's *Hymns on the Lord's Supper*, which was published in 1745 by the Bristol printer, Felix Farley. This collection of 166 hymns would be reprinted a number of times over the next forty or so years, with a ninth edition appearing in 1786, two years before Charles Wesley's death. In the first edition, that of 1745, the brothers also included a lengthy edited extract from a work by Daniel Brevint (1616–1695), *The Christian Sacrament and Sacrifice* (1673). Brevint, whose grandfather Cosme Brevint (1520–1605) had trained for the ministry under Calvin at Geneva, came originally from the Isle of Jersey and was therefore bilingual. After study at the Huguenot seminary of Saumur in France as well as at Jesus College, Oxford, he served Huguenot churches in France and Anglican ones in England, his last charge being the deanship of Lincoln.[10] It is generally believed that John Wesley edited this extract and Charles Wesley authored the hymns. It is noteworthy that a twentieth-century student of Wesley's hymnody, J. Ernest Rattenbury, can state that none of Wesley's hymn collections is "as rich and deep as the hymns on the Lord's Supper."[11]

One final aspect regarding the historical context behind this hymnal needs to be noted. During the 1740s, the Wesleys found themselves engaged in a controversy with men and women who had hitherto played important roles in the revival in which the Wesley brothers were increasingly central figures, namely the English Moravians. The controversy had to do with the role of the ordinances in the believer's life and would come to be called the "Stillness Controversy."[12] Some of the English Moravians were convinced that the means of grace, such as the Lord's Supper, were "a thing of mere indifference" and not at all vital to the Christian life. Some went so far as to say that any comfort drawn from the Lord's Supper, for example, came not from the Holy

---

10 Kenneth W. Stevenson, "Brevint, Daniel," in *Oxford Dictionary of National Biography*, eds. H.C.G.Matthew and Brian Harrison (Oxford: Oxford University Press, 2004), 7:511–512.

11 J. Ernest Rattenbury, *The Evangelical Doctrines of Charles Wesley's Hymns* (London: The Epworth Press, 1942), 216.

12 For more details, see John R. Tyson, ed., *Charles Wesley: A Reader* (Oxford: Oxford University Press, 1989), 260–286, and John R. Tyson, *Assist Me to Proclaim: The Life and Hymns of Charles Wesley* (Grand Rapids: Eerdmans, 2007), 83–98.

Spirit, but from the devil![13] Motivating their thinking was a fear that the ordinances might become a spiritual crutch and thus a hindrance to walking in the Sprit. In a very real sense, the Wesleys collection of Eucharistic hymns was a direct response to this controversy. Consider, for instance, this hymn:

> ...If now I do not *feel*
> The Streams of Living Water flow
>   Shall I forsake the Well?
>
> Because He hides his Face,
>   Shall I no longer stay,
> But leave the Channels of his Grace,
>   And cast the Means away?
>
> Get Thee behind me Fiend,
>   On Others try thy Skill,
> Here let thy hellish Whispers end,
>   To thee I say *Be still!*
>
> Jesus hath spoke the Word,
>   His Will my Reason is,
> *Do this* in Memory of thy Lord,
>   Jesus hath said, *Do this!*
>
> He bids me eat the Bread,
>   He bids me drink the Wine,
> No other Motive, Lord, I need
>   No other Word than Thine.[14]

---

13 Charles Wesley, *Journal* entries, April 3 and 6, 1740, in Tyson, ed., *Charles Wesley: A Reader*, 263, 265.

14 Hymn LXXXVI, stanzas 1–5, *Hymns on the Lord's Supper*, 73–74.

"SACRAMENTAL GLORY"

Of all the various means of grace given by God to his people to further their growth in godliness, Charles Wesley considered the Lord's Supper to be the chief:

> Fasting He doth, and Hearing bless,
>   And Prayer can much avail,
> Good Vessels all to draw the Grace
>   Out of Salvation's Well.
>
> But none like this Mysterious Rite
>   Which dying Mercy gave
> Can draw forth all his promis'd Might
>   And all his Will to save.
>
> This is the richest Legacy
>   Thou hast on Man bestow'd,
> Here chiefly, Lord, we feed on Thee,
>   And drink thy precious Blood.[15]

And in one of the longer hymns in this collection—it has ten stanzas—Wesley compares the "Gospel-Ordinances" to "Stars in Jesu's Church" to help "steer the Pilgrim's Course aright."[16] Then Wesley stresses:

---

15 Hymn XLII, stanzas 2-4, *Hymns on the Lord's Supper*, 31. I owe the reference to this hymn to Ole E. Bergen, *John Wesley on the Sacraments: A Theological Study* (Grand Rapids: Francis Asbury Press, 1985), 15. This study by Bergen has been tremendously helpful in the following portion of this paper. See also Hymn LIV, stanza 4, *Hymns on the Lord's Supper*, 39:

> The Prayer, the Fast, the Word conveys,
>   When mixt with Faith, thy Life to me,
> In all the Channels of thy Grace,
>   I still have Fellowship with Thee,
> But chiefly here my Soul is fed
>   With fullness of Immortal Bread.
>
> Communion closer far I feel,
>   And deeper drink th' Atoning Blood,
> The Joy is more unspeakable…

16 Hymn LXII, stanzas 3, 5, *Hymns on the Lord's Supper*, 46.

But first of the Celestial Train
Benignest to the Sons of Men,
The *Sacramental Glory* shines,
And answers all our God's designs.[17]

It is, therefore, not at all surprising that Wesley regarded the Table as more than memorial. That it is a memorial Wesley is not slow to point out in this hymn loosely based on the Paraclete passages in the farewell discourse of John 14 to 16:

Come, Thou everlasting Spirit,
 Bring to every thankful Mind
All the Saviour's dying Merit
 All his Suffering for Mankind:
...
Come, Thou Witness of his Dying,
 Come, Remembrancer Divine,
Let us feel thy Power applying
 Christ to every Soul and mine...[18]

But it is not simply a place to remember—"'Tis not a dead external sign"[19]—for Wesley fully expected to meet Christ at the Table.

We come with Confidence to find
 Thy special Presence here.[20]

And as he prayed in these two hymns:

To every faithful Soul appear,
 And shew thy Real Presence here.[21]

---

17 Hymn LXII, stanza 6, *Hymns on the Lord's Supper*, 46. Italics original.

18 Hymn XVI, stanzas 1–2, *Hymns on the Lord's Supper*, 13.

19 Hymn LV, stanza 1, *Hymns on the Lord's Supper*, 39. See also Hymn LXXXIX, stanza 1, *Hymns on the Lord's Supper*, 76.

20 Hymn LXXXI, stanza 1, *Hymns on the Lord's Supper*, 69. See also Hymn LXXXIX, stanza 3, *Hymns on the Lord's Supper*, 76.

21 Hymn CXVI, stanza 5, *Hymns on the Lord's Supper*, 99. See also Hymn LXVI,

Jesu, dear, redeeming Lord,
   Magnify thy dying Word,
In thine Ordinance appear,
   Come, and meet thy Followers here.[22]

And urged communicants:

Sinner with Awe draw near,
   And find thy Saviour here,
In his Ordinances still,
   Touch his Sacramental Cloaths…[23]

On the other hand, it is vital to recognize, as Ole Bergen has shown in his study *John Wesley on the Sacraments*, that for neither of the Wesleys is Christ's presence at the Table a *physical* presence.[24] Bergen refers us to this hymn to make his point:

…Christ the Crucified appear,
Come in thy Appointed Ways,
   Come, and meet, and bless us here.

No local Deity
We worship, Lord, in Thee:
Free thy Grace and unconfin'd,
   Yet it here doth freest move;
In the Means thy Love enjoin'd
   Look we for thy richest Love.[25]

---

stanza 2, *Hymns on the Lord's Supper*, 48:
  …do Thou my Heart prepare,
    To find thy real Presence there.

22 Hymn XXXIII, stanza 1, *Hymns on the Lord's Supper*, 24–25.
23 Hymn XXXIX, stanza 1, *Hymns on the Lord's Supper*, 29.
24 Bergen, *John Wesley on the Sacraments*, 58–69.
25 Hymn LXIII, stanzas 1–2, *Hymns on the Lord's Supper*, 47.

Bergen rightly points out that the phrase "No local Deity" is meant to guard against a corporeal understanding of the presence of Christ. Wesley "refuses to accept any local presence of Christ in the elements."[26]

Similarly, Wesley can state in the hymn that compares the ordinances to stars, that while "with Joy" believers feel the "Sacred Power" communicated by the elements at the Table, they "neither Stars nor Means adore."[27]

Wesley is thus neither a Zwinglian nor a Lutheran in his understanding of the presence of Christ at the Table. Is he then a Calvinist in his understanding of the Table? It certainly seems so.

"COME, HOLY GHOST"

In line with the Calvinist understanding of the presence of Christ at the Table, Wesley can say:

> Come Holy Ghost, set to thy Seal,
>   Thine inward Witness give,
> To all our waiting Souls reveal
>   The Death by which we live.[28]

And:

> Come, Holy Ghost, thine Influence shed,
>   And realize the Sign,
> Thy Life infuse into the Bread,
>   Thy Power into the Wine.[29]

Or again:

> Come in thy Spirit down,
>   Thine Institution crown,

---

26 Bergen, *John Wesley on the Sacraments*, 62–63. See also Rattenbury, *Evangelical Doctrines of Charles Wesley's Hymns*, 217.
27 Hymn LXII, stanza 8, *Hymns on the Lord's Supper*, 46.
28 Hymn VII, stanza 1, *Hymns on the Lord's Supper*, 6.
29 Hymn LXXI, stanza 1, *Hymns on the Lord's Supper*, 51.

Lamb of God as slain appear,
   Life of all Believers Thou,
Let us now perceive Thee near,
   Come Thou Hope of Glory now.[30]

In Wesley's thinking, the Spirit's work *vis-à-vis* the Supper especially relates to his giving to believers a sense of the forgiveness of their sins as they partake of the bread and the wine. Wesley's linguistic description of this work of the Spirit is drawn from the Pauline description of the Spirit as a seal in the believer's life.[31] Thus Wesley prays:

The Sp'rit's Attesting Seal impart,
   And speak to every Sinner's Heart
The Saviour died for Thee![32]

Or he can ask the Spirit directly:

Spirit of Faith, come down,
   Thy Seal with Power set to,
The Banquet by thy Presence crown,
   And prove the Record true:

Pardon, and Grace impart:
   Come quickly from above.
And witness now in every Heart
   That God is perfect Love.[33]

It is due to the presence of the Spirit the Sealer that the bread and the wine, though "Badge and Token," can be called the "Sure confirming Seal."[34] One final text in this regard throbs with the revival context in which Wesley penned these hymns:

---

30 Hymn LIII, stanza 3, *Hymns on the Lord's Supper*, 38.
31 See 2 Corinthians 1:22; Ephesians 1:13; 4:30.
32 Hymn X, stanza 4, *Hymns on the Lord's Supper*, 9.
33 Hymn LXXV, stanza 3, *Hymns on the Lord's Supper*, 65.
34 Hymn XII, stanza 2, *Hymns on the Lord's Supper*, 11.

> 'Tis done; the Lord sets to his Seal.
>   The Prayer is heard, the Grace is given,
> With joy unspeakable we feel
>   The Holy Ghost sent down from Heaven.
> The Altar streams with sacred Blood,
>   And all the Temple flames with God![35]

Little wonder the Wesley scholar Frank Baker has commented that "the subsequent lowering of the spiritual temperature, even within Methodism, made it somewhat difficult after a few generations to sing many of Wesley's greatest hymns without either hypocrisy or at least a faintly uneasy self-consciousness."[36]

It is the Spirit then who is the One who communicates the forgiving presence of Christ to the believer at the Table. But how he does this, Wesley rightly admits, he cannot explain. Wesley is confident that grace is indeed conveyed to the believer at the Table, though he cannot say how:

> Let the wisest Mortal shew
>   How we the Grace receive:
> Feeble elements bestow
>   A power not theirs to give:
> Who explains the Wondrous Way?
>   How thro' these the Virtue came?
> These the Virtue did convey,
>   Yet still remain the same.[37]

Yes, "the Sign transmits the Signified,"[38] though "the Manner be unknown"[39]:

---

35 Hymn LXXXIX, stanza 4, *Hymns on the Lord's Supper*, 76. See the comments of Rattenbury, *Evangelical Doctrines of Charles Wesley's Hymns*, 221, regarding the revival context in which these hymns were penned.

36 Frank Baker, *Representative Verse of Charles Wesley* (New York: Abingdon Press, 1962), xvi.

37 Hymn LVII, stanza 2, *Hymns on the Lord's Supper*, 41.

38 Hymn LXXI, stanza 1, *Hymns on the Lord's Supper*, 50.

39 Hymn LVII, stanza 4, *Hymns on the Lord's Supper*, 41.

How the Means transmit the Power
Here He leaves our Thought behind,
And Faith inquires no more.⁴⁰

Thus the Table remains Christ's "Mysterious Supper,"⁴¹ with its "Mysterious Bread"⁴² and "Mystick Wine."⁴³

A CONCLUDING EXAMPLE

Although Charles Wesley's poetic genius is on display in the hymnody we have looked at, the root of these hymns lies in the hymnwriter's personal knowledge of the "Sacramental Glory"⁴⁴ of the Lord Jesus' Supper. About four years after the appearance of the hymnal we have been considering, Charles Wesley was married to Sarah (a.k.a. Sally) Gwynne (1726–1822) on Saturday April 8, 1749, at a small chapel in the Welsh village of Llanlleonfel. Sally was the daughter of a Welsh Calvinistic Methodist, Marmaduke Gwynne (1692–1769), who had been converted in 1737 under the preaching of Howel Harris).⁴⁵ Charles' entry in his *Journal* about the wedding reveals his delight in his new bride, his bent for poetry and his Eucharistic piety, for he closes the entry with these words: "It was a most solemn season of love! Never had I more of the divine presence at the sacrament."⁴⁶

---

40 Hymn LIX, stanza 1, *Hymns on the Lord's Supper*, 43.
41 Hymn XII, stanza 1, *Hymns on the Lord's Supper*, 10; Hymn CLXV, stanza 2, *Hymns on the Lord's Supper*, 138.
42 Hymn XXIX, stanza 1, *Hymns on the Lord's Supper*, 22.
43 Hymn XL, stanza 1, *Hymns on the Lord's Supper*, 30.
44 Hymn LXII, stanza 6, *Hymns on the Lord's Supper*, 46. Italics original.
45 Geraint Tudor, "Gwynne Family," in John A. Vickers, ed., *A Dictionary of Methodism in Britain and Ireland* (Peterborough: Epworth Press, 2000), 145.
46 Cited Tabraham, *Brother Charles*, 52.

4

"Guide me, O thou great Jehovah"

William Williams, Pantycelyn and his hymn[1]

> Guide me, O thou great Jehovah,
> Pilgrim through this barren land.
> I am weak, but thou art mighty;
> Hold me with thy powerful hand.
> —WILLIAM WILLIAMS

In 1738, a twenty-one year old medical student named William Williams was returning home to Carmarthenshire when he happened to pass through a little village called Talgarth in Breconshire. It was Sunday;

---

[1] This chapter first appeared as "William Williams, Pantycelyn (1717–91) and his 'Guide me, O thou great Jehovah,'" *La revue Farel*, 5 (2010): 97–104. Used by permission.

the village church bell was calling the village parishioners to worship and Williams joined them. But the service that morning was spiritually cold and lifeless. As he came out of the church, however, he was amazed to see another young man standing on top of a table tomb. It was the evangelist Howel Harris, the Welsh evangelist who left an indelible mark on Welsh evangelicalism, and who has been called "the greatest Welshman of the eighteenth century."[2] Harris had been prevented from preaching within the church and thus had resorted to the graveyard. It was a sermon, Williams would later recall, that was "unusually terrifying." Around him the words of the evangelist were being driven home by the Spirit of God to sinful hearts, and sinners were coming to Christ. It was the time of the Great Awakening in Wales, when, as Harris told the English preacher George Whitefield:

> The outpouring of the Blessed Spirit is now so plentiful and common, that I think it was our deliberate observation that not one sent by Him opens his mouth without some remarkable showers. He comes either as a Spirit of wisdom to enlighten the soul, to teach and build up, and set out the works of light and darkness, or else a Spirit of tenderness and love, sweetly melting the souls like the dew, and watering the graces; or as the Spirit of hot burning zeal, setting their hearts in a flame, so that their eyes sparkle with fire, love, and joy; or also such a Spirit of uncommon power that the heavens seem to be rent, and hell to tremble.[3]

Not surprisingly, Williams never forgot that day. "It was a morning," he wrote many years later, "which I shall always remember, for it was then that I heard the voice of heaven."[4] Henceforth Williams regarded himself as a pilgrim on the way to the celestial city.[5]

---

2 R. Tudur Jones, "The Evangelical Revival in Wales: A Study in Spirituality," in James P. Mackey, ed., *An Introduction to Celtic Christianity* (Edinburgh: T&T Clark, 1989), 238.

3 Cited Eifion Evans, *Daniel Rowland and the Great Evangelical Awakening in Wales* (Edinburgh: The Banner of Truth Trust, 1985), 243.

4 Cited Tim Shenton, *Christmas Evans: The Life and Times of the One-Eyed Preacher of Wales* (Darlington: Evangelical Press, 2001), 34.

5 Eifion Evans, "'A most gifted, respected and useful man': Part 1: A Survey of

When William Williams, Pantycelyn,[6] died in 1791, he had written some 860 hymns and over 90 books, and had travelled nearly 112,000 miles as an itinerant preacher during the stirring days of the Great Awakening in Wales.[7] D. Martyn Lloyd-Jones considered Williams to be "the theologian of Welsh Calvinistic Methodism," which was born in that Welsh revival.[8] His great contribution to that revival was in the realm of "experimental hymnody and revival apologetic."[9] His hymns were a central vehicle in the extension of the revival and also in creating a hunger for literacy.[10] Thomas Charles (1755–1814) of Bala said of him at the time:

> He was one of the most gifted, respected and useful men of his age. His gift of poetry was naturally and abundantly given him by the Lord.... His hymns wrought a remarkable change in the religious aspect of Wales, and in public worship. Some verses in his hymns are like coals of fire, warming and firing every passion when sung.[11]

Again Lloyd-Jones can say of William's hymn-writing:

> The hymns of William Williams are packed with theology and experience.... William Williams was the greatest hymn-writer of them all. You get greatness, and bigness, and largeness in Isaac Watts; you get the experimental side wonderfully in Charles Wesley. But in William Williams you get both at the same time.[12]

Williams' Life," in his trans. of William Williams, *Pursued by God* (Bryntirion: Evangelical Press of Wales, 1996), 17.

6 "Pantycelyn" was the name of his mother's old home, where he lived from 1748 onwards after his marriage. Descendants of his family still inhabit the home.

7 Evans, *Daniel Rowland*, 63.

8 "William Williams and Welsh Calvinistic Methodism," in D. Martyn Lloyd-Jones, *The Puritans: Their Origins and Successors. Addresses Delivered at the Puritan and Westminster Conferences 1959–1978* (Edinburgh: The Banner of Truth Trust, 1987), 192.

9 Evans, *Daniel Rowland*, 63.

10 W. Glanffrwd Thomas, "Welsh Hymnody," in John Julian, ed., *Dictionary of Hymnology* (1907 ed.; repr. Grand Rapids: Kregel, 1985), 2:1251.

11 Cited Evans, *Daniel Rowland*, 63.

12 Cited Evans, *Daniel Rowland*, 296.

OVERVIEW OF WILLIAMS LIFE AND MINISTRY

After his conversion Williams studied at a Nonconformist Academy under a Rev. Vavasor Griffiths (d.1741), learning Greek, Hebrew, Latin and the Puritan classics.[13] Of the latter, he was deeply influenced by John Owen (1616–1683), Thomas Goodwin (1600–1679), and, interestingly enough, John Gill (1697–1771), who had some hyper-Calvinistic tendencies. Many years later, in 1779, he would publish a translation of the life of Thomas Goodwin.[14] Ordained a deacon in 1740, he was appointed to a parish with an unsympathetic vicar and a people who considered him a fanatic. By 1743, the local bishop had deep concerns about Williams, who was preaching beyond the parish bounds, and he refused him ordination as a priest. But God owned Williams' preaching. As Howel Harris said of him at this time:

> Hell trembles when he comes and souls are taken daily in the Gospel net. ...He is eminently owned by his heavenly Master in His service; he is indeed a flaming instrument in his hands.[15]

In 1748 he married Mary Francis, and he and his new bride went to live in his mother's old home at Pantycelyn. Mary would often accompany him on his preaching tours. When they stayed in an inn, Williams would ask his wife to sing one of his compositions. A crowd would gather to hear, and Williams would have a group to which to preach.[16] Between 1756 and 1779, Williams wrote extensively so as to give the Welsh Calvinistic Methodists a theological framework. Among the key works of these years was his definitive rebuttal of Sandemanianism, *The Crocodile of Egypt's River Seen on Mount Zion* (1767). His final

---

13 Stephen J. Turner, "Theological Themes in the English Works of Williams, Pantycelyn" (M.Th. thesis, 1981), 324 and n. 33. The best biography of Williams is undoubtedly Eifion Evans, *Bread of Heaven: The life and work of William Williams, Pantycelyn* (Bryntirion: Brynitirion Press, 2010).

14 Cited Evans, "Survey of Williams' Life" in his trans. of Williams, *Pursued by God*, 22.

15 Cited Evans, "Survey of Williams' Life" in his trans. of Williams, *Pursued by God*, 19.

16 Cited Evans, "Survey of Williams' Life" in his trans. of Williams, *Pursued by God*, 21.

**William Williams, Pantycelyn
(1717–1791)**

years saw no slackening of the pace, as he continued to preach and itinerate.

WILLIAMS THE HYMNWRITER

His first book of hymns—*Aleluia: Collection of hymns on various themes* containing 248 hymns—came out in the mid-1740s in Welsh. It proved to be very popular and went through three editions. In 1759 he had published an English hymnal, *Hosannah to the Son of David: or, Hymns of Praise to God for our glorious redemption by Christ*, in which there are 51 hymns, 11 of which Williams had especially translated from Welsh for this hymnal. Three years later, he published a second major Welsh hymnal. Its title in translation is *The songs of those on the crystal sea*. Containing 149 hymns, it soon went through five editions. Between this hymnal, which appeared in 1762 and his death in 1791, he published another four Welsh hymnals. A second English hymnal, *Gloria in Exclesis: or, Hymns of Praise to God and the Lamb*—published at the request of George Whitefield and Selina Hastings, the Countess of Huntingdon for use in Whitefield's orphanage in Georgia—appeared in 1772 with 72 hymns.[17]

Williams' hymns "often express longing for Christ" and employ the Song of Songs as a favoured source of images relating to this longing.[18] For example, there is this well-known hymn from 1776:

> Jesus, Jesus, all sufficient,
>   Beyond telling is thy worth;
> In thy Name lie greater treasures
>   Than the richest found on earth.
> Such abundance
>   Is my portion with my God.
> In thy gracious face there's beauty
>   Far surpassing every thing

---

[17] W. Glanffrwd Thomas, "Williams, William," in Julian, ed., *Dictionary of Hymnology*, 2:1284.

[18] Eifion Evans, "'A most gifted, respected and useful man': Part 2: A Survey of Williams' Published Work," in his trans. of Williams, *Pursued by God*, 30.

Found in all the earth's great wonders
    Mortal eye hath ever seen.
Rose of Sharon,
    Thou thyself art heaven's delight.[19]

Or this from his 1759 hymnal *Hosannah to the Son of David*:

One drop of that o'erflowing stream
    That angels taste above,
One smile from my Rdeemer's face
    Would kindle all to love.[20]

For Williams, hymns had two key purposes: first, to fix Scripture truth in the mind and memory, and second, to kindle spiritual affections, especially that of love for the Triune God.[21]

GUIDE ME, O THOU GREAT JEHOVAH

Now, one of the dominant, if not *the* dominant, images of his written work, both prose and verse, was that of the pilgrim.[22] At least fifty of his hymns explore this theme of pilgrimage.[23] Thus, his best-known hymn in English, "Guide me, O thou Great Jehovah" is quintessential Williams.

There were abundant sources by earlier Christian authors to influence him in this regard. One thinks of John Bunyan's *Pilgrim's Progress*, for example, which a number of writers think was deeply influential

---

19 Cited Evans, "Survey of Williams' Published Work," in his trans. of Williams, *Pursued by God*, 30.
20 Cited Evans, "Survey of Williams' Published Work," in his trans. of Williams, *Pursued by God*, 32.
21 Evans, "Survey of Williams' Published Work," in his trans. of Williams, *Pursued by God*, 32.
22 Turner, "Theological Themes in the English Works of Williams, Pantycelyn," 311–382.
23 Ted A. Campbell, "'Guide Me, O Thou Great Jehovah': Contributions of Welsh and English Calvinists to Worship in Eighteenth-Century England," *Proceedings of the Charles Wesley Society*, 1 (1994): 74.

on Williams' thinking.[24] But it was Scripture in particular that influenced him in this emphasis. So, for example, there is the story of the expulsion of the man and the woman from the Garden of Eden. Or there is the call of Abram to leave his home in Ur of the Chaldees and journey to a new land. Abraham would subsequently speak of his life as a pilgrimage.[25] Or there is the Exodus story of Israel leaving Egypt and wandering in the desert for forty years. In the New Testament, it is the book of Hebrews that especially picks up this theme.[26]

The geography of Wales would also have influenced Williams in this regard: its rugged, mountainous terrain with its rough and stormy coastline made travel very difficult at times. Here is Williams writing in a letter one September: "…intended to go to Langeitho next Sunday, but the weather is so cold, the wind so high and, the frost so severe that I fear I can't go."[27]

"Guide me, O thou great Jehovah" was originally written in Welsh and published in 1745. It was entitled in Welsh, "A Prayer for strength to go through the Wilderness of the World" and had five stanzas.[28] In 1771, Peter Williams of Carmarthen translated into English stanzas 1, 3 and 5 of this Welsh version. The following year, when Selina Hastings and George Whitefield requested a hymnal, Williams used Peter Williams' translation of the first stanza. He then made his own translation of stanzas 3 and 4 of the Welsh version, considerably revising them, and added a fourth stanza not in the Welsh version.

The tune to which this hymn is normally sung, *Cwm Rhondda*, was written in 1905 for a Baptist song festival by John Hughes, a deacon of and precentor for Salem Baptist Chapel, Pontypridd.[29]

---

24 Turner, "Theological Themes in the English Works of Williams, Pantycelyn," 319, n. 22.

25 Genesis 23:4. See also Hebrews 11:8–10.

26 See, for example, Hebrews 3–4 and 11:8–16.

27 Cited Turner, "Theological Themes in the English Works of Williams, Pantycelyn," 320.

28 J.R. Watson, ed., *An Annotated Anthology of Hymns* (Oxford: Oxford University Press, 2002), 228.

29 Frank Colquhoun, *Hymns That Live: Their Meaning and Message* (London: Hodder and Stoughton, 1980), 193.

STANZA 1
Guide me, O thou great Jehovah,
    Pilgrim through this barren land.
I am weak, but thou art mighty;
    Hold me with thy powerful hand.
Bread of heaven,
    Feed me till I want no more.

The first line was originally as it stands here, not "Guide me, O thou great *Redeemer*" as it has been altered in some hymnals.[30] The change is regrettable since it loses the Old Testament text that is the operative passage behind the hymn: Exodus.[31] The Christian life is likened to the journey of Israel through the wilderness (see Exodus 16:1), which Williams calls a "barren land." But Christian pilgrims are weak and in need of guidance. Thus, Williams beseeches God: "Guide me, O thou great Jehovah/Pilgrim through this barren land."

But Christians need not only *guidance* but also *protection* in this wilderness, for there are dangers and hazards to be faced. Thus, Williams prays: "I am weak, but thou art mighty;/Hold me with thy powerful hand." But there is yet more. We need guidance. We need to be guarded. And we need *nourishment*. So Williams now prays: "Bread of heaven, bread of heaven,/Feed me till I want no more." Here, Williams is alluding to Exodus 16:4–18. Now, this text is explicitly referred to by Jesus in John 6:48–51 as a reference to himself. Christ, then, is the "Bread of Heaven" to whom we are praying when we sing this hymn.

It needs noting that Williams' use of the term "want" in the final line is the older meaning of that word, which has the idea of "being in want." It is not our modern use of the word which bears the idea of "desire." Hence the line "till I want no more" does not mean "till I desire no more." Rather, it is the idea of "Feed me till I am no more in need, till the hunger of my soul is satisfied." This is why some modern hymnals rephrase this line thus: "Feed me now and evermore."[32]

---

30 Colquhoun, *Hymns That Live*, 194. For the following analysis of the hymn, Colquhoun, *Hymns That Live*, 193–198 has been very helpful.
31 Watson, ed., *Annotated Anthology of Hymns*, 228.
32 Colquhoun, *Hymns That Live*, 195.

STANZA 2
Open thou the crystal fountain,
  Whence the healing stream doth flow;
Let the fire and cloudy pillar,
  Lead me all my journey through.
Strong Deliverer,
  Be thou still my strength and shield.

"Open now the crystal fountain,/Whence the healing stream doth flow" takes us back to Exodus, this time Exodus 17:1–6. Again, there is a Christocentric emphasis, for Paul understands the rock that is smitten here to be Christ, as stated in 1 Corinthians 10:4. "The fire and cloudy pillar" refer to Exodus 13:21, and spoke of God's presence with his people and his guidance of them. Thus, the singer prays: "Lead me all my journey through."

Again, though, there is the realization that not only is guidance needed but also *strength* for the journey. In this regard, it bears recalling that the original title of the hymn in Welsh was "A Prayer for strength to go through the Wilderness of the World." The Christian pilgrimage has a *goal*, though, which Williams now describes in the third stanza:

STANZA 3
When I tread the verge of Jordan,
  Bid my anxious fear subside;
Death of deaths, and hell's destruction,
  Land me safe on Canaan's side.
Songs of praises,
  I will ever give to thee.

At the end of her journey through the wilderness, Israel came to the River Jordan and crossed over into the promised land. Traditionally, this crossing over was seen as a symbol of the end of the Christian pilgrimage and crossing over into heaven. This third stanza then is a prayer in the face of death and the fears that can grip one as one faces that: "When I tread the verge of Jordan,/Bid my anxious fear subside."

Fears are a great challenge to the believer. When George Whitefield died in 1770, Williams could write in his elegy on the preacher: "But anxious fears do still of every kind,/Resistless rush unto my thoughtful mind."[33] In Williams' day, it should be noted, the average life-span in Wales was twenty-seven and death an ever-present reality among the population.[34] Even as an old man, in 1790, Williams asked Thomas Charles to pray that the Lord would "make me Strong to meet death."[35]

Now, what does Williams mean by "Death of death, and hell's destruction"? Surely, this is a reference to Christ, who as the risen Lord has defeated death (see 2 Timothy 1:10) and defeated hell. Such a One can "land" the believer "safe on Canaan's side." And what is our response when there—and if so there, then also here in this world in anticipation? "Songs of praises,/I will ever give to thee."

The final stanza is usually omitted, but it forms a fitting conclusion to the hymn, as Williams reaffirms a central gospel truth: Heaven is a Christ-centred habitation.

STANZA 4
Musing on my habitation,
   Musing on my heav'nly home,
Fills my soul with holy longings:
   Come, my Jesus, quickly come;
Vanity is all I see;
   Lord, I long to be with Thee!

It was with such an other-worldly passion that the hearts of men and women were fired in the time of the Calvinistic revivals of the eighteenth century and they did great exploits for their God in this world.

---

33 Turner, "Theological Themes in the English Works of Williams, Pantycelyn," 355.
34 Turner, "Theological Themes in the English Works of Williams, Pantycelyn," 366.
35 Cited Turner, "Theological Themes in the English Works of Williams, Pantycelyn," 368.

5

"Dissent warmed its hands at Grimshaw's fire"[1]

William Grimshaw of Haworth and the Baptists of Yorkshire

> Glory be to God for free grace. No reason can be assigned for this; only He would have mercy; because He would have mercy. —WILLIAM GRIMSHAW

The Yorkshireman William Crabtree (1720–1811) never forgot the first time that he heard the preaching of William Grimshaw. It was 1743, when Crabtree was twenty-three, and the Anglican evangelical was speaking on the parable of the prodigal son. In the course of the sermon, Grimshaw made the observation that "one sin would damn a

---

1 The quotation comes from Frank Baker, *William Grimshaw 1708–1763* (London: The Epworth Press, 1963), 270.

soul as well as a thousand."² Now, Crabtree had done his apprenticeship as a weaver in what he later described as "a wicked village, next door to hell itself, given to Sabbath breaking, drunkenness, profane cursing and swearing." Nor had he been immune from the sins of his fellow villagers. Upon hearing this one sentence, driven home to his heart by the Spirit of God, he said that he thought his situation was "deplorable." But such was the drawing power of the Spirit of God that he continued to go to Haworth to listen to Grimshaw. In time he was soundly converted and eventually became the first pastor of Westgate Baptist Chapel in Bradford, as well as planting three other West Yorkshire Baptist causes at Halifax, Farsley and Leeds.³

Crabtree was one of thousands who blessed God for the day that they first heard Grimshaw and whose powerful preaching was the means of their conversion. Here we will explore some aspects of Grimshaw's life and ministry, as well as indicating how God used this Anglican cleric to help revive the Baptist interest in Yorkshire.

EARLY DAYS IN LANCASHIRE AND CAMBRIDGE

William Grimshaw was born on September 3, 1708, at Brindle, Lancashire, not far from Preston. There is very little reliable data about his early years, though there is some evidence that his parents, nominal Christians at the time, raised him with a sense of moral responsibility to a holy God.⁴ At the age of seventeen, Grimshaw went up to Cambridge, where he was admitted to Christ's College—the college of John Milton (1608–1674)—as a sizar (poor student), in April 1726. The population of Cambridge at the time was 6,000, a fraction of today's population. It is important to realize that academic standards at Cambridge during the eighteenth century were not that high. The majority of the professors did not lecture or tutor the students, but spent their time writing and left the direction of the students' academic studies to tutors or tutorial assistants. Academic requirements

---

2 Faith Cook, *William Grimshaw of Haworth* (Edinburgh: The Banner of Truth Trust, 1997), 232.

3 Baker, *William Grimshaw*, 270; Cook, *William Grimshaw*, 232 ("Farley" should be "Farsley").

4 Baker, *William Grimshaw*, 16–17.

for completing a degree course were minimal. Moreover, as John Wesley noted about the moral state of the universities of Cambridge and Oxford: "the moment a young man sets foot in either Oxford or Cambridge he is surrounded by company of all kinds...with loungers and triflers of every sort; with men who no more concern themselves with learning than religion."[5]

During his first couple of years at Cambridge, Grimshaw, however, applied himself to his studies and later described himself at this time as "sober and diligent."[6] But this soon changed as Grimshaw gave way to the moral turpitude of university life. In his own words, he fell in "with bad company" and "learned to drink, swear, and what not."[7] Given his style of living, it is amazing that throughout the latter period of time he hoped to become a clergyman upon graduation. As he put it, he aimed at such because it would give him a steady source of income, a roof over his head and bread upon his plate.[8] What theology he had was of the Deistic variety, in which the robust Christianity of the Reformers and Puritans was subjected to the scrutiny of human reason, and all that seemingly could not pass the test of rationality was rejected or played down. Thus the very concept of revelation was discarded along with Trinitarianism and the deity of Christ.[9]

Despite his evident lack of qualifications to be a minister in the Church of England, Grimshaw was ordained in April 1731, and proceeded to his first charge, what was then the hamlet of Littleborough, three miles north of Rochdale, Lancashire. He was in this parish but a few months. In September of the same year he moved six miles further north to Todmorden, where he was ordained a priest in the Anglican Church in 1732. The men and women in this parish were described by one contemporary as "wild, uncouth, rugged as their native hills."[10] But it was here, at Todmorden, that Grimshaw began to be awakened to the fact that he was in a desperate spiritual state.

---

5 Cited J. H. Whiteley, *Wesley's England* (London: Epworth Press, 1945), 269.
6 Baker, *William Grimshaw*, 23.
7 Cited Baker, *William Grimshaw*, 24.
8 Cited Baker, *William Grimshaw*, 24.
9 Cook, *William Grimshaw of Haworth*, 12–13.
10 Cited Baker, *William Grimshaw*, 28.

AWAKENED TO "THE PARDONING LOVE OF GOD"

The godlessness of Grimshaw's life was all too typical of eighteenth-century clerics. Like many other ministers throughout the length and breadth of England, Grimshaw spent his time fishing and hunting, drinking and playing cards. Instead of being times of spiritual nurture, his pastoral visits were occasions for heavy drinking.[11] And like other ministers of this ilk, he thought nothing of the vows he had made when ordained to preach the gospel and to be the spiritual guide of those in the parish. John Newton, who wrote an early biography of Grimshaw, noted that he did "his duty, as the phrase is, in the church, once on the Lord's day. ...With this his conscience was satisfied. Whether his flock was satisfied, he neither knew nor cared."[12]

How then was he awakened and converted? In part, the cause of his awakening was the death of a five-week-old girl, the first child of a young couple in the parish, James and Susan Scholfield. The mother awoke one awful morning to find the child she dearly loved stone dead. For a period of time, Susan's mind became unhinged and she continued to tend to the child as if it were alive. Grimshaw was called for, but could only advise the parents "to put away all gloomy thoughts, and to get into merry company, and divert themselves, and all would soon be right."[13] Not surprisingly, this advice proved utterly ineffective to help the parents overcome their grief. Grimshaw was again sent for and this time admitted he did not know what to say to help them.

This realization of a profound lack of spirituality was a first step on the road to change. He now tried to reform his life and began to urge his congregation to lead moral lives. He started praying four times a day, a practice he would continue after his conversion. But as he later admitted, all of this was but an earnest "working out a righteousness of his own," in which he tried to balance the sins of his life with good deeds. He actually kept a folio volume, in which he would record his sins on one page and his good deeds on another, with the hope that at

---

11 Paul and Faith Cook, *Living the Christian Life: Selected Thoughts of William Grimshaw of Haworth* (Darlington: Evangelical Press, 2008), 13.

12 *Memoirs of the Life of the Late Rev. William Grimshaw, A.B.* (London: T. Hamilton, 1814), 8.

13 Baker, *William Grimshaw*, 29–30.

year's end they would balance.[14] Although accurate dating is not possible, it seems he went on like this for seven years, from 1734 to 1741. Sometimes, though, the futility of trying to find salvation through the pathway of good works would overwhelm him and he would despair. Once he actually cried out in the middle of a service: "My friends, we are in a damnable state, and I scarcely know how we are to get out of it."[15] He was beginning to realize, in the words of Frank Baker, that "he could not put himself right with God by a multitude of devotional exercises, however arduous."[16]

During this period of time, in 1735, Grimshaw was married to a widow named Sarah Sutcliffe (1710–1739), whom he loved dearly, but who, after bearing him two children, died at the very young age of twenty-nine.[17] Grimshaw was shattered. He went through months of deep depression—not only mourning for his wife but also sorrowing over his sinful state. He was harassed with sexual temptations, which he resisted, but which left him deeply troubled. Old Deistic notions reappeared. On one occasion, for example, he "was tempted to believe Christ to be but a meer [sic] man." On another, the thought entered his mind that the God of the Bible was "a cruel implacable Being."[18]

But in the midst of his despair God sent him deliverance through "the agency of a man and a book."[19] Although Grimshaw does not specifically identify the man, it may well have been the Yorkshire evangelist, Benjamin Ingham (1712–1772) a friend of John Wesley and the brother-in-law of that wealthy patroness of Evangelical causes, Selina Hastings.[20] Ingham had been ordained in 1735 and had accompanied John and Charles Wesley as a missionary to the American colony of Georgia. In 1737, after his return to his native town of Ossett in Yorkshire and upon an evangelical conversion, Ingham started to establish what has become known as the Inghamite Methodists, after being banned in 1739 from preaching in Anglican churches. By 1755 there

---

14 Baker, *William Grimshaw*, 37.
15 Cited Cook, *William Grimshaw*, 20.
16 Cited Baker, *William Grimshaw*, 39.
17 Baker, *William Grimshaw*, 34–39; Cook, *William Grimshaw*, 20–22.
18 Baker, *William Grimshaw*, 41.
19 Baker, *William Grimshaw*, 44.
20 For this identification, see Baker, *William Grimshaw*, 44.

were over eighty Inghamite congregations, mainly in Yorkshire and Lancashire. Whether it was Ingham or not, this minister used to ride over to see Grimshaw and rebuke him for his attempts to earn salvation, "Mr. Grimshaw, you are a Jew, you are no believer in Jesus Christ, you are building on the sand."[21]

The book was *The Doctrine of Justification by Faith Through the Imputation of the Righteousness of Christ, Explained, Confirmed, & Vindicated* by the Puritan divine John Owen.[22] Visiting a friend in 1741, Grimshaw happened to see the book lying on a table. Seeing from the title on the spine that it was a theological work, he picked it up and went to open it to the title page. Then, a strange event happened. As he was opening the book he felt "an uncommmon heat" flush his face. Thinking that the flash of heat must have come from a fire in the fireplace of the room, he turned towards it but realized that it was too far away to have caused the flash of heat. He opened the book again and experienced a second heat flash. He took these flashes of heat to be divine signs that this book would be of special help to him.[23] And so it proved.

In this classic study of the imputed righteousness of Christ, Owen argued that justification meant that the sinner who was justified no longer sought to commend himself to God through his own good deeds, but rested in the fact that the righteousness of Christ was reckoned to him, giving him a spotless holiness purer than an angel's. Reading Owen, Grimshaw was enabled, as he later put it, to "renounce myself, every degree of fancied merit and ability, and to embrace Christ only for my all in all. O what light and comfort did I now enjoy in my own soul, and what a taste of the pardoning love of God!"[24]

A couple of decades later, when the London Evangelical William Romaine (1714–1795) asked Grimshaw for a statement of his doctrinal

---

21 Cited Baker, *William Grimshaw*, 44. On Ingham, see especially H.M. Pickles, *Benjamin Ingham: Preacher Amongst the Dales of Yorkshire, the Forests of Lancashire, and the Fells of Cumbria* (Coventry: H.M. Pickles, 1995).

22 *The Doctrine of Justification by Faith Through the Imputation of the Righteousness of Christ, Explained, Confirmed, & Vindicated* (London: R. Boulter, 1677).

23 Cook, *William Grimshaw*, 26–27.

24 Cited Baker, *William Grimshaw*, 46. For a summary of Owen's work, see A. Skevington Wood, *William Grimshaw*, The Annual Lecture of the Evangelical Library (London: The Evangelical Library, 1963), 12–13.

**William Grimshaw
(1708–1763)**

convictions, Grimshaw stated the following with regard to Christ's imputed righteousness:

> ...this very righteousness is sufficient to redeem all mankind; but it only is, and will be imputed to every penitent, believing soul... Glory be to God for free grace. No reason can be assigned for this; only He would have mercy; because He would have mercy. ...in this righteousness, every member of Christ stands, and will stand, complete, irreprovable,[25] and acceptable in God's sight, both at death and judgement.[26]

THE HAWORTH REVIVAL

Grimshaw's preaching now began to change as he heralded forth the good news of salvation by faith alone. Within a year of his conversion, in 1741, Grimshaw moved to a new parish, that of Haworth in West Yorkshire. Haworth was an isolated town in what is a very hilly and bleak part of Yorkshire. Daily existence was rough and hard, with life expectancy being around twenty-five. Almost half of all the children in the town died before the age of six. Raw sewage flowed down the main street and contaminated the drinking water, and not surprisingly dysentery and typhus were rampant, along with that killer of the eighteenth century, smallpox.[27] People sought refuge in drink, gambling and violence. According to John Newton, the inhabitants of the town "had little more sense of religion than their cattle, and were wild and uneducated like the mountains and rocks which surrounded them."[28] Hard and independent, few of Grimshaw's parishioners exhibited any Christian virtues.[29] But Grimshaw was just the man to reach them.

Heralding the changes about to take place in the village was the installation of a new pulpit in the parish church, St. Michael and All

---

25 i.e. blameless.

26 William Grimshaw's Creed, Articles XVI-XVII (Letter to William Romaine, December 8, 1762, in Erasmus Middleton, *Biographia Evangelica* [London: W. Justins, 1786], IV, 411). The spelling and punctuation have been modernized. For the full creed, see also Cook, *William Grimshaw*, 315–322.

27 Faith Cook, "William Grimshaw—Man of faith and action" (Unpublished paper presented to The Carey Conference, Swanwick, Derbyshire, January 9, 2008), 2.

28 Newton, *Memoirs*, 13–14, 43–44.

29 Cook, *Living the Christian Life*, 18–19.

Angels. On the sounding board above the pulpit can still be read the two verses of Scripture that Grimshaw had engraved on it to graphically display the heart of his ministry: "I am determined to know nothing among you, save Jesus Christ and him crucified" (1 Corinthians 2:2) and "For to me to live is Christ, and to die is gain" (Philippians 1:21).[30]

Grimshaw was an extremely gifted preacher who could hold the attention of a congregation for up to two hours while he preached.[31] In part, this was due to the fact that during the course of the sermon he would use what his critics called "market language" to appeal to his hearers' consciences. He was not afraid of using colloquial words in the pulpit or of even coining new ones. Filled with pithy phrases and striking images, his style of preaching was well suited to drive home the gospel to the hearts of rough and ready Yorkshire men and women. But the success of his preaching was also due to the sense of the presence of God as he would denounce sin, warn of the dreadful consequences of continuing in it, and urge all and sundry to accept Christ as their only hope of salvation.

Only a handful of Grimshaw's sermons survive. A section of his unpublished treatise "The Admonition of a Sinner" gives one a taste of his preaching style:

> My neighbour, my friend, my heart longs over you. Your manner of life is actually, openly and evidently such that if not seasonably prevented, it will shortly and certainly terminate in your inevitable, intolerable, eternal ruin and destruction. ...Don't be angry with me, please don't. It's because I love you that I thus address you...I want you without delay to repent of your sins, "to seek the Lord while he may be found, to call upon him while he is near" (Isaiah 55:6–7). Acquaint yourself with him, be at peace with him, through his blood, that thereby good may come to you: pardon, peace, grace, heaven, glory, glory for evermore.[32]

---

30 Cook, *William Grimshaw*, 58.
31 Cook, *William Grimshaw*, 91; Baker, *William Grimshaw*, 128.
32 "The Admonition of a Sinner" (Unpublished manuscript held in the John Rylands University Library of Manchester). Cited Esther Bennett, *Heavenly Fire: The life and ministry of William Grimshaw of Haworth (1708–1763)* (Dundas: Joshua Press, 2000), 8.

As people began to be converted, Grimshaw was at first unaware that the Haworth Revival was a rivulet in a much larger stream of revival inundating the British Isles in the mid-eighteenth century. But soon he made contact with Whitefield and the Wesley brothers, and became a central figure in the awakening. Frank Baker has maintained that apart from the evangelists just mentioned, Grimshaw exercised "probably a more potent influence than that of almost any other religious leader of his time."[33] John Wesley was so taken with Grimshaw's love for Christ and his passion for the salvation of sinners that he once wrote, "A few such as him would make a nation tremble. He carries fire wherever he goes."[34] In fact, Wesley nominated Grimshaw as his successor in leading the Arminian Methodist movement if he and Charles were to predecease Grimshaw.[35]

Within a few months of Grimshaw's arrival in Haworth, the church began to fill with people and conversions become increasingly common. When he had first come to the church in 1742, he had had a dozen or so people taking communion in a church that could seat 1,200. Five years later, the church was full and 1,200 took communion.[36] By the late 1740s and early 1750s, summer congregations might reach as high as 6,000! When Whitefield preached at the church in September 1749, for example, over 1,000 took communion and 6,000 gathered to hear him preach.[37]

The people came from all around the countryside. Some were reached by Grimshaw himself as he travelled throughout the week to nearby towns and villages outside of the boundaries of his own parish. Others came through the preaching of lay preachers whom he began to employ from 1744 onward.[38] In any given month in 1751, for example, Grimshaw reckoned that he might preach some sixty times.[39] From the point of view of Anglicanism, this was highly irregular and a source of worry to neighbouring parish ministers. To prevent Grimshaw act-

---

33 Baker, *William Grimshaw*, 268.
34 Cited Cook, *William Grimshaw*, 1.
35 Cook, *William Grimshaw*, 1, 172, 247.
36 Cook, *William Grimshaw*, 66.
37 Baker, *William Grimshaw*, 182.
38 Cook, *William Grimshaw*, 85.
39 Cook, "William Grimshaw—Man of faith and action," 4.

ing irregularly, some of them had recourse to aiding and abetting violent persecution. George White (d.1751), the nearby vicar of Colne, actually raised an army of local thugs, who were pledged "for the defence of the Church of England" and who were determined to wreak violence upon either Grimshaw or one of his lay preachers if they preached in the adjoining parishes.[40] Consider the experience, for example, of Grimshaw's lay preacher Thomas Lee (1727–1786):

> In the year 1752, and during the winter following, the work of God prospered exceedingly; but persecution raged on every side. …One day, as I was going through Pateley [Bridge], the captain of the mob [there], who was kept in constant pay, pursued me, and pulled me off my horse. The mob then soon collected about me; and…dragged me into a house by the hair of the head; then pushed me back, with one or two upon me, and threw me with the small of my back upon the edge of the stone stairs. This nearly broke my back; and it was not well for many years after. Thence they dragged me to the common sewer, which carries the dirt of the town to the river. They rolled me in it for some time; then dragged me to the bridge and threw me into the water. They had me mostly on the ground, my strength being quite spent.
> My wife, with some friends, now came up. Seeing her busy about me, some asked: "What, are you a Methodist?"—gave her several blows which made her bleed at the mouth, and swore they would put her into the river. All this time I lay upon the ground, the mob being undetermined what to do. Some cried out: "Make an end of him"—others were for sparing my life; but the dispute was cut short by their agreeing to put some others into the water. So they took them away, leaving me and my wife together. She endeavoured to raise me up; but, having no strength, I dropped to the ground again, and supported me about a hundred yards; then I was set on horseback, and made a shift to ride softly as far as Michael Granger's house. Here I was stripped from head to foot, and was washed. I left my wet clothes

---

40 Cook, *William Grimshaw*, 127. On the persecution, see Baker, *William Grimshaw*, 130–138.

here, and rode to Greenhow Hill, where many were waiting for me; and though much bruised and very weak, preached a short sermon from Psalm xxxiv.19: "Many are the troubles of the righteous; but the Lord delivereth him out of them all."[41]

"MAD GRIMSHAW"

In addition to solid biblical proclamation, Grimshaw's methods for raising the spiritual temperature of the Haworth parish also included what Frank Baker has termed "holy pranks," by reason of which some called the Haworth minister "Mad Grimshaw."[42] For example, John Newton recorded that during Sunday worship Grimshaw sometimes had the congregation sing a psalm—later embellishment made it Psalm 119—while he went out and checked the inns in the town to see if there were any drinking there who should have been in church.[43]

Once he apparently sent two of his churchwardens to round up such loiterers. They were slow in returning, so Grimshaw went in search of them. The psalm was long over when footsteps were heard and the two churchwardens appeared shamefaced with Grimshaw behind them. As Grimshaw came into the church, he cried out, "What think you! The churchwardens who went out to detect others and prevent them from sinning I have found in the inn drinking a pint of ale! For shame! For shame! For shame!"[44]

On another occasion Grimshaw was striding over the moors to preach in a village some distance from Haworth. Two ruffians met him on the way and sizing him up as one like themselves—for he was a big man physically, broad-chested and exceptionally strong[45]—they informed him that they were off "to hear Mad Grimshaw. We shall have some rare sport tonight!" Grimshaw pretended to be heading for another destination, but eventually agreed to accompany them. They had no idea who he truly was until he got to the place where he was

---

41 In Bennett, *Heavenly Fire*, 13.

42 Baker, *William Grimshaw*, 13.

43 Newton, *Memoirs*, 93–94. For the embellishment, see Cook, *William Grimshaw*, 140–141.

44 Baker, *William Grimshaw*, 212.

45 Baker, *William Grimshaw*, 259.

to preach and he went into the pulpit. The two would-be hecklers were silenced, "first by fear, then by shame, and lastly by the conviction of their own sinfulness, as he rallied them with the words: 'Come on! We shall have some rare sport tonight!'"[46]

Newton also tells the account of how Grimshaw put an end to the horse racing that was an annual feature of a fair normally held in mid-October. It was, in Grimshaw's words, "a scene of the grossest and most vulgar riot, profligacy, and confusion." Grimshaw sought in vain to end the races; he did not succeed until 1759 when he made it a matter of extended prayer. That year, quite contrary to the usual pattern of weather for October, it rained incessantly for five days, from October 12 to October 17. Newton said that it was reported that "old Grimshaw put a stop to the races by his prayers."[47]

"DISSENT WARMED ITS HANDS AT GRIMSHAW'S FIRE"[48]

Grimshaw's impact on the Particular Baptist cause in Yorkshire was profound. Like other centres of Baptist witness in England during the eighteenth century, many of the Yorkshire Baptists were moribund prior to Grimshaw's ministry, owing to such things as hyper-Calvinism and traditionalism. A goodly number of Grimshaw's converts became Baptists, including such Baptist leaders as William Crabtree, Richard Smith (1710–1764) of Wainsgate, James Hartley (1722–1780) of Haworth and John Parker (1725–1793) of Barnoldswick.[49] Grimshaw, though, took it all in his stride and was even able to joke about the fact that "so many of my chickens turn ducks!"[50]

---

46 Baker, *William Grimshaw*, 13.

47 Newton, *Memoirs*, 103–104. See also Baker, *William Grimshaw*, 213–214.

48 Baker, *William Grimshaw*, 270.

49 For details on Smith and Hartley, see Robin Greenwood, "The Evangelical Revival Among Particular Baptists: The Early History of West Lane and Hall Green Baptist Chapels in Haworth, during the Involvement of the Greenwood Family (Unpublished ms., 2000), 18–29. For Smith, also see Pickles, *Benjamin Ingham*, 40–42. For Parker, see John Fawcett, "A Sketch of the Life and Character of the Late Mr. John Parker," in John Parker, *Letters to his Friends* (Leeds, 1794), 3–48.

50 Cited Baker, *William Grimshaw*, 243.

Grimshaw's greatest influence on Baptist life and witness in Yorkshire, however, came through one who was not converted under his preaching, but who regularly went to hear him for a time, namely John Fawcett (1740–1817). Fawcett was born on January 6, 1740, at Lidget Green, a small village near Bradford in the West Riding of Yorkshire.[51] The death of his father, Stephen Fawcett, when he was but twelve and to whom he was deeply attached, made a deep impression upon him. For some time afterward he was, his son relates, "deeply agitated by fears" concerning his father's final state, and he prayed much about it.[52] Reinforcing this early openness to spiritual matters was Fawcett's ardent reading of the Scriptures and a variety of Puritan classics, including Bunyan's *Pilgrim's Progress*, *A Call to the Unconverted to Turn and Live* by Richard Baxter (1615–1691) and the works of John Flavel (c.1630–1691). It was not until September 1755, however, that Fawcett understood and owned as his own the biblical way of salvation by "a God reconciled through the atonement of a suffering Saviour."[53] The key influence at this point was not another author from the Puritan era, but one who has been rightly described as a "revived Puritan," namely George Whitefield.[54]

Over the next two years, Fawcett frequently trudged the nine or so miles over the moors from Bradford to hear Grimshaw, and especially made a point of going when the Lord's Supper was to be administered.[55] In 1764, Fawcett was called to succeed Richard Smith as pastor of Wainsgate Baptist Church in Hebden Bridge, where many of the early members, including Smith, had come to Christ under Grimshaw's powerful ministry. Located but five or six miles from Haworth, this church is considered to be a direct result of the Haworth Revival.

---

51 The main source for the life of Fawcett is that drawn up by his son, [John Fawcett, Jr.], *An Account of the Life, Ministry, and Writings of the Late Rev. John Fawcett, D.D.* (London: Baldwin, Cradock, and Joy, 1818). See also "Memoir of the Author," in *The Miscellaneous Works of the Late John Fawcett, D.D.* (London: W. Jones, 1824), 3–34 and Ian Sellers, "Other Times, Other Ministries: John Fawcett and Alexander McLaren," *The Baptist Quarterly*, 32 (1986–1987): 181–187.

52 [Fawcett, Jr.], *Life, Ministry, and Writings*, 6–7.

53 [Fawcett, Jr.], *Life, Ministry, and Writings*, 16.

54 [Fawcett, Jr.], *Life, Ministry, and Writings*, 15–17.

55 [Fawcett, Jr.], *Life, Ministry, and Writings*, 30–31.

Fawcett's ministry here and then later in a work right in the town of Hebden Bridge was marked by an irenic Calvinism and catholicity—both marks of the life of Grimshaw as well—a robust commitment to theological education—he began an academy for training Baptist ministers—and missions—William Ward (1769–1823), who went out to India to join William Carey at Serampore, was trained under Fawcett.[56] In fact, without a gift of £200 that Fawcett gave to the fledgling Baptist Missionary Society in 1793, it is quite possible that Carey would not have been able to sail to India that year.[57] In a way, then, Grimshaw played a small role in the onset of the modern missionary movement. And how the Anglican minister of Haworth would have rejoiced to think of the Baptist minister Carey preaching Christ in India, for, as Grimshaw wrote in the creed he sent to William Romaine, Christ's imputed "righteousness is sufficient to redeem all mankind."[58]

---

56 Baker, *William Grimshaw*, 271.

57 George R. Cragg, *Grimshaw of Haworth: A Study in Eighteenth Century Evangelicalism* (London: Canterbury Press, 1947), 102.

58 Cragg, *Grimshaw of Haworth*, 103.

6

"The great spiritual director of souls through the post"
John Newton as a spiritual mentor[1]

> Heaven will make abundant amends, for all that we can suffer or lose upon Earth. And even while we are here, our crosses are appointed to work together for our good. —JOHN NEWTON[2]

In a ground-breaking article on the way that letter-writing connected the various steams of revival in the early years of the eighteenth-

---

[1] This chapter first appeared as "John Newton (1725–1807) as a spiritual guide— 'The great spiritual director of souls through the post': an appreciation in the bicentennial year of his entry into glory," *Sovereign Grace Journal*, 11, no. 1 (January 2008): 4–15.

[2] Letter to Sarah Pearce, November 4, 1799 (Angus Library, Regent's Park College, University of Oxford).

century awakening, Susan O'Brien identified ten ministers who were central to this network of letters, including Jonathan Edwards, Isaac Watts, Philip Doddridge (1702–1751) and George Whitefield.[3] If her study had taken in the latter half of the eighteenth century, she would have found a similar network of Evangelical letter-writers, and central among them John Newton.[4] By the 1790s Newton was regularly devoting significant amounts of time to letter-writing, although he considered himself to be perpetually behind in answering letters, usually having, he estimated, fifty to sixty unanswered pieces of mail at any given time.[5] And it was through this medium of the letter that Newton exercised a central part of his calling as a minister and spiritual guide. Before we consider some aspects of Newton as a mentor in detail, we give a brief sketch of Newton's life, his conversion and Christian ministry.

A SKETCH OF THE LIFE OF JOHN NEWTON

Newton's first exposure to biblical Christianity was in the circles of English Nonconformity. Newton's mother, Elizabeth (d.1732), worshipped at the Independent chapel on Old Gravel Lane, Wapping, just outside of London, where the minister was David Jennings. Newton

---

   3 Susan O'Brien, "A Transatlantic Community of Saints: The Great Awakening and the First Evangelical Network, 1735–1755," *The American Historical Review*, 91, no. 4 (October 1986): 819.

   4 The definitive study of Newton and his theology is D. Bruce Hindmarsh, *John Newton and the English Evangelical Tradition between the Conversions of Wesley and Wilberforce* (Oxford: Clarendon Press, 1996). For other biographies of Newton, especially see Josiah Bull, *John Newton of Olney and St. Mary Woolnoth* (1868 ed.; repr. Edinburgh: The Banner of Truth Trust, 1998); Bernard Martin, *John Newton: A Biography* (Melbourne: William Heinemann, 1950); and Jonathan Aitken, *John Newton: From Disgrace to Amazing Grace* (Wheaton: Crossway Books, 2007).

   For shorter studies of his life, see also the excellent sketch by Donald E. Demaray, *The Innovation of John Newton (1725–1807): Synergism of Word and Music in Eighteenth Century Evangelism* (Lewiston: The Edwin Mellen Press, 1988), 5–39 and the dictionary article by D. Bruce Hindmarsh, "Newton, John," in H.C.G. Matthew and Brian Harrison, eds., *Oxford Dictionary of National Biography* (Oxford: Oxford University Press, 2004), 40:725–729.

   5 Hindmarsh, *John Newton*, 249–250.

remembered her as "a pious experienced Christian,"[6] from whom he learned the rudiments of piety that he was never completely able to erase despite his later dissolute years.[7] Four years after the death of his mother in 1732, Newton's father, also called John Newton (d.1750) a captain in the merchant marine, took his son to sea with him. Over the next twelve years as a sailor, Newton sought to rid himself entirely of his mother's godly instruction. He embraced the viewpoint of a free-thinking Deist, came to be adept in ridiculing Christianity and liberally peppered his speech with coarse language and blasphemies. In his words:

> My whole life, when awake, was a course of most horrid impiety and profaneness. I know not that I have since met with so daring a blasphemer. Not content with common oaths and imprecations, I daily invented new ones.[8]

But during a fearsome storm on the Atlantic on March 21, 1748, when it seemed impossible that the ship on which he was a sailor would not founder, Newton was shocked to hear a cry to God for mercy issue from his own mouth, his first real prayer in many years. The ship did not sink and Newton would later remark: "About this time, I began to know that there is a God who hears and answers payer."[9]

Newton was set now on the path of seeking to find the true God, though it was not until 1754 that he was firmly committed to the perspective of evangelical Christianity. A providential meeting with Alexander Clunie (d.1770), a naval captain who was a solid believer, on the Caribbean island of St. Kitts was critical in Newton's spiritual growth. According to Newton's later recollection:

---

6 *The Life and Spirituality of John Newton*, introd. Bruce Hindmarsh (Vancouver: Regent College Publishing, 2003), 17. This work contains Newton's *Authentic Narrative of Some Remarkable and Interesting Particulars in the Life of*—— (1764), which recounts the story of Newton's early years and conversion. For a study of this work, see David Lyle Jeffrey, *People of the Book: Christian Identity and Literary Culture* (Grand Rapids: Eerdmans, 1996), 288–300.

7 Hindmarsh, *John Newton*, 52–54.

8 Bull, *John Newton*, 23.

9 Bull, *John Newton*, 27.

[Clunie] not only improved my understanding, but inflamed my heart. He encouraged me to open my mouth in social prayer. He put me upon an attempt to make my profession more public, and to venture to speak for God. From him, or, rather, from the Lord, by his means, I received an increase of knowledge, my conceptions became clearer and more evangelical, and I was delivered from a fear which had long troubled me—the fear of relapsing into my former apostasy. But now I began to understand the security of the covenant of grace, and to expect to be preserved, not by my own power and holiness, but by the mighty power and promise of God through faith in an unchangeable Saviour.[10]

Sensing a call to vocational ministry, Newton was ordained to the Anglican ministry in 1764 and became the curate-in-charge in the market-town of Olney, Buckinghamshire. Newton ministered at Olney until 1780, when he accepted an offer to move to St. Mary Woolnoth, London, where he was till his death in 1807. In both the Church of St. Peter & St. Paul in Olney and St. Mary Woolnoth, Newton regularly preached to large crowds, though, compared to other preachers of his day—men like Whitefield, Daniel Rowland or even Newton's neighbour, the eccentric John Berridge (1716–1793) of Everton—his preaching was not remarkable.[11] His close friend and fellow hymn-writer William Cowper (1731–1800) once described his preaching as simply "plain and neat."[12]

Newton did excel as a hymnwriter, and it is as such that he is mainly remembered today for what has become an iconic song of North American culture, "Amazing Grace," originally entitled "Faith's review and expectation."[13] However, his key contribution to eighteenth-century

---

10 Bull, *John Newton*, 58.

11 Ernest Gordon Rupp, *Religion in England 1688–1791*, Oxford History of the Christian Church (Oxford: Clarendon Press, 1986), 482; Tony Baker, *1807–2007: John Newton and the Twenty-First Century*, St Antholin's Lectureship Charity Lecture (London: Latimer Trust, 2007), 15–18.

12 Martin, *John Newton*, 231–232.

13 Newton's hymns can be found in *Olney Hymns, in Three Books* (London, 1779). A facsimile edition of this work was published by The Cowper and Newton Museum, Olney, Buckinghamshire, in 1979. It bears noting that the hymnal was not entirely

John Newton
(1725–1807)

evangelicalism was in the realm of spiritual mentoring and guidance, especially through the medium of the letter. As Anglican historian G.R. Balleine once expressed it, Newton was "the great spiritual director of souls through the post."[14] Newton's use of written correspondence as a conduit of spiritual formation was facilitated first by the increased efficiency of the post office and mail delivery in Newton's day. Then, the development of a writing style that was simpler and less convoluted than the baroque prolixity of seventeenth-century theologians like John Owen made spiritual letters like those of Newton a joy to read.[15] In what follows, we look at two men whom Newton mentored: the evangelical politician William Wilberforce (1759–1833) and the Baptist pastor John Ryland, Jr. (1753–1825).

"A CHRISTIAN AND A STATESMAN": DIRECTING WILLIAM WILBERFORCE

Without a doubt, the most famous of Newton's correspondents was William Wilberforce, well-known for the key role that he played in the abolition of the slave trade.[16] Newton's mentoring of the English politi-

---

Newton's work. Of the 348 hymns in this volume, William Cowper wrote sixty-seven.

For studies of the hymns, see Erik Routley, *I'll Praise My Maker: A study of the hymns of certain authors who stand in or near the tradition of English Calvinism 1700–1850* (London: Independent Press, 1951), 145–178; Robin A. Leaver, "Olney Hymns 1779: 1. The book and its origins," *Churchman* 93 (1979): 327–342; Robin A. Leaver, "Olney Hymns 1779: 2. The hymns and their use," *Churchman* 94 (1980): 58–66; Robin A. Leaver, "Olney Hymns: a documentary footnote," *Churchman* 97 (1983): 244–245; Hindmarsh, *John Newton and the English Evangelical Tradition*, 257–288; J.R. Watson, *The English Hymn: A Critical and Historical Study* (Oxford: Clarendon Press, 1997), 282–299; and William E. Phipps, *Amazing Grace in John Newton: Slave-Ship Captain, Hymnwriter, and Abolitionist* (Macon: Mercer University Press, 2001), 115–158.

14 G.R. Balleine, *A History of the Evangelical Party in the Church of England* (London: Longmans, Green, and Co., 1908), 107.

15 Baker, *John Newton and the Twenty-First Century*, 22–23.

16 For two older studies of the life of Wilberforce, see especially Robin Furneaux, *William Wilberforce* (London: Hamish Hamilton, 1974) and John Pollock, *Wilberforce* (1977 ed.; repr. Eastbourne: Kingsway, 2001). In a review of Pollock's book, Richard V. Pierard judged it to be a slightly better biography than that of Furneaux: "The Greatness of Wilberforce," *Christianity Today*, 24, no. 1 (January 4, 1980): 36. For more recent biographies of his life, see Kevin Belmonte, *Hero for Humanity. A Biography of*

cian began when Wilberforce, shortly after his conversion, approached Newton about the rectitude of a Christian being in politics. In the fashionable circles in which Wilberforce moved Newton and evangelicals like him were regarded with utter disdain and contempt. Writing to Newton on December 2, 1785, Wilberforce stressed that any visit to the well-known evangelical minister had to be kept secret.[17] In fact, when Wilberforce did call on Newton five days later, he walked around the block twice before knocking on Newton's door. The meeting between the two men would be a true turning point in the social and political history of Great Britain.

Wilberforce was contemplating leaving the realm of politics. For a number of eighteenth-century evangelical communities, particularly the Methodist followers of John Wesley and some of the Calvinistic Baptists, politics was a "worldly" occupation from which the believer was best to separate himself or herself.[18] Anglican evangelicals like Newton, however, did not view their Christian discipleship in such a counter-cultural light and Newton wisely encouraged Wilberforce to stay in the world of politics. Some words that Newton wrote to him a couple of years later well capture the essence of his advice to the young convert: "It is hoped and believed that the Lord has raised you up for the good of His church and for the good of the nation."[19] Newton was well aware of the challenge of being a Christian and a politician. As he wrote of Wilberforce to his good friend William Cowper the year after Wilberforce came to see him: "I hope the Lord will make him a blessing both as a Christian and a statesman. How seldom do these characters coincide!! But they are not incompatible."[20]

Nor did Newton simply direct Wilberforce into the calling God had chosen for him, but over the next couple of decades Newton proved

---

William Wilberforce (Colorado Springs: NavPress, 2002); Eric Metaxas, *Amazing Grace: William Wilberforce and the Heroic Campaign to End Slavery* (New York,: HarperCollins, 2007); and William Hague, *William Wilberforce: The Life of the Great Anti-Slave Trade Campaigner* (London: HarperCollins, 2007). See also chapter 6.

17 For the letter, see Metaxas, *Amazing Grace*, 56–57.

18 See, for example, Murray Andrew Pura, *Vital Christianity: The Life and Spirituality of William Wilberforce* (Fearn: Christian Focus, 2003), 37–38.

19 Cited Pollock, *Wilberforce*, 38.

20 Cited Hague, *William Wilberforce*, 88.

to be the ablest and most devoted of spiritual mentors. For example, in 1785, Newton stated he hoped and trusted Wilberforce would derive his wisdom "from your attention to the Word of God and the throne of his Grace."[21] Nevertheless, when pressed by Wilberforce, Newton did give Wilberforce advice on such matters as how far a Christian might accommodate himself "to the prejudices of those about us, with a hope of winning upon them." He warned Wilberforce that "an upright, conscientious man" could not wholly avoid "the censure and dislike of the world, so far as his religious principles are concerned," but urged him "to square his life according to the precepts and spirit of the Gospel." Newton then outlined the areas of godly living from which he perceived a believer in a public position dare not recede.[22] Newton thus helped Wilberforce to develop a profound awareness of life *sub specie æternitatis* and the importance of using his time on earth for good. "A man who acts from the principles I profess," Wilberforce could thus write in 1789, "reflects that he is to give an account of his political conduct at the Judgment seat of Christ."[23]

It needs noting that there were occasions when Newton turned to Wilberforce for help. For instance, he occasionally told Wilberforce about the needs of fellow believers or clergy in dire straits if he thought Wilberforce might be able to help them. For instance, when he learned that William Carey was seeking assistance for his proposed passage out to Bengal, he wrote to Wilberforce on May 27, 1793:

---

21 Letter to William Wilberforce, November 1, 1787 (MS Wilberforce c. 49, fols. 14–15; Bodleian Library, Oxford University).

22 Letter to William Wilberforce, November 1, 1787.

23 Cited David Bebbington, "Abolition: William Wilberforce and the Slave Trade," in John D. Woodbridge, ed., *More Than Conquerors: Portraits of Believers from All Walks of Life* (Chicago: Moody Press, 1992), 242. For a synopsis of Wilberforce's religious views, see Pollock, *Wilberforce*, 149–153 and Pura, *Vital Christianity*, passim. Pollock classifies him theologically as an Arminian (Pollock, *Wilberforce*, 152–153). However, he was most indebted to the seventeenth-century Puritans, especially John Owen, John Howe, John Flavel and Richard Baxter, and to men influenced by them, such as Philip Doddridge and Jonathan Edwards. See Murray A. Pura and Donald M. Lewis, "On Spiritual Symmetry: the Christian Devotion of William Wilberforce," in J.I. Packer and Loren Wilkinson, eds., *Alive to God: Studies in Spirituality presented to James Houston* (Downers Grove: InterVarsity Press, 1992), 177–181.

My dear Sir:

I expect that a Mr. Cary [sic] will shortly wait upon you, and will probably bring an introductory line from me. Though I do not personally know him, his character and business are such that I could not refuse him this request.

He was the Baptist Minister at Leicester, well known to Mr. [Thomas] Robinson, and much respected by him.[24] Mr. Robinson has often mentioned him to me in terms of strong approbation. He has for some time had a strong desire of preaching the Gospel among the heathen, and the accounts he received from Mr. [John] Thomas...determined his choice to Bengal. Mr. Cary wishes to know if it be practicable to procure the [East India] Company's leave for his passage thither, or if he might be permitted to stay, if he could find his way by a foreign ship. He thought, if you and Mr. [Henry] Thornton approved of his character, motives and ends, your patronage might probably enable him to go. However this may be, if you could afford him a short audience, you could perhaps give him such advice in a quarter of an hour, as might put him in a right path, and be useful to him through life.

I believe what he heard from Mr. Thomas (how true I know not) chiefly determined him to think of India. He said he was ready to go anywhere, to the ends of the earth, so that he might preach the Gospel to the ignorant. I mentioned America, that there was an open door to Canada and Nova Scotia, particularly to New Brunswick; whether he considers himself too far engaged for Bengal, to think of any other place I know not, but perhaps a word from you might have weight. From what Mr. Robinson has said of him, I believe he may be depended upon as a faithful man; and that his zeal to be a missionary is not the flight of a warm fancy, but the desire of a man who is willing to give up, and to hazard everything for the glory of God and the good of souls.

I consider your time, and therefore spare you the addition of anything farther, but my prayers for your guidance and blessing.[25]

---

24 Thomas Robinson (1749–1813) was the vicar of St. Mary's, Leicester. See Arthur Pollard, "Robinson, Thomas," in Donald M. Lewis, ed., *The Blackwell Dictionary of Evangelical Biography 1730–1860* (Oxford: Blackwell Publishers, 1995), II, 948.

25 Letter to William Wilberforce, May 27, 1793 (MS Wilberforce c. 49, fol. 46;

Years later Wilberforce would play a critical role in securing freedom for Carey and other Baptist missionaries to labour in India.

As the years passed, Newton continued to encourage Wilberforce in his calling as a politician. For example, in 1796, Newton wrote to Wilberforce: "I believe you are the Lord's servant, and are in the post which He has assigned you; and though it appears to me more arduous, and requiring more self-denial than my own, I know that He who has called you to it can afford you strength according to your day."[26] Newton also helped Wilberforce by recalling those in Scripture who had served in the political realm.

> May the wisdom that influenced Joseph and Moses and Daniel rest upon you. Not only to guide and animate you in the line of political duty—but especially to keep you in the habit of dependence upon God, and your communion with him, in the midst of all the changes and bustle around you.[27]

Wilberforce in turn acknowledged his dependence on the support of this faithful friend and mentor. For instance, he asked Newton in September 1788: "O my dear Sir, let not your hands cease to be lifted up, lest Amalek prevail—entreat for me that I may be enabled by divine grace to resist and subdue all the numerous enemies of my salvation."[28]

Nearly two years after Wilberforce went to see Newton about the state of his soul and his calling, the former wrote in his diary these words as he contemplated his future service for God: "God Almighty has placed before me two great objects, the Suppression of the Slave Trade and the Reformation of Manners."[29] The first of these objects would occupy Wilberforce for the next twenty years, and when it was achieved in 1807, it was one of the great moral triumphs of the gospel. And there is little doubt that a significant influence on Wilberforce's

---

Bodleian Library, Oxford University).

26 Cited Hague, *William Wilberforce*, 88.

27 John Newton, Letter to William Wilberforce, May 18, [1786] (MS Wilberforce c. 49, fol. 9; Bodleian Library, Oxford University).

28 Letter to John Newton, September 6, 1788 (MS Wilberforce c. 49 fols. 19–20; Bodleian Library, Oxford University).

29 Cited Pollock, *Wilberforce*, 69.

campaign to abolish the slave trade came from the spiritual direction given by Newton to the Christian politician.

"WISE COUNSEL": THE MENTORING OF JOHN RYLAND, JR.

For a second example of Newton's spiritual mentoring we turn to his friendship with the Calvinistic Baptist, John Ryland, Jr. In 1781, Ryland was invited by College Lane Baptist Church, Northampton, to become co-pastor with his father, John Collett Ryland (1723–1792).[30] Four years later, his father left Northampton for Enfield, near London, and Ryland became the sole pastor. This Northampton pastorate concluded in 1793, when Ryland moved to Bristol, where, until his death in 1825, he pastored Broadmead Baptist Church and was also the principal of Bristol Baptist Academy, the only Baptist theological college at that time in England.[31]

Newton's friendship with Ryland dates from 1768, a few years after the former had become the curate at the parish church in Olney and when the latter was living not far away in Northampton.[32] "We began," Newton wrote to Ryland in 1795, "when you were a lad and I a curate and we have gone on till you are grown into a doctor and I am dignified with the title of rector."[33] Though belonging to different generations, both men deeply valued their friendship. Near the end of his life, Newton could write to his friend:

---

30 On the elder Ryland, see Peter Naylor, "John Collett Ryland (1723–1792)," in Haykin, ed., *British Particular Baptists*, I, 184–201.

31 There is no substantial biography of the younger Ryland. For a brief sketch by his son, see J.E. Ryland, "Memoir," in John Ryland, Jr., *Pastoral Memorials: Selected from the manuscripts of the late Revd. John Ryland, D.D. of Bristol* (London: B.J. Holdsworth, 1826), I, 1–56.

32 John Ryland, "Remarks on the Quarterly Review, for April 1824, Relative to the Memoirs of Scott and Newton," in his *Pastoral Memorials: Selected from the manuscripts of the late Revd. John Ryland, D.D. of Bristol* (London: B.J. Holdsworth, 1828), II, 346. For a discussion of Ryland's friendship with Newton, see especially Grant Gordon, ed., *Wise Counsel: John Newton's letters to John Ryland, Jr.* (Edinburgh: The Banner of Truth Trust, 2009). Also see L.G. Champion, "The Letters of John Newton to John Ryland," *The Baptist Quarterly*, 27 (1977–1978): 157–163 and L.G. Champion, "The Theology of John Ryland: Its Sources and Influences," *The Baptist Quarterly*, 28 (1979–1980): 17–18, 26.

33 Letter to John Ryland, July 28, 1795 (Gordon, ed., *Wise Counsel*, 317).

> If, as is possible, this should be my last letter to you, keep it as a memorial of the love I bear you, and of my thankful remembrance of past times, when being within a few miles, we could see each other often, take sweet counsel together, and go to the house of our God in company.[34]

And in 1824, the year before Ryland died, the Baptist pastor recalled: "Mr. Newton invited me to visit him at Olney in 1768; and from thence to his death, I always esteemed him, and Mr. Hall of Arnsby…as my wisest and most faithful counsellors, in all difficulties."[35]

The truth of Ryland's assertion is readily seen even by a cursory examination of the letters he received from Newton. He frequently consulted Newton about a variety of matters, some theological, some personal, the latter ranging from prospective marriages (Ryland married twice) to his decision to leave his pastorate in Northampton for that of Broadmead in Bristol. One of the matters in which Newton was a great help had to do with Ryland's father.

The elder Ryland was one of the leading Calvinistic Baptist pastors of the eighteenth century, and throughout his life maintained cordial relations with Anglican evangelicals such as George Whitefield and James Hervey (1714–1758)—like Whitefield a one-time member of the Oxford "Holy Club," which had been run by the Wesley brothers According to the Congregationalist preacher, William Jay (1769–1853), John Ryland, Sr. was

> much attached to many other preachers less systematically orthodox than himself; and laboured, as opportunity offered, with them. He was, indeed a lover of all good men…while many talked of candour, he exercised it. Though he was a firm Baptist, he was no friend to bigotry or exclusiveness.[36]

---

34 Letter to John Ryland, January 16, 1801 (Gordon, ed., *Wise Counsel*, 379).

35 "Remarks on the Quarterly Review," 346. The Baptist pastor Robert Hall, Sr. (1728–1791). On his life and ministry see Graham W. Hughes, "Robert Hall of Arnesby: 1728–1791," *The Baptist Quarterly* 10, (1940–1941): 444–447, and Michael A.G. Haykin, "Robert Hall, Sr. (1728–1791)," in his ed., *The British Particular Baptists 1638–1910* (Springfield: Particular Baptist Press, 1998), I, 203–211.

36 *The Autobiography of the Rev. William Jay*, eds. George Redford and John Angell

Yet, the elder Ryland was also a very candid man, often quite incorrigibly impetuous, and sometimes very unwise in his choice of words, all of which gave his son much anguish of heart. It was Ryland, for example, who, at a meeting of the ministers of the Northamptonshire Association in 1785, asked William Carey, who had just become the minister of the Baptist cause in the village of Moulton, Northamptonshire, to offer the meeting a subject for discussion.[37] Carey proposed a subject on which he had been long ruminating: "Whether the command given to the apostles to teach all nations was not binding on all succeeding ministers, to the end of the world, seeing that the accompanying promise was of equal extent." Carey's question grew out of his reflection on Matthew 28:18–20. The promise Carey had in mind is clearly that given by the Lord Jesus in verse 20, and the command that in verse 19a. If, Carey reasoned, Christ's promise of his presence is for all time (verse 20), then what of his command (verse 19a)? There is considerable debate about the older Ryland's response. According to John Webster Morris (1763–1836), pastor of Clipston Baptist Church in Northamptonshire, who was actually present, Ryland responded thus to Carey:

> You are a miserable enthusiast for asking such a question. Certainly nothing can be done before another Pentecost, when an effusion of miraculous gifts, including the gift of tongues, will give effect to the commission of Christ as at first. What, Sir! Can you preach in Arabic, in Persic, in Hindustani, in Bengali, that you think it your duty to send the gospel to the heathens?

John C. Marshman, the son of Carey's respected co-worker in India, Joshua Marshman (1768–1837), reported a more abrupt retort by the elder Ryland: "Young man, sit down. When God pleases to convert the heathen, he will do it without your aid or mine!" John Ryland, Jr., the son, on the other hand, strongly asserted that his father never uttered such sentiments.[38]

James (2nd ed.; London: Hamilton, Adams & Co., 1855), 297.
37 For more details on Carey, see chapter 9.
38 For discussion of this incident, see especially John Ryland, Jr., *The Work of Faith,*

Though the younger Ryland denied the historicity of this particular outburst of his father, which most students of this era acknowledge to have taken place, other similar incidents could not be denied. As William Jay observed, Ryland's speech was marked by "bold sayings and occasional sallies of temperament," and though a man whose "excellencies...more than balanced his defects," he was all in all "a peculiar character, and had many things about him *outré* and *bizarre*, as the French would call them."[39] On one occasion, Jay recorded, Ryland had preached about angels and had mentioned their presence at Christian worship. The congregational singing after his sermon, however, was so bad that Ryland halted the singing mid-stream and told the congregation, "I do not wonder the angels of God do not wrench your necks off."[40] On another occasion, Jay witnessed Ryland's impassioned response to the slave trade:

> One morning I was reading to him some of the reported miseries and cruelties of the middle passage; among others, of a captain who had a fine female slave in his cabin, but, when her infant cried, he snatched him up, and flung him out into the sea; still requiring the wretched creature to remain, as the gratifier of his vile passions. At the recital of this Mr. Ryland seemed frantic, and to lose his usual self-control. He was agitated, and paced up and down the room, "O God, preserve me! O God, preserve me!" and

---

the Labour of Love, and the Patience of Hope, Illustrated; in the Life and Death of the Rev. Andrew Fuller (2nd ed.; London: Button & Son, 1818), 112, note; S. Pearce Carey, *William Carey* (8th ed.; London: The Carey Press, 1934), 54; F. Deaville Walker, *William Carey: Missionary Pioneer and Statesman* (Chicago: Moody Press, 1925), 54–55; Iain H. Murray, *The Puritan Hope: A Study in Revival and the Interpretation of Prophecy* (Edinburgh: The Banner of Truth, 1971), 139 and 280, n. 14; Iain H. Murray, "William Carey: Climbing the Rainbow," *The Banner of Truth*, 349 (October 1992): 18–21; Ruth Tucker, "William Carey: Father of Modern Missions," in John D. Woodbridge, ed., *Great Leaders of the Christian Church* (Chicago Moody Press, 1988), 308; Brian Stanley, *The History of the Baptist Missionary Society 1792–1992* (Edinburgh: T&T Clark, 1992), 6–7; and Michael A.G. Haykin, *One heart and one soul: John Sutcliff of Olney, his friends, and his times* (Darlington: Evangelical Press, 1994), 193–196.

39 *Autobiography of the Rev. William Jay*, eds. Redford and James, 286.
40 *Autobiography of the Rev. William Jay*, eds. Redford and James, 293.

then, unable to contain any longer, burst forth into a dreadful imprecation, which I dare not repeat. It shocked me, and I am far from justifying it; and yet, had the reader been present to witness the excitement and the struggle, he would hardly have been severe in condemning him.[41]

When the younger Ryland thus asked Newton for advice about what he should do with regard to his father's eccentricities, Newton's advice was especially helpful. In a letter dated March 26, 1791, Newton advised Ryland:

I have always admired him [i.e. Ryland Sr.]: his love to the truth and to souls; his zeal and benevolence, have appeared to me, exemplary. His eccentricities and failures have likewise been great, but I think they were constitutional chiefly. He will leave them behind him, with the mortal part, and perhaps the blemishes may be more visible, and his excellencies more clouded the longer he lives.[42]

Again, the following year, on January 31, 1792, when Ryland, Jr. was still disturbed by some of his father's behaviour at times—this time it appears he had publicly criticized his own son—Newton told him:

Poor man, I love and pity him. I am persuaded his most conspicuous failings are strictly constitutional. He acts according to the impetus of his spirits, is hurried away, and I believe he cannot help it. ...I would no more write against such a man, though he is not my father, than I would employ my right hand to wound my left.[43]

Another example of Newton's wise counsel to Ryland is found in relation to Ryland's controversy with the Antinomian author William Huntington (1745–1813), who helped foment a dissension in Ryland's

---

41 *Autobiography of the Rev. William Jay*, eds. Redford and James, 290–291.
42 Letter to John Ryland, March 26, 1791 (Gordon, ed., *Wise Counsel*, 241–242).
43 Letter to John Ryland, January 31, 1792 (Gordon, ed., *Wise Counsel*, 255–256).

church. A popular London preacher whose preaching was a curious and heady mix of bombast, Tory politics and rancorous denunciation of any who dared to criticize him,[44] Huntington played a significant role in the propagation of Antinomian principles in the late eighteenth century. Though he was not a Baptist, numerous Baptists imbibed his argument that the moral law should not be considered as a pattern for the Christian life and that any, like the two Rylands, who did regard it as such were simply nothing more than "Pharisees" and guilty of "undervaluing Christ's imputed righteousness."[45] In the early 1790s, Huntington viciously attacked the elder Ryland and Caleb Evans (1737–1791), principal of Bristol Baptist Academy, in pamphlets. A Mr. Adams from Ryland's congregation sided with Huntington against his pastors and invited him to Northampton to preach. Huntington even had the effrontery to ask Ryland if he could speak from his pulpit! When Adams was eventually disfellowshipped, Huntington wrote an 84-page booklet against the younger Ryland, and the latter's congregation ended up losing slightly more than 20 members—it decreased from 206 in 1782 to 183 in 1792[46]—due to the controversy.

What should Ryland do—should he respond to Huntingdon's pamphlet? Newton's advice was sage and sound. On January 25, 1792, he wrote to Ryland:

---

44 For contrasting perspectives on Huntington, see George M. Ella, *William Huntington: Pastor of Providence* (Darlington: Evangelical Press, 1994) and Robert W. Oliver, *History of the English Calvinistic Baptists 1771–1892: From John Gill to C.H. Spurgeon* (Edinburgh: The Banner of Truth Trust, 2006), 119–145. Huntington went so far as to imply that any who strenuously opposed him would be struck dead by God. See John Ryland, *Serious Remarks on the Different Representations of Evangelical Doctrine by the Professed Friends of the Gospel* (Bristol, 1817), 2:39–41.

45 Robert W. Oliver, "The Emergence of a Strict and Particular Baptist Community among the English Calvinistic Baptists, 1770–1850" (Ph.D. thesis, London Bible College, 1986), 130; John Ryland, *The Practical Influence of Evangelical Religion* (London, 1819), 38. Oliver's thesis is essentially the same as his book, *History of the English Calvinistic Baptists*, though not all of the material in the thesis appears in the book and vice versa.

46 College Lane Churchbook, 134 (Northamptonshire Record Office, Northampton, England).

When you speak, as not being fully determined whether to answer this doughty pamphlet, or not, I am a little alarmed. And as it seems there are some who advise it, I am willing to throw my mite into the opposite scale. But I think if you regard your own character you will pity and pray for the writer in silence. If a chimney-sweeper insulted you in the street, would you demean yourself so low as to fight him? Let him alone, and he will expose himself more effectually than you can expose him. And his performance will soon die and be forgotten, unless you keep the memory of it alive, by an answer. I believe scarcely any thing has conduced [i.e. contributed] so much to perpetuate disputes and dissensions in the professing church, as the ambition of having the last word.

His fan is in his hand [cp. Matthew 3:12]. He has sent a fan to Northampton, to rid you of some chaff. Why should this grieve or displease you? If any simple people whose hearts are better than their heads are drawn away at first, give them time, and the Lord will show them their folly, and deliver them. He knows them that are his.[47]

The following week, Newton gave further advice about the matter:

The embers at Northampton will soon go out, if you do not keep them alive, and blow them up. I have such a love for you and for peace, that, if money would prevent it, I would give something out of my pocket rather than see you degrade yourself, and perplex your people, by answering a performance which deserves no other treatment than silent contempt.[48]

"YOUR AFFECTIONATE FRIEND": COUNSELLING SARAH PEARCE

Finally, let us conclude this chapter with considering what it was like to get a letter from Newton. Well, consider this one that he wrote to Sarah Pearce (d.1805), the widow of Samuel Pearce (1766–1799), the

---

47 Letter to John Ryland, January 25, 1792 (Gordon, ed., *Wise Counsel*, 251–252).
48 Letter to John Ryland, January 31, 1792 (Gordon, ed., *Wise Counsel*, 258).

Birmingham Calvinistic Baptist pastor, a close friend of Ryland and William Carey, and a man for whom Newton had great respect.

Pearce died in October. Newton wrote to his wife on November 4. He had been unable to finish the letter till then due to numerous commitments and various interruptions. He wrote in part:

> My dear Madam,
> I call you Dear, tho' I never saw you, and probably never may in this world; but I trust we shall meet in a better...
> I am well qualified to sympathize with you, under your present affliction, for I likewise had the desire of my Eyes taken away with a stroke. And then I learnt practically what I indeed believed and had often told my hearers, that Our God and Saviour is All-sufficient; but in the time of my trouble, *I found him* so. What before was a Truth in my judgment, then became a truth in my Experience—and since that time, having been so wonderfully supported myself, I almost take it for granted that He will give all who love Him, & walk before him simply in the exercise of Faith and a Good Conscience, strength according to their day.
> I know your trial is great; so was mine. The flesh will feel, & indeed if we did not feel, it would be no trial. The Lord who knows our frame, & whereof we are made, allows to us, by his Apostle, that these things, at the time, are not joyous but grievous; but we are encouraged to hope, that even now they are tokens of his Love, and shall hereafter, by his blessing, yield the peaceful fruit of Righteousness to our souls.
> You are a Widow—yet not strictly so, for Your Maker, Your Redeemer, the Lord of Hosts is still your Husband. Whoever dies He lives. He is unchangeably the same, and because He lives, you shall live also. My friend Ryland informs me that you have five children, but your living Husband knows their Number, and the names of them all. I doubt not but you, and your husband who has lately exchanged Earth for Heaven, and a bed of languishing for a seat near the Throne, offered up many prayers for them, both jointly and separately, and you know the Lord our God is a hearer of prayer. ...Depend upon his promises, Madam, they will bear you up. He has not bid his people seek his face in vain. All

hearts & means are in his hands, and He could as easily provide for fifty children, if you had so many, as for five, or for one.

...Many eyes will now be upon you, and many prayers I doubt not will be offered for you. You are not forgotten in mine. Tho' a stranger to you in the flesh, I trust we are members of the same spiritual Body—as such I feel for you. Seasons of great affliction are especially suitable to experience...and to manifest to others, the power of the Gospel and the Faithfulness [of our] Lord to his promises. When the Bush was on fire, and not consumed, it was a proof that the Lord was there. Thus may He be glorified, & his people encouraged, by your peaceful submission to his Will, and the general tenor of your conduct. Heaven will make abundant amends, for all that we can suffer or lose upon Earth. And even while we are here, our crosses are appointed to work together for our good. Rom. 8.18; 2 Cor. 4.17, 18.

...Your affectionate friend, John Newton.[49]

There is more to the letter, but what a gem of pastoral love and counsel! Little wonder that Newton was recognized in his own day as a spiritual mentor *par excellence*.

A CONCLUDING WORD

John Newton can help us enormously, for this surely is one of our great needs: true shepherds who will mentor and disciple God's people. I personally rejoice in the great recovery in biblical theology, expository preaching and worship that has transpired in the past fifty years. But all of this must be accompanied by a passion for mentoring and shepherding, which will help secure the integrity of these other vital areas of the life of the church.

---

49 Letter to Sarah Pearce, November 4, 1799 (Angus Library, Regent's Park College, University of Oxford).

7

"Co-equal, co-essential, and co-eternal"
Introducing Anne Dutton and her reflections on the Trinity[1]

> [The] Word brake in... upon my heart, with such a ray of glorious light, that directed my soul to the true and proper object of its joy, even the Lord himself.
> —ANNE DUTTON

With the passing of the Act of Toleration on May 24, 1689, religious liberty was guaranteed for various communities outside of the Anglican

---

1 The heart of this lecture was delivered as "The 2017 Baldwin Puritan Lecture," hosted by the J. William Horsey Library at Tyndale University College & Seminary on January 25, 2017. This was subsequently printed as "'Co-Equal, Co-Essential, and

state church, such as the Congregationalists and Particular Baptists, and a religious pluralism was enshrined within the make-up of English society. Although the Act did not provide such liberty for Anti-Trinitarians, the following decade of the 1690s saw the beginning of a profound Trinitarian controversy that raged on and off throughout the "long" eighteenth century. Contrary to the impression given by various recent historical overviews of the doctrine of the Trinity, the late seventeenth and eighteenth centuries were actually replete with critical battles over Trinitarianism.[2]

The ancient church's doctrine of the Trinity, encapsulated in the Niceno-Constantinopolitan Creed of A.D. 381, had remained basically unchallenged until the seventeenth century. Even during the theological tumult of the Reformation, this vital area of Christian belief did not come into general dispute, though there were a few, like Michael Servetus (1511–1553) and the Italians, Lelio Francesco Sozzini (1525–1562) and his nephew Fausto Sozzini (1539–1604), who rejected Trinitarianism for a Unitarian perspective on the Godhead. However, as Sarah Mortimer has argued in her ground-breaking study of seventeenth-century English Socinianism, in the century after the Reformation the Socinian understanding of human beings as "inquiring, reasoning and active individuals who must take responsibility for their own spiritual lives" did come to play a critical role in undermining the way that Trinitarian communities in England had established theological boundaries for themselves.[3] This was part of a growing tide of rationalism in the seventeenth and eighteenth centuries that led to what Philip Dixon has termed a "fading of the trinitarian imagination"

Co-Eternal': Introducing Anne Dutton and her Reflections on the Trinity," *Midwestern Journal of Theology*, 16, no. 2 (Fall 2017): 79–93. Used by permission.

Most of Dutton's works have survived in only a few copies. Thankfully her works are currently available in a series of volumes compiled by JoAnn Ford Watson, *Selected Spiritual Writings of Anne Dutton: Eighteenth-Century, British-Baptist, Woman Theologian*, 7 vols. (Macon: Mercer University Press, 2003–2015).

2   For an exception, see Stephen R. Holmes, *The Quest for the Trinity: The Doctrine of God in Scripture, History, and Modernity* (Downers Grove: IVP Academic, 2012), 170–181.

3   Sarah Mortimer, *Reason and Religion in the English Revolution. The Challenge of Socinianism* (Cambridge: Cambridge University Press, 2010), 240–241.

and to the doctrine coming under heavy attack.⁴ Informed by the Enlightenment's confidence in the "omnicompetence" of human reason, increasingly the intellectual *mentalité* of this era either dismissed the doctrine of the Trinity as a philosophical and unbiblical construct of the post-apostolic church, and turned to classical Arianism as an alternate perspective, or simply ridiculed it as utterly illogical and argued for Deism or Socinianism.⁵

Now, a number of key Particular Baptist authors like John Gill, Caleb Evans and Andrew Fuller, were deeply involved in this controversy about God's being and penned significant treatises in defence of his Triunity. However, one Particular Baptist author, who also wrote on this subject and who has been generally overlooked, is Anne Dutton. Following an introduction to Dutton's life and writing, this article will focus on her discussion of Trinitarian ontology in her tract *A Letter on the Divine Eternal Sonship of Jesus Christ: As the Second Person in the Ever-blessed Three-one God* (1757), written in response to a work by the Anglican evangelical William Romaine.⁶

INTRODUCING ANNE DUTTON

Anne Dutton was born Anne Williams to godly Congregationalist parents in 1692 in Northampton, the East Midlands.⁷ Her conversion

---

4 See especially William C. Placher, *The Domestication of Transcendence. How Modern Thinking about God Went Wrong* (Louisville: Westminster John Knox Press, 1996), 164–178; Philip Dixon, *'Nice and Hot Disputes': The Doctrine of the Trinity in the Seventeenth Century* (London: T&T Clark, 2003). The quote from Dixon can be found at 'Nice and Hot Disputes', 212.

5 G.L. Bray, "Trinity," in *New Dictionary of Theology*, eds. Sinclair B. Ferguson, David F. Wright, and J.I. Packer (Downers Grove: InterVarsity Press, 1988), 694.

6 Anne Dutton, *A Letter on the Divine Eternal Sonship of Jesus Christ: As the Second Person in the Ever-blessed Three-one God* (London: J. Hart, 1757).

7 For Dutton's life and thought, see especially J.C. Whitebrook, "The Life and Works of Mrs. Ann Dutton," *Transactions of the Baptist Historical Society*, 7, nos. 3–4 (1921): 129–146; Stephen J. Stein, "A Note on Anne Dutton, Eighteenth-Century Evangelical," *Church History*, 44 (1975): 485–491; Michael D. Sciretti, Jr., " 'Feed My Lambs': The Spiritual Direction Ministry of Calvinistic British Baptist Anne Dutton During the Early Years of the Evangelical Revival" (PhD thesis, Baylor University, 2009).

The sketch of her early life that follows is dependent in part on Sciretti, "Feed My Lambs," 48–115. For her own account of her conversion, which she detailed in her *A*

came at the age of thirteen after a serious illness.[8] Two years later, in 1707, she joined the Congregationalist church, although she wrestled with doubt and various fears as a young believer. Subsequently, though, she experienced a significant encounter with the Holy Spirit that she interpreted as the sealing of the Spirit—a phrase derived from such Pauline texts as Ephesians 1:13 and 4:30. As she later recalled the experience, the Spirit used Philippians 4:4 ("Rejoice in the Lord always: and again I say rejoice," KJV) in his sealing of her heart:

> [This] Word brake in...upon my heart, with such a ray of glorious light, that directed my soul to the true and proper object of its joy, even the Lord himself. I was pointed thereto, as with a finger: In the *Lord*, not in your *frames*. *In* the Lord, not in what you enjoy *from* him, but in what you are in *him*. And the Lord seal'd my instruction, and fill'd my heart brim-full of joy, in the faith of my eternal interest, and unchangeable standing in *him*; and of *his* being an infinite fountain of blessedness, for me to rejoice in alway; even when the streams of sensible enjoyments fail'd. Thus the Blessed Spirit took me by the arms, and taught me to go.
>
> ...the Lord the Spirit went on to reveal Christ more and more to me, as the great foundation of my faith and joy. He shew'd me my everlasting standing in his person, grace and righteousness: and gave me to see my security in his unchangeableness, under all the changes which pass'd over me. And then I began to rejoice in my dear Lord Jesus, as always the *same*, even when my frames *alter'd*.[9]

In other words, Dutton learned to put her faith in Christ alone, and not in her experience of him. Her beliefs about the sealing of the Spirit were probably derived from reading the works of the Puritan Thomas Goodwin.[10]

Brief Account of the Gracious Dealings of God, with a Poor, Sinful, Unworthy Creature (1743), see Watson, comp., *Selected Spiritual Writings of Anne Dutton*, 3:8–27.

8 Sciretti, "Feed My Lambs," 51–53.

9 Dutton, *A Brief Account of the Gracious Dealings of God* in Watson, comp., *Selected Spiritual Writings of Anne Dutton*, 3:27–28. I have modernized Dutton's capitalization of words in her writings, which Watson retained.

10 On Goodwin's influence on Dutton, see Sciretti, "Feed My Lambs," 62.

Anne Dutton
(1692–1765)

In 1710, she transferred her church affiliation to an open-membership Baptist church in Northampton, pastored at the time by John Moore (1662–1726).[11] There, in her words, she found "fat, green pastures," for, as she went on to explain, "Mr. Moore was a great doctrinal preacher: and the special advantage I receiv'd under his ministry, was the establishment of my judgment in the doctrines of the gospel."[12] It was in this congregation that she was baptized as a believer around 1713.[13]

When she was twenty-two in 1715, she married a Thomas Cattell, and moved with her husband to London. While there she worshipped with the Calvinistic Baptist church that met at a premises on Wood Street in the Cripplegate region.[14] Founded by Hanserd Knollys (1599–1691), this work had known some rough times in the days immediately prior to Dutton's coming to the church. David Crosley (1669–1744), an evangelist from the Pennine hills in Northern England, had been the pastor of the work from 1705 to 1709, but he had been disfellowshipped for drunkenness, unchaste conduct with women and lying to the church about these matters when accused.[15] The sorrow and sense of betrayal, disappointment and consternation in the church would have run deep. It was not until 1714 that the church succeeded in finding a new pastor. John Skepp (d.1721), a member of the Cambridge

---

11 On Moore, see Sciretti, "Feed My Lambs," 59–60, n. 42.

12 Dutton, *A Brief Account of the Gracious Dealings of God*, in Watson, comp., *Selected Spiritual Writings of Anne Dutton*, 3:47, 50.

13 Sciretti, "Feed My Lambs," 64–65.

14 On this church's history during this period, see Murdina D. MacDonald, "London Calvinistic Baptists 1689–1727: Tensions within a Dissenting Community under Toleration" (DPhil thesis, Regent's Park College, Oxford, 1982), 109–131.

15 For his story, see the small study by B.A. Ramsbottom, *The Puritan Samson: The Life of David Crosley 1669–1744* (Harpenden: Gospel Standard Trust Publications, 1991). See also details in MacDonald, "London Calvinistic Baptists 1689–1727," 118–119. Crosley genuinely repented, and years later, having lived a life in accord with genuine repentance, he would know some usefulness again in the Lord's work. He carried on a correspondence with George Whitefield, who noted that their "sentiments as the essential doctrines of the gospel, exactly harmonize[d]" and who wrote a commendatory preface for a sermon Crosley published on Samson. See George Whitefield, "Preface to the Reader," in David Crosley, *Samson a Type of Christ* (London 1744 ed.; repr. Newburyport: William Barrett, 1796), iii.

Congregationalist church of Joseph Hussey (1659–1726), was called that year to be the pastor.

Now, Hussey is often seen as the father of hyper-Calvinism, insomuch as he argued in his book *God's Operations of Grace but no Offers of Grace* (1707) that offering Christ indiscriminately to sinners is something that smacks of "creature-co-operation and creature-concurrence" in the work of salvation. Skepp published but one book, and that posthumously, which was entitled *Divine Energy: or The Efficacious Operations of the Spirit of God upon the Soul of Man* (1722). In it he appears to have followed Hussey's approach to evangelism. It is sometimes argued that Anne Dutton's exposure to hyper-Calvinism at a young age shaped her thinking for the rest of her life. If so, it is curious to find her rejoicing in the ministry of free-offer preachers like George Whitefield in later years.

Skepp, though, was an impressive preacher, owing in part to what Dutton called his "quickness of thought, aptness of expression, suitable affection, and a most agreeable delivery."[16] Despite his refusal to freely offer the gospel to all and sundry, the overall trend in the church during his ministry was one of growth. There were 179 members when he came as pastor in 1714. When he died in 1721, the church's membership had grown to 212.[17]

In the early months of 1719, though, Dutton's life underwent a deep trial as her husband of but five or six years died.[18] She returned to her family in Northampton, and found herself wrestling with spiritual depression. In her words, Dutton sought God "in his ordinances, in one place and another; but alas! I found him not."[19] She was not long single, however. A second marriage in the middle months of 1720 was to Benjamin Dutton (1691–1747), a clothier who had studied for vocational ministry in various places, among them Glasgow University.

---

16 Dutton, *A Brief Account of the Gracious Dealings of God*, in Watson, comp., *Selected Spiritual Writings of Anne Dutton*, 3:51.

17 MacDonald, "London Calvinistic Baptists 1689–1727," 124.

18 Dutton, *A Brief Account of the Gracious Dealings of God*, in Watson, comp., *Selected Spiritual Writings of Anne Dutton*, 3:63–64.

19 Dutton, *A Brief Account of the Gracious Dealings of God*, in Watson, comp., *Selected Spiritual Writings of Anne Dutton*, 3:70.

Anne and Benjamin had met in the final months of 1719 and within a year they were wed.[20]

Ministry took the couple to such towns as Whittlesey and Wisbech in Cambridgeshire, before leading them finally in 1731 to a Particular Baptist congregation in Great Gransden, Huntingdonshire, in 1733.[21] It is noteworthy that prior to this call to Great Gransden, Benjamin Dutton had wrestled with alcoholism. But the Lord delivered him completely around the time of the move to Great Gransden. In his own words, he said that he now "stood not in need of wine, or strong drink. The Lord also, of his great goodness, took away my inclination thereto; so that I had no more *inclination* to it, or desire after it, than if I had never tasted any in my whole life."[22]

Under Benjamin Dutton's preaching the church flourished so that on any given Sunday the congregation numbered anywhere between 250 and 350, of whom roughly 50 were members. This growth led to the building of a new meeting-house, which can still be seen in the village. Benjamin decided to go to America to help raise funds to pay off the debt incurred in the building of the meeting-house but the ship on which he was returning foundered not far from the British coast in 1747, and Dutton was drowned. He had sent the money he had raised by means of another ship, however, so that at least was not lost.

"A TALENT FOR WRITING"
Widowed now for the second time, Anne Dutton was to live another eighteen years. During that time "the fame of her…piety," as Baptist historian Joseph Ivimey (1773–1834) once referred to her spirituality,[23] became known in evangelical circles on both sides of the Atlantic and that through various literary publications.

Dutton had been writing for a number of years before her second husband's demise. After his death a steady stream of tracts and treatises, collections of selected correspondence and poems poured forth

---

20 Sciretti, "Feed My Lambs," 76–77.
21 For a brief history of the church, see Joseph Ivimey, *A History of the English Baptists* (London: Isaac Taylor Hinston and Holdsworth & Ball, 1830), 4:509–510.
22 Cited Sciretti, "Feed My Lambs," 91–92.
23 Ivimey, *History of the English Baptists*, 4:510.

from her pen. Among her numerous correspondents were a number of key figures in the eighteenth-century evangelical revival: the Welsh preacher Howel Harris, the redoubtable Selina Hastings, the Countess of Huntingdon, and George Whitefield.[24] Harris was convinced that the Lord had entrusted her "with a talent of writing for him."[25] When William Seward (1711–1740), an early Methodist preacher who was killed by a mob in Wales, read a letter she had written to him in May, 1739, he found it "full of such comforts and direct answers to what I had been writing that it filled my eyes with tears of joy."[26] And Whitefield, who helped promote and publish Dutton's writings, once said after a meeting with her: "her conversation is as weighty as her letters."[27]

By 1740 she had written seven books. Another fourteen followed between 1741 and 1743, and fourteen more by 1750.[28] And there were yet more, for she continued to write up until her death in 1765. She was clearly the most prolific female Baptist author of the eighteenth century. But she wrestled with whether it was biblical for her to be an authoress. In a tract entitled *A Letter To such of the Servants of Christ, who May have any Scruples about the Lawfulness of Printing any Thing written by a Woman* (1743), she maintained that she wrote not for fame, but for "only the glory of God, and the good of souls."[29] To those who might accuse of her violating 1 Timothy 2:12, she answered that her books were not intended to be read in a public setting of worship, which the 1 Timothy text was designed to address. Rather, the instruction that her books gave was private, for they were read by believers in "their own private houses."[30] She asked those who opposed women

---

24 See the discussion of these links by Stein, "A Note on Anne Dutton," 485–490, and Sciretti, "Feed My Lambs," 198–280.

25 Cited Stein, "A Note on Anne Dutton," 487–488.

26 Cited Stein, "A Note on Anne Dutton," 488.

27 George Whitefield, Letter to Mr. [Jonathan] B[ryan], July 24, 1741 in *Letters of George Whitefield For the period 1734–1742* (1771 ed.; repr. Edinburgh: The Banner of Truth Trust, 1976), 280.

28 Sciretti, "Feed My Lambs," 100–101.

29 Anne Dutton, *A Letter To such of the Servants of Christ, who May have any Scruples about the Lawfulness of Printing any Thing written by a Woman*, in Watson, comp., *Selected Spiritual Writings of Anne Dutton*, 3:254.

30 Dutton, *Printing any Thing written by a Woman*, in Watson, comp., *Selected Spiritual Writings of Anne Dutton*, 3:254.

writers to "Imagine then...when my books come to your house, that I am come to give you a visit" and to "patiently attend" to her infant "lispings."[31] What if some other authoresses had used the press for "trifles"? Well, she answered, "shall none of that sex be suffer'd to appear on Christ's side, to tell of the wonders of his love, to seek the good of souls, and the advancement of the Redeemer's interest?"[32]

TALKING/WRITING ABOUT THE TRINITY

Dutton was not slow to critique theological positions she felt erroneous or inadequate. In 1757, for example, she happened to read William Romaine's *A Discourse upon the Self-Existence of Jesus Christ* (1755). Romaine, at the time the only evangelical Anglican clergyman in the English capital,[33] had preached this sermon on John 8:24 ("I said therefore unto you, that ye shall die in your sins: for if ye believe not, that I am, ye shall die in your sins") two years earlier and had it published the same year. In the published version Romaine gave a powerful defence of the essential deity of Jesus Christ—and thus a rebuttal of two major heresies of the eighteenth century, Socinianism and Deism—and was also insistent that the "doctrine of the Trinity is the most necessary article of the Christian religion."[34] It went through at least five editions in the 1750s and was still being reprinted as late as 1788 (the seventh edition).

In one portion of the sermon, though, Dutton believed that Romaine's language smacked of Sabellianism, or modalism. Romaine

---

31 Dutton, *Printing any Thing written by a Woman*, in Watson, comp., *Selected Spiritual Writings of Anne Dutton*, 3:257.

32 Dutton, *Printing any Thing written by a Woman*, in Watson, comp., *Selected Spiritual Writings of Anne Dutton*, 3:256.

33 On Romaine, see especially Tim Shenton, *'An Iron Pillar': The Life and Times of William Romaine* (Darlington: Evangelical Press, 2004). See also the classic account of Romaine's life and ministry by J.C. Ryle, *The Christian Leaders of the Last Century; or, England a Hundred Years Ago* (London: T. Nelson and Sons, 1880), 149–179.

34 William Romaine, *A Discourse upon the Self-Existence of Jesus Christ* (4th ed.; London: J. Worrall and E. Withers, 1756), 19. For the historical context of the sermon, see Shenton, *'An Iron Pillar'*, 127–129. I first read this sermon by Romaine in November of 2003, and felt then that Romaine did not clearly distinguish his conception of the Godhead from modalism.

was replying to critics of the nomenclature used to describe the persons of the Godhead, namely, Father, Son and Holy Spirit:

> They suppose, with ignorance common to infidelity, that these names were to give us ideas of the manner, in which the persons exist in the essence [of God], but the Scripture had quite a different view in using them. The ever blessed Trinity took the names of Father, Son, and Holy Spirit, not to describe in what manner they exist as divine persons, but in what manner the divine persons have acted for us, and for our salvation. These names were to give us ideas of the distinct offices, which the Trinity had agreed to sustain in the œconomy of our redemption. The Scripture informs us...that the covenant of grace was made before the world, and the gracious plan of man's salvation was settled before he had his being. According to the plan of this covenant one of the divine persons agreed to demand infinite satisfaction for sin, when mankind should offend, and to be the Father of the human nature of Jesus Christ, and our Father through him; and therefore he is called God the Father, not to describe his nature, but his office. Another of the divine persons covenanted to become a son, to take our nature upon him, and in it to pay the infinite satisfaction for sin, and therefore he is called Son, Son of God, and such like names, not to describe his divine nature, but his divine office. Another of the divine persons covenanted to make the infinite satisfaction of the Son of God effectual, by inspiring the spirits of men, and disposing them to receive it, and therefore he is called the holy Inspirer, or Holy Spirit, and the Spirit of God, not to describe his divine nature but his divine office. The terms Father, Son, and Holy Spirit, are terms of œconomy and are accordingly used in Scripture, to describe the distinct parts, which the ever blessed and adorable Trinity sustained in our redemption.
> ...The Scripture makes no difference between the divine persons, except what is made by the distinct offices, which they sustain in the covenant of grace. The persons are equal in every perfection and attribute; none is before or after other; none is greater or less than another; but the whole three persons are

> co-eternal together and co-equal. And consequently Christ, who was from eternity co-equal with the Father, did not make himself inferior, because he covenanted to become a Son, nor did the Holy Spirit, who was from eternity co-equal with the Father and the Son, make himself inferior, because he covenanted to make the spirits of men holy by his grace and influence. Son and Holy Spirit are names of office, and the names of their offices certainly cannot lessen the dignity of their nature, but should rather exalt them in our eyes, for whose salvation they condescended to sustain these offices. [35]

This text more than adequately displays Romaine's commitment to the affirmation that there are three persons within the Godhead and that these three persons are absolutely co-equal and co-eternal. But it is noteworthy that Romaine does not attempt to distinguish the divine persons by classical patristic terms, namely, the Father's ingenerateness, the Son's eternal generation and the Holy Spirit's eternal procession. In fact, he appears to argue against this way of distinguishing the divine persons. The divine persons are to be differentiated on the basis of the roles that they play in the economy of salvation. The term "Son," for example, says nothing about his divine nature, but about the office he bore to effect the salvation of sinners. Likewise, the name "Holy Spirit" says nothing about his relationship to the other two persons of the Godhead, but has to do with the way he persuades sinners to believe in Christ.

When Dutton read Romaine's sermon, she was "loth to think" that Romaine was not truly Trinitarian, but she was convinced that he had "given great countenance to the Sabellian error." The above-cited text essentially distinguished the divine persons solely on the basis of their work in salvation.[36] Dutton thus asked whether or not "the three divine persons...were not Father, Son, and Spirit, prior to their agreeing to act" in eternity past for the salvation of fallen humanity?[37]

---

35 Romaine, *Discourse upon the Self-Existence of Jesus Christ*, 18–20.
36 Dutton, *Divine Eternal Sonship of Jesus Christ*, 4–5.
37 Dutton, *Divine Eternal Sonship of Jesus Christ*, 6.

She then indicated how she would distinguish the persons by means of classical Nicene Trinitarian terminology:

> Those proper names, by which these divine persons are described in the Holy Scriptures, are doubtless descriptive, if not of their nature, as God; yet of their distinct subsistences in, and as possessing of the divine essence, with their mutual relations to each other therein. So that the first divine person, with respect to his begetting the second divine person, is called the Father, and to beget his Son, is the peculiar property of God the Father. The second divine person, with respect to his ineffable and eternal generation, in the divine essence, is called the Son; and to be the only-begotten of the Father, is the peculiar property of God the Son. And the third divine person with respect to his proceeding from the Father and the Son, in the divine essence, is called the Spirit; and to proceed from both, as the Spirit of the Father and the Son, is the peculiar property of God the Spirit. And tho' there is no priority, nor posteriority, among these divine persons: so that one was before, and another after the other, and a third after both, with regard to the order of time; but each of these three divine subsistences, did together and at once necessarily exist in the eternal self-existent essence of Jehovah. Yet I humbly think, that we may, yea, must conceive, according to the Scripture-names given to these divine persons, with their relative properties, that there was priority, and posteriority, with respect to the order of nature. And yet this infers not any superiority, nor inferiority, among the divine persons: in that the three distinct subsistences, do jointly possess, all the immense and eternal glories, of the one undivided, infinite essence of Jehovah...in which these three divine persons are co-equal, co-essential, and co-eternal.[38]

Like Romaine, Dutton affirmed her conviction that the three divine persons are "co-equal, co-essential, and co-eternal." The three are "undivided" and share to the full the "infinite essence" of deity. Unlike Romaine, however, Dutton was not chary about using the patristic

---

38 Dutton, *Divine Eternal Sonship of Jesus Christ*, 6–7, 8.

language of generation and procession to distinguish the three persons. The different names used in the Bible of the three persons speak of eternal relationships in which there is no sense of lesser or greater, but which nonetheless speak of an order: only the Father could beget the Son, only the Son could be begotten, and only the Spirit could proceed from both the Father and the Son. Contrary to the implications of Romaine's explanation of the divine names, these relationships are not arbitrary. As Dutton sums up her position:

> …the Son's being begotten of the Father, and the Spirit's proceeding from both, makes no superiority, nor inferiority, among the divine persons, as each possess the same infinite essence; but only denotes the particular manner and order, in which the divine essence necessarily exists.[39]

To Dutton's way of thinking, to deny that the divine names describe the "distinct subsistences in the divine essence" is "nothing less than to rob them of their personality; and so, of their divine glory."[40]

TWO OTHER BAPTIST CRITIQUES

It is noteworthy that Dutton's younger Baptist contemporary, Benjamin Beddome (1717–1795), the pastor of the Particular Baptist cause in Bourton-on-the-Water, was also familiar with this idiosyncrasy of Romaine's Trinitarian theology. In a sermon on Mark 12:28–31 that Romaine published in 1760, the Anglican minister had stated:

> The right knowledge of God then consists in believing, that in Jehovah the self-existence essence there are three co-equal and co-eternal persons, between whom there is no difference or inequality, but what is made by the covenant of grace. Their names Father, Son, and Holy Spirit, are not descriptive of their nature, but of their offices, they are not to teach us in what manner they exist in Jehovah, but they are covenant names, belonging to the offices, which the divine persons sustain in the covenant.

---

39 Dutton, *Divine Eternal Sonship of Jesus Christ*, 14.
40 Dutton, *Divine Eternal Sonship of Jesus Christ*, 8.

The scripture does not use these names to teach us, how the divine persons exist, but how they act; how they stand related to the heirs of promise, and not what they are in themselves, as persons in Jehovah. This is a truth of great importance, which I have endeavoured to defend both from the pulpit and from the press, and particularly in a printed discourse upon the self-existence of Jesus Christ. The true object of worship then, to whom our obedience and love are due, is Jehovah Alehim,[41] according to what is said in the Creed, "the unity in Trinity and the Trinity in unity is to be worshipped."[42]

In an undated sermon entitled *Christ manifested to the soul*,[43] Beddome cited this very passage and then noted that "others contend"—was he aware of Dutton's critique of Romaine?—that the term "Son" is

a title belonging to Christ as the second Person in the ever-blessed Trinity, and expressive of both of equality of essence, and the peculiar relation in which he stands to the Divine Father; and that this is an article of faith which enters into the experience and worship of God's people.[44]

Beddome himself was of the opinion that the term "Son" could "be understood in both these senses" in "different passages of Scripture."[45]
The doyen of Baptist theology in this era, John Gill,[46] was also quite

---

41 Alehim here would appear to be Romaine's term for what is now transliterated as *Elohim*.
42 William Romaine, "Upon the right Love of the Lord God," in his *Twelve Discourses upon the Law and the Gospel. Preached at St. Dunstan's Church in the West, London* (London: J. Worrall and M. Withers, 1760), 262–263.
43 In Benjamin Beddome, *Sermons Printed from the Manuscripts of the Late Rev. Benjamin Beddome, A.M.* (London: William Ball, 1835), 119–127. I owe this reference to my doctoral student, Rev. Daniel Ramsey of Cleveland, Ohio.
44 *Sermons Printed from the Manuscripts of the Late Rev. Benjamin Beddome*, 119.
45 *Sermons Printed from the Manuscripts of the Late Rev. Benjamin Beddome*, 119.
46 The standard biographical sketch of Gill is John Rippon, *A Brief Memoir of the Life and Writings of the late Rev. John Gill, D. D.* (repr. Harrisonburg: Gano Books, 1992). For more recent studies of Gill and his theology, see Graham Harrison, *Dr. John Gill and His Teaching*, Annual Lecture of The Evangelical Library (London: The Evangelical

critical of the sort of Trinitarian reflection proposed by Romaine. He did not mention him by name, but it is unlikely he was not acquainted with his views as both men ministered in the English capital during the 1750s and 1760s. In fact, on one occasion during the early to mid-1750s, Gill had breakfast with Romaine, along with Gill's friend James Hervey, George Whitefield and John Wesley.[47] For Gill, the eternal sonship of Christ, and thus his eternal generation, "is an article of the greatest importance in the Christian religion," even its "distinguishing criterion," without which "the doctrine of the Trinity can never be supported."[48] As Gill argued in his systematic theology, published in 1769, without eternal sonship (and the eternal spiration of the Spirit), there is nothing to distinguish the different persons within the Godhead in eternity past:

> Those men I have now respect to, hold that there are three distinct persons in the Godhead, or divine nature; and therefore it must be something in the divine nature, and not any thing out of it, that distinguishes them; not any works *ad extra*, done by them; nor their concern in the economy of man's salvation; nor office bore by them, which are arbitrary things, which might, or might not have been, had it pleased God...[49]

Gill especially took aim at the thinking of the Congregationalist Thomas Ridgley (1667–1734), who maintained a position identical to that of Romaine: sonship has to do with the office of mediator, not the

---

Library, 1971); Tom Nettles, *By His Grace and for His Glory: A Historical, Theological, and Practical Study of the Doctrines of Grace in Baptist Life* (Grand Rapids: Baker Book House, 1986), 73–107, *passim*; George M. Ella, *John Gill and the Cause of God and Truth* (Eggleston: Go Publications, 1995); Michael A.G. Haykin, ed., *The Life and Thought of John Gill (1697–1771): A Tercentennial Appreciation* (Leiden: E.J. Brill, 1997); and Timothy George, "John Gill," in his and David S. Dockery, ed., *Theologians of the Baptist Tradition* (rev. ed.; Nashville: Broadman & Holman, 2001), 11–33.

47 Aaron C. H. Seymour, *The Life and Times of Selina Countess of Huntingdon* (London: William Edward Painter, 1840), 1:162.

48 John Gill, *A Complete Body of Doctrinal and Practical Divinity* (new ed.; London: W. Winterbotham, 1796), 1:209, 210.

49 Gill, *Body of Doctrinal and Practical Divinity*, 1:205, 207.

internal relationship of the first and second persons of the Godhead.[50] As Gill responded to Ridgley—and he would have said the same to Romaine: without the Son's eternal generation "no proof can be made of his being a distinct divine person in the Godhead."[51]

CODA

There were at least three reprints of Romaine's *A Discourse upon the Self-Existence of Jesus Christ* after Dutton's robust critique, but his argument remained unaltered. It is possible he was unaware of her letter, but her friendship with fellow evangelicals like Whitefield, who also knew Romaine well, makes this unlikely.[52] Did the Anglican preacher believe then that Dutton's criticism was not worth answering? If so, he would have been very mistaken. Dutton was indeed right to critique his failure to use classic terminology to differentiate the three within the Godhead. In his sermon, Romaine had rightly asserted: "The doctrine of the Trinity is the most necessary article of the Christian religion, and we cannot take one step in the way to heaven, without being clear in it."[53] Dutton's letter provided a clarity that Romaine's sermon—and one might add, current quarters of evangelicalism—greatly needed.

---

50 See Gill, *Body of Doctrinal and Practical Divinity*, 1:210–212. For the text that Gill is criticizing, see Thomas Ridgley, *A Body of Divinity* (London: Daniel Midwinter, Aaron Ward, John Oswald; and Richard Hett, 1731), 121–131.
51 Gill, *Body of Doctrinal and Practical Divinity*, 1:210.
52 For Romaine's friendship with Whitefield, see Shenton, 'An Iron Pillar', 167–169.
53 *Romaine, Discourse upon the Self-Existence of Jesus Christ*, 19.

8

"Eminent spirituality" & "eminent usefulness"
True spirituality according to Andrew Fuller

> Truth learned only at second-hand will be to us what Saul's armour was to David; we shall be at a loss how to use it in the day of trial.—ANDREW FULLER[1]

The most common interpretative grid for understanding English Calvinistic Baptist life and theology in the eighteenth century is an ecclesial one. Due to the ecclesiological differences between the Calvinistic Baptists and other Dissenting communities, like those of the Presbyterians and Congregationalists, it is often assumed that the

---

1 Andrew Fuller, *Intimate Knowledge of Divine Truth* in *The Complete Works*, ed. Joseph Belcher (3rd London ed.; repr. Harrisonburg: Sprinkle Publications, 1988), I, 64.

best way to understand these Baptists is by focusing on issues of church polity. Ecclesiological distinctives did set the Calvinistic Baptists apart from these other Christian communities during this era, but these distinctives were penultimate. As B.B. Warfield and others have stressed, the Puritans and their heirs—that is, the Calvinistic Baptists, Presbyterians and Congregationalists—were men and women whose ultimate ardency was about the Christian experience of the Holy Spirit. As such, pneumatological concerns and spirituality are at the core of eighteenth-century English Calvinistic Baptist experience.[2]

"THE DIVINE SPIRIT" AND "DIVINE ORDINANCES"

Many Calvinistic Baptists in this era were thus adamant that keeping in step with the Spirit was *the* vital matter when it came to the nourishment of the believer's soul or the sustenance of a congregation's inner life. As John Sutcliff (1752–1814) of Olney, Buckinghamshire, observed:

> …the outpouring of the divine Spirit…is the grand promise of the New Testament.… His influences are the soul, the great animating soul of all religion. These withheld, divine ordinances are empty cisterns, and spiritual graces are withering flowers. These suspended, the greatest human abilities labour in vain, and the noblest efforts fail of success.[3]

On another occasion Sutcliff made the same point thus:

---

2 B.B. Warfield, "Introductory Note" to Abraham Kuyper, *The Work of the Holy Spirit* (1900 ed.; repr. Grand Rapids: Eerdmans, 1956), xxxv, xxviii. See also the discussions by Irvonwy Morgan, *Puritan Spirituality* (London: Epworth Press, 1973), 53–65; Dewey D. Wallace, Jr., *The Spirituality of the Later English Puritans: An Anthology* (Macon: Mercer University Press, 1987), xi–xiv; Garth B. Wilson, "Doctrine of the Holy Spirit in the Reformed Tradition: A Critical Overview," in George Vandervelde, ed., *The Holy Spirit: Renewing and Empowering Presence* (Winfield: Wood Lake Books, 1989), 57–62; J.I. Packer, *A Quest for Godliness: The Puritan Vision of the Christian Life* (Wheaton: Crossway Books, 1990), 37–38. In an older work on the Holy Spirit, published in 1882, George Smeaton observed: "Except where Puritan influences are still at work, we may safely affirm that the doctrine of the Spirit is almost entirely ignored." George Smeaton, *The Doctrine of the Holy Spirit* (1882 ed.; repr. London: The Banner of Truth Trust, 1958), 1.

3 John Sutcliff, *Jealousy for the Lord of Hosts Illustrated* (London: W. Button, 1791), 12.

Be earnest with God for the gift of his Holy Spirit, in an abundant measure. Seek his divine influences, to furnish you with *spiritual* ability, in order that you may be found in the discharge of that which is your indispensible [sic] duty. Highly prize his sacred operations. These are the real excellency of all religious duties.[4]

Eighteenth-century Calvinistic Baptist life and thought was clearly marked by what Richard Lovelace has termed "a theology of radical dependence on the Spirit."[5]

Yet, these Baptists were also certain that to seek the Spirit's strength apart from the various means through which the Spirit normally worked was both unbiblical and foolish. Benjamin Keach, the most significant Baptist theologian at the cusp of the eighteenth century, put it this way in 1681, when, in an allusion to the Quakers, who dispensed with the ordinances of baptism and the Lord's Supper, he declared:

> Many are confident they have the Spirit, Light, and Power, when 'tis all meer [sic] Delusion. ...Some Men boast of the Spirit, and conclude they have the Spirit, and none but they, and yet at the same time cry down and villify his blessed Ordinances and Institutions, which he hath left in his Word, carefully to be observed and kept, till he comes the second time without Sin unto Salvation. ...The Spirit hath its proper Bounds, and always runs in its spiritual Chanel [sic], viz. The Word and Ordinances, God's publick [sic] and private Worship...[6]

Keach mentions three central vehicles that the Holy Spirit uses to shape God's people: the Word and the ordinances of baptism and the Lord's Supper. Benjamin Beddome, pastor of the Baptist cause in Bourton-on-the-Water, Gloucestershire, and whose life spanned most

---

4 John Sutcliff, *The Authority and Sanctification of the Lord's-Day, Explained and Enforced* (Circular Letter of the Northamptonshire Association, 1786), 8.

5 Richard Lovelace, "Pneumatological Issues in American Presbyterianism," *Greek Orthodox Theological Review*, 31 (1986): 345–346.

6 Benjamin Keach, *Tropologia: A Key to Open Scripture-Metaphors* (London: Enoch Prosser, 1681), II, 312, 314.

of the eighteenth century, discerned in the phrase "Draw nigh unto my soul" (Psalm 69:18) five ways in which God draws near to his people, three of which are identical to the means of spiritual formation listed by Keach. God draws near to us and we to him, Beddome said, in prayer, in "hearing the Word," in the ordinances of baptism and the Lord's Supper, and also, he added, in "the time of affliction" and death.[7]

"THE FIRE OF DEVOTION"

These twin foci of Calvinistic Baptist spirituality—the Holy Spirit and the means of grace or spiritual formation—are also prominent in the works of the leading Baptist divine of the late eighteenth century, Andrew Fuller. The nineteenth-century Welsh author David Phillips aptly described Fuller as the "elephant of Kettering,"[8] an allusion to his weighty theological influence in both his own day and throughout the century following his death. Charles Haddon Spurgeon (1834–1892) considered him to be "the greatest theologian" of his century,[9] and the Southern Baptist historian A.H. Newman, who taught church history at McMaster University from 1881 to 1901, on one occasion commented that Fuller's "influence on American Baptists" was "incalculable" for good.[10]

Fuller wrote major theological works on a variety of issues, many of them in the area of apologetics. For instance, he wrote refutations of such eighteenth-century theological aberrations as Socinianism (or Unitarianism) and Sandemanianism, and in 1799 published the definitive eighteenth-century Baptist response to Deism.[11] But it was through

---

7 Benjamin Beddome, *Communion with God our Security and Bliss* in his *Sermons printed from the manuscripts of the late Rev. Benjamin Beddome, A.M.* (London: William Ball, 1835), 399–401.

8 David Phillips, *Memoir of the Life, Labors, and Extensive Usefulness of the Rev. Christmas Evans* (New York: M.W. Dodd, 1843), 74.

9 Cited Gilbert Laws, *Andrew Fuller, Pastor, Theologian, Ropeholder* (London: Carey Press, 1942), 127.

10 "Fuller, Andrew," in Samuel Macauley Jackson, et al. ed., *The New Schaff-Herzog Encyclopedia of Religious Knowledge* (New York: Funk and Wagnalls Co., 1909), 4:409.

11 Fuller's main refutation of Socinianism may be found in *The Calvinistic and Socinian Systems Examined and Compared, as to their Moral Tendency* in *Complete Works*, II, 108–242. For his reply to Sandemanianism, see *Strictures on Sandemanianism, in*

Andrew Fuller
(1754–1815)

his rebuttal of hyper-Calvinism that he made his most distinctive contribution.

Philip Roberts, one-time president of Midwestern Baptist Theological Seminary, has noted in a study of Fuller as a theologian:

> [Fuller] helped to link the earlier Baptists, whose chief concern was the establishment of ideal New Testament congregations, with those in the nineteenth century driven to make the gospel known worldwide. His contribution helped to guarantee that many of the leading Baptists of the 1800s would typify fervent evangelism and world missions. ...Without his courage and doctrinal integrity in the face of what he considered to be theological aberrations, the Baptist mission movement might have been stillborn.[12]

Fuller's life thus reveals a great truth linked with times of revival and awakening, namely, the vital role played by key leaders. To be sure, no great work for God is accomplished by men working in isolation. And Fuller had the ability to nurture and sustain deep, long-lasting, and satisfying friendships that enabled him and his friends to serve God powerfully in their generation and to be the vehicles of a tremendous revival. One sees the depth of this relationship in three simple words that William Carey said when he heard of Fuller's death in 1815: "I loved him."

But it was Fuller's theology, known as Fullerism, that was central to this entire movement of revitalization. And undergirding his theology

---

Twelve Letters to a Friend, in *Complete Works*, II, 561–646. His chief response to Deism, especially that of the popularizer Thomas Paine (1737–1809), is *The Gospel Its Own Witness* (*Complete Works*, II, 1–107). For examinations of Fuller's reply to these theological aberrations, see Michael A.G. Haykin, "'The Oracles of God': Andrew Fuller and the Scriptures," *Churchman*, 103 (1989): 60–76; idem, Michael A.G. Haykin, "A Socinian and Calvinist Compared: Joseph Priestley and Andrew Fuller on the Propriety of Prayer to Christ," *Dutch Review of Church History*, 73 (1993): 178–198; Thomas Jacob South, "The Response of Andrew Fuller to the Sandemanian View of Saving Faith" (Th.D. thesis, Mid-America Baptist Theological Seminary, 1993).

12 Phil Roberts, "Andrew Fuller," in Timothy George and David S. Dockery, ed., *Theologians of the Baptist Tradition* (rev. ed.; Nashville: Broadman & Holman, 2001), 46–47.

was his personal walk with God and his commitment to the Scriptures. Consider in this regard the sermon that Fuller delivered at the installation of Robert Fawkner as the pastor of Thorn Baptist Church, Bedfordshire, on October 31, 1787, which was later entitled *The Qualifications and Encouragement of a faithful Minister illustrated by the Character and Success of Barnabas*.[13] Fuller took Acts 11:24 for his text, where the early Christian leader Barnabas is said to have been "a good man, and full of the Holy Spirit, and of faith" and that as a result of his ministry "much people was added to the Lord" in Antioch. Although Fuller's remarks regarding spiritual formation were delivered in the context of a charge to a pastor, there is much here, as he would have readily agreed, that has more general application.

Fuller began by expressing his conviction that the example of other people's lives can have "a great influence upon the human mind" for good, and especially the examples of those illustrious figures found in the Scriptures. The latter, "drawn with the pencil of inspiration," have what Fuller called "an assimilating tendency," that is, the record of their lives has a way of inspiring emulation and imitation.[14] Like most in his Baptist community, Fuller deeply valued Christian biography for its instructive value. As he noted in another context: "It is good to read

---

13 The sermon was first published in 1787: Andrew Fuller and John Ryland, *The Qualifications and Encouragement of a faithful Minister, illustrated by the Character and Success of Barnabas. And, Paul's Charge to the Corinthians respecting their Treatment of Timothy, applied to the Conduct of Churches toward Their Pastors. Being the Substance of Two Discourses, Delivered at The Settlement of The Rev. Mr. Robert Fawkner, in the Pastoral Office, Over the Baptist Church at Thorn, in Bedfordshire, October 31, 1787* (London: Published for Thorn Baptist Church, 1787). It can be conveniently found in *The Complete Works*, I, 135–144.

For a discussion of this sermon, see Nigel David Wheeler, "Eminent Spirituality and Eminent Usefulness: Andrew Fuller's (1754–1815) Pastoral Theology in his Ordination Sermons" (PhD thesis, University of Pretoria, 2009), 189–203.

14 *Qualifications and Encouragement of a Faithful Minister*, in *Complete Works*, I, 135. See also Andrew Fuller, *Preaching Christ*, in *Complete Works*, I, 505; Andrew Fuller, *On An Intimate and Practical Acquaintance with the Word of God*, in *Complete Works*, I, 483: "Example has a strong tendency to excite us to emulation." The Calvinistic Baptist minister James Fanch (1704–1767) once referred to deep friendships as having "a marvelous transforming assimilating nature" (*Ten Sermons on Practical Subjects* [London: G. Keith, 1768], 30).

the lives of holy men; and the more holy they have been the better."[15]

Fuller proceeded to examine the three characteristics mentioned in the description of Barnabas' character. First of all, Barnabas was a good man. Fuller extolled the importance of being marked by the virtue of goodness and noted various spheres in which goodness must be expressed. First and foremost in Fuller's mind was the home:

> Value [goodness]…at home in your family. If you walk not closely with God there, you will be ill able to work for him elsewhere. You have lately become the head of a family. Whatever charge it shall please God, in the course of your life, to place under your care, I trust it will be your concern to recommend Christ and the gospel to them, walk circumspectly before them, constantly worship God with them, offer up secret prayer for them, and exercise a proper authority over them.[16]

The desire to be a good man must also be seen both in one's public demeanour—"prove by your spirit and conduct that you are a lover of all mankind," Fuller told Fawkner—and as a main priority in one's life.[17]

THE BIBLE AND PRAYER

But how is such goodness to be obtained? Alluding to another passage from Acts, namely, Acts 6:4, Fuller emphasized two key means of spiritual formation and spiritual vitality: Fawkner was to give himself to personal study of "the word of God, and to prayer." With regard to the Scriptures, right from the very beginning of his ministry Fuller built his life and thought on the Word of God—as he said in the first draft (1778) of *The Gospel Worthy of All Acceptation*: "O Lord, impress thy Truth upon my heart with thine own seal. Fuller was an ardent reader of the Scriptures that he regarded as "the book by way of emi-

---

15 Andrew Fuller, "Memoirs of Rev. James Garie," in *Complete Works*, III, 756.
16 Fuller, *Qualifications and Encouragement of a Faithful Minister*, in *Complete Works*, I, 136.
17 Fuller, *Qualifications and Encouragement of a Faithful Minister*, in *Complete Works*, I, 137–138.

nence, the book of books."[18] It occupied such a place of pre-eminence in his mind because, unlike all other books, it is "unerring"[19] and is characterized by "Divine inspiration and infallibility."[20] As Fuller commented:

> Many religious people appear to be contented with seeing truth in the light in which some great and good man has placed it; but if ever we enter into the gospel to purpose, it must be by reading the word of God for ourselves, and by praying and meditating upon its sacred contents. It is "in God's light that we must see light" [cf. Psalm 36:9]… The writings of great and good men are not to be despised, any more than their preaching: only let them not be treated as oracular. The best of men, in this imperfect state, view things *partially*, and therefore are in danger of laying an improper stress upon some parts of Scripture, to the neglect of other parts of equal, and sometimes of superior importance. … If we adopt the principles of fallible men, without searching the Scriptures for ourselves, and inquiring whether or not these things be so [Acts 17:11], they will not, even allowing them to be on the side of truth, avail us, as if we had learned them from a higher authority. Our faith, in this case, will stand in the wisdom of man, and not in the power of God. …Truth learned only at second-hand will be to us what Saul's armour was to David; we shall be at a loss how to use it in the day of trial.[21]

Fuller here differentiated between the books of fallible men, albeit good thinkers, and the truth of God in Scripture. The writings of fallible men are, at best, unable to provide the nourishment necessary for genuine spiritual growth. And because they stem from fallible minds, they are inevitably partial perspectives on the truth and inadequate to

---

18 Andrew Fuller, "The Apostolic Office," in *Complete Works*, III, 498–499.
19 Andrew Fuller, *On Spiritual Declension and the Means of Revival*, in *Complete Works*, III, 629.
20 Andrew Fuller, *The Nature and Importance of an Intimate Knowledge of Divine Truth*, in *Complete Works*, I, 160).
21 Fuller, *Intimate Knowledge of Divine Truth*, in *Complete Works*, I, 164.

support the believer in a time of trial. By contrast, Scripture is a sure guide for the believer, it brings godly balance and perspective to his life, and provides him with a wholly adequate support in the face of life's challenges.

The importance Fuller accorded to the Scriptures as a vehicle of spiritual vitality is also evident from the fact that he made essentially the same point in an ordination or installation sermon based on Ezra 7:10. "Learn your religion from the Bible," Fuller told the prospective minister:

> Let that [i.e. the Bible] be your decisive rule. Adopt not a body of sentiments, or even a single sentiment, solely on the authority of any man—however great, however respected. Dare to think for yourself. Human compositions are fallible. But the Scriptures were written by men who wrote as they were inspired by the Holy Spirit.[22]

Also significant in the sermon for Robert Fawkner are Fuller's remarks about prayer:

> Beware also, brother, of neglecting secret prayer. The fire of devotion will go out if it be not kept alive by an habitual dealing with Christ. Conversing with men and things may brighten our gifts and parts; but it is conversing with God that must brighten our graces. Whatever ardour we may feel in our public work, if this is wanting, things cannot be right, nor can they in such a train come to a good issue.[23]

Enabling true ministry, as Fuller conceived it, was to be "the fire of devotion." And such devotion needed the fuel of prayer to keep it bright and aflame. Fuller is usually remembered today for either his activism in the genesis of the modern missionary movement or his

---

[22] Andrew Fuller, *On An Intimate and Practical Acquaintance with the Word of God*, in *Complete Works*, I, 483.

[23] Fuller, *Qualifications and Encouragement of a Faithful Minister*, in *Complete Works*, I, 137.

acumen as an apologist for the Christian faith.[24] But undergirding both his activism and his apologetics was a recognition that prayer had to be a priority in his own life and ministry if he were ever going to be useful for God. As he stressed in a charge given to John West at the latter's ordination to the pastorate of the Baptist cause in Carlton, Bedfordshire, in the same year as his Thorn sermon:

> Let all your private meditations [on the Bible] be mingled with prayer. You will study your Bible to wonderful advantage, if you go to it spiritually-minded. It is this which causes us to see the beauty and to feel the force of many parts of Scripture…[25]

Other passages from Fuller's corpus show that he was convinced that a prayerful life was requisite for all Christians if they were to know spiritual growth. For instance, in a series of articles he wrote on the Sermon on the Mount, he noted regarding Jesus' words on prayer in Matthew 6:5–8:

> …it is taken for granted that Christ's disciples are praying men. What he says is not to persuade them to prayer, but to direct them in it. Infidels may imagine that God does not concern himself with the affairs of mortals, and may excuse themselves by pretending that it were presumption in them to solicit the Supreme Being to do this or that; formalists may say their prayers, and be glad when the task is over; but Christians cannot live without communion with God.[26]

---

24 Both of these marks of Fuller's character and ministry were noticed during his lifetime. In an obituary at the time of his death in 1815, the question was asked: "for clearness of conception, for strength and vigour of mind, for decision of character, for laborious exertion, for punctuality and promptness in all his measure, where shall we find his equal?" ("Obituary," *The New Evangelical Magazine and Theological Review*, 1 [1815]: 192).

25 Fuller, *Intimate and Practical Acquaintance*, in *Complete Works*, I, 484. On West, see Michael A.G. Haykin, ed., *The Armies of the Lamb: The spirituality of Andrew Fuller* (Dundas: Joshua Press, 2001), 114, n.2.

26 Andrew Fuller, "Sermon on the Mount: Alms-giving, and Prayer," in *Complete Works*, I, 576.

And again, in a circular letter that he drew up in 1785 for the Northamptonshire Association of Baptist Churches and which was sent out to all of its members, he urged his readers:

> Finally, brethren, let us not forget to intermingle prayer with all we do. Our need of God's Holy Spirit to enable us to do any thing, and everything, truly good, should excite us to do this. Without his blessing all means are without efficacy, and every effort for revival will be in vain. Constantly and earnestly, therefore, let us approach his throne. Take all occasions especially for closet prayer. Here, if anywhere, we shall get fresh strength, and maintain a life of communion with God.[27]

And in one of his final sermons, preached at the funeral of his close friend, John Sutcliff, in 1814, Fuller hammered home the same point: "There is no intercourse with God without prayer. It is thus that we walk with God."[28]

"FULL OF THE HOLY SPIRIT AND OF FAITH"

Barnabas was also a man, according to Luke's description of him in Acts 11, who was "full of the Holy Spirit," which Fuller understood to mean that Barnabas was full of the fruit of the Spirit mentioned in Galatians 5:22–23. In his words:

> To be full of the Holy Spirit is to be full of the dove, as I may say; or full of those fruits of the Spirit mentioned by the apostle to the Galatians; namely, "love, joy, peace, long-suffering, gentleness, goodness." …A person that is greatly under the influence of the love of this world is said to be drunken with its cares or pleasures. In allusion to something like this, the apostle exhorts that we "be not drunken with wine, wherein is excess; but filled with the Spirit" [Ephesians 5:18]. The word "filled," here, is very expressive; it denotes, I apprehend, being overcome, as it were,

---

27 Andrew Fuller, *Causes of Declension in Religion, and Means of Revival*, in *Complete Works*, III, 324.

28 Andrew Fuller, *Principles and Prospects of a Servant of Christ*, in *Complete Works*, I, 344.

with the holy influences and fruits of the blessed Spirit. How necessary is all this, my brother, in your work! Oh how necessary is "an unction from the Holy One" [1 John 2:20]![29]

Fuller's interpretation here of the term "unction" from 1 John 2:20 was taken directly from John Gill, the voluminous eighteenth-century Baptist exegete. In his commentary on this passage, Gill had delineated that the "unction" or "anointing" that believers received from the Holy One, that is, the Lord Jesus, was the "Spirit, and his graces."[30]

Fuller was further convinced that the doctrinal divisions between Christians was owing to a lack of such fullness of the Spirit: "It is no breach of charity to say," he declared forthrightly, "that if the professors of Christianity had more of the Holy Spirit of God in their hearts, there would be a greater harmony among them respecting the great truths which he has revealed."[31] Above all things, therefore, Fawkner should make Psalm 51:11 his prayer, "Take not thy Holy Spirit from me."[32] For, Fuller stressed: "If we are destitute of the Holy Spirit, we are blind to the loveliness of the Divine character, and destitute of any true love to God in our hearts."[33] Again, we see the radical need of the Spirit's help in the Christian life: It is he who opens out eyes to unsurpassable beauty of God, and it is he who fills our hearts with love for God.

The final characteristic of Barnabas' life was that he was full of faith. Fuller took this to be expressive of three ideas: Barnabas had a mind "stored with divine sentiment," that is, he had deep personal convictions about the vital truths of the Bible; then he was "rooted and grounded in the truth of the gospel," and finally, he was "daily living upon it."[34]

---

29 Fuller, *Qualifications and Encouragement of a Faithful Minister*, in *Complete Works*, I, 138, 139.

30 John Gill, *An Exposition of the New Testament* (London: George Keith, 1776), 355–356.

31 Fuller, *Qualifications and Encouragement of a Faithful Minister*, in *Complete Works*, I, 139.

32 Fuller, *Qualifications and Encouragement of a Faithful Minister*, in *Complete Works*, I, 139.

33 Fuller, *Qualifications and Encouragement of a Faithful Minister*, in *Complete Works*, I, 139.

34 Fuller, *Qualifications and Encouragement of a Faithful Minister*, in *Complete Works*, I, 141.

"EMINENT USEFULNESS"

Fuller's spirituality was that of an activist. After the formation of the Baptist Missionary Society in October 1793, Fuller became the first secretary of the society until his death in 1815. The work of the mission consumed an enormous amount of Fuller's time as he regularly toured the country, representing the mission and raising funds. On average he was away from home three months of the year. Between 1798 and 1813, for instance, he made five lengthy and arduous trips to Scotland for the mission as well as undertaking journeys to Wales and Ireland.[35] For example, on a trip he made to Scotland in 1805, Fuller travelled 1,300 miles and preached fifty sermons in around sixty days. As the mission secretary he also carried on an extensive correspondence both to the missionaries on the field and to supporters at home. And finally, he supervised the selection of missionary appointees and sought to deal with troubles as they emerged on the field. In short, he acted as the pastor of the missionaries sent out.[36] The amount of energy and time this took deeply worried his friends. As one of his friends, Robert Hall, Jr. (1764–1831), put it in a letter to John Ryland, Jr., Fuller's first biographer:

> ...if he [i.e. Fuller] is not more careful he will be in danger of wearing himself out before his time. His journeys, his studies, his correspondcies [sic] must be too much for the constitution of any man.[37]

It is not surprising, therefore, that Fuller concluded his sermon for Fawkner with a reference to serving Christ and his kingdom. As he put it, "eminent spirituality in a minister is usually attended with eminent usefulness."[38] Fuller stressed that this affirmation was not

---

35 On Fuller's trips to Scotland, see Dudley Reeves, "Andrew Fuller in Scotland," *The Banner of Truth*, 106–107 (July/August 1972): 33–40.

36 Doyle L. Young, "Andrew Fuller and the Modern Mission Movement," *Baptist History and Heritage*, 17 (1982): 17–27.

37 Letter to John Ryland, Jr., May 25, 1801, cited Geoffrey F. Nuttall, "Letters from Robert Hall to John Ryland 1791–1824," *The Baptist Quarterly* 34 (1991–1992): 127.

38 Fuller, *Qualifications and Encouragement of a Faithful Minister*, in *Complete Works*, I, 143. See also Andrew Fuller, *Affectionate Concern of a Minister for the Salvation of his*

meant to imply that piety automatically guaranteed success:

> I do not mean to say our usefulness depends upon our spirituality, as an effect depends upon its cause; nor yet that it is always in proportion to it. God is a Sovereign; and frequently sees proper to convince us of it, in variously bestowing his blessing on the means of grace.[39]

On the other hand, Fuller was certain that "our want of usefulness is often to be ascribed to our want of spirituality, much oftener than to our want of talents." Men, who seemed destined to be greatly used by God because of their gifts, have turned out otherwise and that because their inner lives were marred by "such things as pride, unwatchfulness, carnality, and levity."[40]

Why did Fuller hold that usefulness in God's service cannot be divorced from spirituality or what he called "eminency in grace"? First, he argued that where there is true spirituality the soul burns "with holy love to Christ and the souls of men." It gives the possessor an unquenchable passion to see God and Christ glorified and men and women converted. Fuller pointed to a number of men who were great examples in this regard: Old Testament saints like Hezekiah, Ezra and Nehemiah and various figures in the history of the church, men such as Peter and Paul, John Wycliffe, Martin Luther and John Calvin, as well as "[John] Elliot [sic], and [Jonathan] Edwards, and [David] Brainerd, and [George] Whitefield."[41] It is noteworthy that in the group of Christian worthies from the seventeenth and eighteenth centuries, three of them—Eliot, Brainerd and Whitefield—were admired in Fuller's day for their activism, their ceaseless missionary endeavours to reach the lost with the gospel. The fourth figure, Edwards—rightly described by Miklós Vetö as "the greatest Christian theologian of the

---

Hearers, in Complete Works, I, 508.

39 Fuller, Qualifications and Encouragement of a Faithful Minister, in Complete Works,, I, 143. See also Wheeler, "Eminent Spirituality and Eminent Usefulness," 202.

40 Fuller, Qualifications and Encouragement of a Faithful Minister, in Complete Works, I, 143.

41 Fuller, Qualifications and Encouragement of a Faithful Minister, in Complete Works, I, 143.

eighteenth century"[42]—was Fuller's main theological and spiritual guide after the Scriptures.[43]

Fuller's second reason was that when a believer grows in spirituality he or she also becomes focused on two great goals, "the glory of God and the welfare of men's souls," both of which God himself is pursuing. Thus, one can hope for God's "blessing to attend our labours." Finally, Fuller believed that a person who is marked by "eminency in grace" will also be a person of genuine humility, and it is safe for him or her "to be much owned of God." Success will not go to his or her head.[44]

"UNCTION FROM THE HOLY ONE"

Fuller's sermon was so well received that the church at Thorn urged its publication, along with one given by Fuller's friend, John Ryland on the same day. The following summer, in July 1788, Fuller wrote to Benjamin Francis (1734–1799), the pastor of a Calvinistic Baptist congregation in Horsley, Gloucestershire, and mentioned that his Thorn sermon had been published. Recalling what he had preached, though, caused Fuller to reflect on the way in which he personally fell short of living according to what he had said on that October day:

> My greatest difficulties arise from within. I am not what a servant of Christ should be. I want an unction from the Holy One. I have lately preached an ordination sermon or two, (that at Thorn, which is printed, for one[45]) in which I have endeavoured to come as home to the heart and conscience of my brethren as I knew how. But, oh, what shame covers my face when I turn my attention

---

42 "Book Reviews: America's Theologian: A Recommendation of Jonathan Edwards. By Robert W. Jenson," *Church History*, 58 (1989): 522.

43 Fuller, *Qualifications and Encouragement of a Faithful Minister*, in *Complete Works*, I, 144. For the influence of Edwards on Fuller, see Chris Chun, *The Legacy of Jonathan Edwards in the Theology of Andrew Fuller*, Studies in the History of Christian Traditions, vol. 162 (Leiden/Boston: Brill, 2012).

44 Fuller, *Qualifications and Encouragement of a Faithful Minister*, in *Complete Works*, I, 144.

45 The other sermon, based on Ezra 7:10, was *Intimate and Practical Acquaintance*, in *Complete Works*, I, 483–486.

inward! I am the man who am too, too guilty of many of those things which I have cautioned them to avoid.[46]

The clause "unction from the Holy One" is, of course, a reference to 1 John 2:20, which, as has been noted, Fuller understood to be a reference to the Holy Spirit. By lamenting his perceived lack of such a fullness of the Spirit, Fuller was obviously indicating his ardency for and prizing of such a blessing. Without such an unction, or fullness of the Spirit, he knew that he could not be a useful servant of Christ, for, as he had put it in his Thorn sermon, "eminent spirituality in a minister is usually attended with eminent usefulness."

---

46 Andrew Fuller, Letter to Benjamin Francis, July 13, 1788, in *The Baptist Magazine* 34 (1842): 637–638. This letter is also reprinted in Haykin, ed., *Armies of the Lamb*, 111–113.

9

Becoming William Carey
A sketch of his life, thought and ministry[1]

> "...it is absolutely necessary that we set an infinite value upon immortal souls." —SERAMPORE TRIO

HOW TO INTERPRET CAREY'S LIFE

For English-speaking people, the eighteenth century was an era of highly significant achievements. Through conquest and exploration, for instance, they established themselves as the masters of a far-flung empire that encircled the globe. It was in the middle of this century that British troops under the command of Robert Clive (1725–1774) defeated a French army in India at the Battle of Plassey, which paved the way for the British conquest of Bengal and later all of India. Two years later on September 13, 1759, General James Wolfe (1727–1759)

---

[1] Most of this chapter appeared as monthly installments throughout 2011 in the magazine, *The Gospel Witness*, published by Jarvis Street Baptist Church, Toronto. Used by permission.

defeated the French General Louis Joseph Montcalm (1712–1759) at the Battle of the Plains of Abraham, then outside the walls of the city of Quebec. Though Wolfe was killed in this engagement, the British victory meant the end of French rule in Canada. Ten or so years later, Captain James Cook (1728–1779), a British naval officer, entered upon his world-changing discoveries in the South Pacific, discovering and mapping the coastlines of New Zealand and Australia.

Running parallel to this empire-building by the British, though distinct from it, came the kingdom-building by English-speaking missionaries. Up until the latter part of the eighteenth century, evangelical Christianity was primarily confined to northern Europe and the Atlantic seaboard of North America. But suddenly in the last decade of the century these evangelicals launched out from these two geographical regions and began to establish churches throughout Asia, Africa and Australasia. At the heart of this missionary movement was William Carey.

The year 2011 was the sestercentennial (250th anniversary) of the birth of Carey, who first saw the light of day on August 17, 1761. In light of Carey's subsequent lionization by evangelicals as "the father of modern missions," it is entirely appropriate to evaluate his legacy.

NOT AN APOSTLE, BUT A PLODDER

"Such a man as Carey is more to me than bishop or archbishop: he is an apostle." This was the estimate that the evangelical Anglican John Newton once expressed about Carey while the latter was still alive. On another occasion, Newton wrote that he did not look for miracles in his own day on the order of those done in the apostolic era. Yet, he went on, "if God were to work one in our day, I should not wonder if it were in favour of Dr. Carey."[2] Interestingly enough, when, in 1826, two missionaries by the names of George Bennet and Daniel Tyerman happened to visit Carey in India (by that time he had been labouring there over thirty years), they were struck by what they called his "apostolic appearance."[3]

---

2 *The Autobiography of William Jay*, eds. George Redford and John Angell James (1854 ed.; repr. Edinburgh: The Banner of Truth Trust, 1974), 275; S. Pearce Carey, *William Carey* (London: Hodder and Stoughton, [1923]), 134.

3 Tom Hiney, *On the Missionary Trail* (London: Chatto & Windus, 2000), 222.

But Carey's opinion of himself was quite different. He once told his nephew Eustace Carey (1791–1855) that he was essentially "a plodder." In other words, his achievements were not the work of an inspired apostle, but the product of grit, gumption, and, he would have wanted to add, divine grace. Carey was quite conscious that he did not merit being decked out with a halo like some medieval saint, something that the later Baptist and evangelical tradition—following Newton's lead?— has done. In the final analysis, Carey was convinced that he had simply done his duty as a servant of Christ.[4] And for Carey that duty had begun about fifty-five years prior to his death, when he first fled to Christ for "strength and righteousness."

CAREY'S FAMILY BACKGROUND

William Carey was born of poor parents in 1761 in a tiny village called Paulerspury in the heart of Northamptonshire. Carey's parents were staunch Anglicans. His father, Edmund (d.1816), the schoolmaster of Paulerspury, was what was known as the parish clerk. According to William Cowper, the evangelical hymnwriter and close friend of John Newton, the parish clerk had to "pronounce the amen to prayers and announce the sermon," lead the chants and the responses during the church service, keep the church register of baptisms, marriages and burials, and chase "dogs out of church and force…unwilling youngsters in."[5] Thus, young William was regularly taken to church. Of this early acquaintance with the Church of England, Carey later wrote:

> Having been accustomed from my infancy to read the Scriptures, I had a considerable acquaintance therewith, especially with the historical parts. I…have no doubt but the constant reading of the Psalms, Lessons, etc. in the parish church, which I was obliged to attend regularly, tended to furnish my mind with a general Scripture knowledge. [But] of real experimental religion I scarcely heard anything till I was fourteen years of age.[6]

---

4 A. Christopher Smith, "The Legacy of William Carey," *International Bulletin of Missionary Research*, 16, no. 1 (January 1992): 2.

5 Mary Drewery, *William Carey: A Biography* (London: Hodder and Stoughton, 1978), 10.

6 Eustace Carey, *Memoir of William Carey, D.D.* (London: Jackson and Walford,

A PASSION FOR FLOWERS

Also living in Paulerspury was William's uncle, Peter Carey. Peter had served with General James Wolfe in Canada during the French and Indian War (a.k.a. the Seven Years' War), and had seen action at the British capture of the citadel of Quebec in 1759, two years before William was born. Peter subsequently returned to England, and worked in Paulerspury as a gardener. His tales of Canada no doubt awakened in young William an unquenchable interest in far-off lands.

Peter also implanted in young William a love of gardens and flowers that remained with him all of his life. When, years later, Carey was established in India, he had five acres of garden under cultivation. Cultivating this garden served as a welcome means of relaxation amid the stresses and strains of ministry in India. It was of this garden that his son Jonathan later remarked that "here he [i.e., his father] enjoyed his most pleasant moments of secret meditation and devotion."[7]

JOHN WARR

Not surprisingly, so much did young Carey love gardening that he wanted to become a gardener like his uncle Peter. At this point in his life, however, Carey suffered from a skin disease that made it very painful for him to spend large amounts of time in the full sun. It is interesting to note that when Carey went to India, he spent a considerable amount of time in the sun, but with no recurrence of this skin disease. And so, in his mid-teens, his father apprenticed him to a shoemaker by the name of Clarke Nichols who lived in Piddington, about seven miles away from his home.

This apprenticeship was to have very significant consequences for William, for one of his fellow apprentices was a Christian. His name was John Warr. He was a Congregationalist and was used of God to bring Carey to Christ. It was known for a long time that Carey's salvation had come partly as the result of the witness of one of his fellow apprentices. Until the First World War, however, the name of this apprentice had been completely lost. During that war it was found in a letter of Carey's that only then came to light. It is a powerful illustration of how the faithful witness of one believer can have immense significance.

1836), 7 [henceforth cited as Carey, *Memoir of William Carey*].

7   Carey, *Memoir of William Carey*, 398.

**William Carey
(1761–1834)**

THE ROAD TO CHRIST

At first, when Warr shared his faith with Carey, Carey resisted. It is vital to recall that he was the product of a staunch Anglican home, and that he had learned to look down on, indeed despise, anyone who was not an Anglican, that is, not part of the state church. For many, to be English was to be Anglican. But John persisted in his attempts to win Carey for Christ. He lent him books and then invited him to attend on a regular basis the mid-week gathering of Congregationalists in Hackleton, a nearby village, for prayer and Bible study. Carey went and came under deep conviction. He tried to reform his life: to give up lying and swearing, and to take up prayer. But at this point in his life he did not realize that a definite change in his lifestyle in this regard could only occur when he had been given, in the language of Scripture, a new heart.

Coupled with Warr's testimony was an important lesson that young Carey learned from a traumatic incident that took place at Christmas 1777. It was the custom for apprentices at that time of the year to be given small amounts of money from the tradespeople with whom their masters had business. Carey had had to go to Northampton to make some purchases for his master as well as for himself. At one particular shop, that of an ironmonger—that is, a hardware dealer—called Hall, he was personally given a counterfeit shilling as a joke. When Carey discovered the worthless coin he decided, not without some qualms of conscience, to pass it off to his employer. Appropriating a good shilling from the money that Nichols had given him, he included the counterfeit shilling among the change for his master. On the way back to Piddington, he even prayed that if God enabled his dishonesty to go undetected he would break with sin from that time forth!

But, Carey commented many years later, "a gracious God did not get me through."[8] Carey's dishonesty was discovered, he was covered with shame and disgrace, and he became afraid to go out in the village where he lived for fear of what others were thinking about him. By this means, Carey was led, he subsequently said, to "see much more of myself than I had ever done before, and to seek for mercy with

---

8 Carey, *Memoir of William Carey*, 12.

greater earnestness."[9] That mercy he found as over the next two years he came to "depend on a crucified Saviour for pardon and salvation."[10]

BAPTIST CONVICTIONS AND MEETING JOHN RYLAND

William Carey continued to go with John Warr to the prayer meetings in Hackleton, but it was not until February 10, 1779, that he actually attended a worship service. On that particular day a man named Thomas Chater (d.1811), a resident of Olney, was preaching. The text on which Chater was preaching has not been recorded, but in his sermon he did quote that powerful exhortation in Hebrews 13:13: "Let us go forth therefore unto him [i.e. Jesus] without the camp, bearing his reproach" (KJV). On the basis of this verse, Chater urged upon his hearers "the necessity of following Christ entirely." As Carey listened to Chater's exhortation, the interpretation that he made of this text and Chater's words was one that he would later describe as "very crude." He distinctly felt that God was calling him to leave the Church of England, where, in his particular parish church, he was sitting under "a lifeless, carnal ministry," and to unite with a Dissenting congregation. Since the Church of England was established by the law of the land, he reasoned, its members were "protected from the scandal of the cross."[11] So Carey became what he had long despised—a Dissenter.

During the first few years after his conversion, Carey struggled "to crystallize his beliefs, to establish foundations on which to build his faith."[12] "Having so slight an acquaintance with ministers," he later wrote, "I was obliged to draw all from the Bible alone."[13] His study of the Scriptures soon led him to the realization that infant baptism, as practiced by Anglicans and Congregationalists, had no real scriptural authority behind it. So, in the course of 1783, he approached a Baptist pastor named John Ryland, Sr., pastor of College Lane Baptist Church in Northampton, for baptism. Ryland, in turn, asked his son, John Ryland, Jr., to baptize Carey.

---

9 Carey, *Memoir of William Carey*, 12.
10 Carey, *Memoir of William Carey*, 14.
11 Carey, *Memoir of William Carey*, 12.
12 Drewery, *William Carey*, 23.
13 Carey, *Memoir of William Carey*, 14, 16.

The younger Ryland was co-pastor with his father of the College Lane cause. When his father moved to Enfield, near London, in 1786, Ryland became the sole pastor of this work. During his early ministerial experience Ryland read deeply in the writings of Jonathan Edwards. Indeed, after the Scriptures, Edwards' writings exerted the strongest theological influence on Ryland. In particular, the works of Edwards helped Ryland to see how classical Calvinism could speak to the men and women of the late-eighteenth and early-nineteenth centuries, as well as giving him a hunger for corporate revival, personal renewal and mission. These three aspects of Edwards' theological reflection provided both shape and substance not only for Ryland's theology but also for that of Carey.

Thus, in the early hours of October 5, 1785, the younger Ryland baptized Carey in the River Nene that then flowed through Northampton. Obviously at the time, neither of these two men realized what the future would hold, and how they would become firm friends and co-labourers in a great work of God.

A GROWING PASSION FOR MISSIONS

Around the time of his baptism Carey came across the accounts of the voyages of discovery undertaken by James Cook in the Pacific, which involved, among other things, the discovery of Tahiti and the charting of the unknown shores of New Zealand and Australia. Iain H. Murray has rightly observed that "the end of Cook's geographical feat [was] the beginning of missionary enterprise."[14] Carey would later say regarding his perusal of these volumes: "Reading Cook's voyages was the first thing that engaged my mind to think of missions."[15] Through these accounts, Carey's boyhood desire to know about other lands was given substance and shape. More importantly, through the written account of Cook's voyages, Carey began to gaze upon wider spiritual horizons than the fields of Northamptonshire, and to reflect on the desperate spiritual plight of those who lived in the countries that Cook had discovered. Many of them had no written language, certainly none of them had the Scriptures in their own tongues, and there were nei-

---

14 "Divine Providence and Captain Cook," *The Banner of Truth*, 274 (July 1986): 7.
15 Carey, *Memoir of William Carey*, 18.

ther local churches nor resident ministers to share with them the good news of God's salvation. "Pity, therefore, humanity, and much more Christianity," he wrote only a few years after reading Cook's journals, called "loudly for every possible exertion to introduce the gospel amongst them."[16] Over the next eight years one of his main preoccupations was the collection of information, especially geographical and religious, about these nations, including the many other nations of the world that had never heard a word of the gospel.

Carey's growing passion for the evangelization of nations outside of Europe did not cause him to forget the need of the many at his own back door. Through his witness, for example, his two sisters, Mary and Ann, were won to Christ. As is often the case with the members of one's own family, William had not found it at all easy to speak to them concerning their need of Christ. But he persevered in praying for them, and when Mary Carey thought back on this period of her life, she could only exclaim, "O what a privilege to have praying relations, and what a mercy to have a God that waits to be gracious!"[17] The two sisters were baptized in 1783.

By the time his sisters were baptized, William Carey had begun preaching. He first preached at the Congregationalist church in Hackleton, a few miles south-east of Northampton, where he had been baptized as a believer. He then began speaking in a village called Moulton, a few miles to the north-east of Northampton, where he was called to be the pastor of the Baptist church in 1785.[18]

FORMING LIFE-LONG FRIENDSHIPS

Carey's formal ordination occurred on August 1, 1787, in the village of Moulton. Taking part in his ordination that day were three Baptist pastors who would become life-long friends and who would be the pillars of the Baptist Missionary Society (BMS) that sent him to India: John Ryland, Jr., Andrew Fuller, later secretary of the BMS, and John

---

16 *An Enquiry into the Obligations of Christians, To Use Means for the Conversion of the Heathens* (1792 ed.; repr. Didcot, Oxfordshire: The Baptist Missionary Society, 1991), 40–41.

17 Carey, *Memoir of William Carey*, 32–33.

18 The church where he ministered, and the cottage in which he lived, can still be seen at the west end of West Street in the village today.

Sutcliff, pastor of Olney Baptist Church, where Carey had his membership for a couple of years. It is quite misleading to suppose that it was Carey's single-handed effort that brought about the founding of the Baptist Missionary Society and enabled him to accomplish all that he did in India from 1793 till his death over forty years later. Carey was part of a close-knit circle of like-minded friends, without whom little of what he longed for would have been realized. A Scottish Baptist by the name of Christopher Anderson (1782–1852), who was well acquainted with a number of Carey's close friends, maintained during Carey's lifetime that it was the "strong personal attachment" of these friends to one another that lay behind the "usefulness" of the BMS: Carey, Joshua Marshman and William Ward—the Serampore Trio—abroad in India; Sutcliff, Fuller and Ryland at home.[19]

Another significant friendship, one that is frequently overlooked, was that of Carey with Robert Hall Sr. (1728–1791), pastor of the Baptist cause in Arnesby, Leicestershire, a friendship that Carey later described as "a jewel I could not too highly prize."[20] Carey was helped enormously by Hall's *Help to Zion's Travellers* (1781), which had started out as a sermon to the Northamptonshire Baptist Association. This work tackled such key issues of that day as hyper-Calvinism and the sad tendency among some Baptists toward Antinomianism. Of the impact of this work on his thinking, Carey later noted, "I do not remember ever to have read any book with such raptures as I did that. If it was poison, as some then said, it was so sweet to me that I drank it greedily to the bottom of the cup; and I rejoice to say, that those doctrines are the choice of my heart to this day."[21] In time, as Austin Walker has noted, "Hall…became Carey's spiritual father. He helped him with the composition of his sermons, and gave him advice about the pastoral

---

19 *The Christian Spirit which is essential to the triumph of the Kingdom of God* (London, 1824), 22–27.

20 Quoted Michael A.G. Haykin, *One Heart and One Soul: John Sutcliff of Olney, his friends and his time* (Darlington: Evangelical Press, 1994), 193.

21 Carey, *Memoir of William Carey*, 16-17. See also the comments of John Ryland, Recommendatory Preface to the Second London Edition, in Robert Hall, *Help to Zion's Travellers* (Boston: Lincoln, Edmunds and Co., 1833), x. For this reference to Ryland, and for this paragraph on the elder Hall, I am indebted to Austin Walker, "William Carey (1761–1834) and his books" (Evangelical Library Annual Lecture, Monday, June 6, 2011).

ministry and about his own walk with God. Carey always spoke about his relationship with Hall with deep emotion."[22]

Carey's pastorate at Moulton admitted him to meeting periodically with other Baptist ministers who pastored churches in what was called the Northamptonshire Baptist Association.[23] This association provided a forum for the exchange of ideas, a meetingplace for fellowship as well as mutual spiritual encouragement. As was noted in chapter 6, it was at a meeting of the pastors of this association on September 30, 1785, that one of the senior pastors of the group, John Ryland, Sr.—who, the reader will recall, Carey had approached regarding baptism—is said to have asked Carey and another young pastor, John Webster Morris, pastor of Clipston Baptist Church in Northamptonshire—to offer those gathered that day some topics for conversation. Carey suggested a question that had been running through his mind for some time: "Whether the command given to the apostles to teach all nations was not binding on all succeeding ministers, to the end of the world, seeing that the accompanying promise was of equal extent." Carey's question obviously grew out of meditation upon Matthew 28:18–20. If, Carey reasoned, Christ's promise of his presence with his people is for all time (verse 20), what then of his command to "teach all nations" about Christ (verse 19a)? Was it not a requirement for the church till the end of history as we know it? And as was noted earlier, Carey did indeed receive some sort of stinging rebuke from the elder Ryland.

CONTENDING WITH HYPER-CALVINISM

Now, the standard interpretation of the elder Ryland's reasoning has been to trace it back to the influence of hyper-Calvinism.[24] Although this author doubts that this is an adequate theological explanation of

---

22 Walker, "William Carey (1761–1834) and his books."
23 For Ryland's rebuke of Carey, see chapter 6.
24 See, for example, F. Deaville Walker, *William Carey: Missionary Pioneer and Statesman* (1925 ed.; repr. Chicago: Moody Press, n.d.), 55, who attributes Ryland's remarks to "ultra-Calvinistic theories"; Timothy George, *Faithful Witness: The Life and Mission of William Carey* (Birmingham: New Hope, 1991), 54–55; Malcolm B. Yarnell, III, *The Heart of A Baptist*, White Paper, No. 2 (Fort Worth: The Center for Theological Research, Southwestern Baptist Theological Seminary, 2005), 2–3.

Ryland's outburst,[25] there is little doubt that hyper-Calvinism was a major challenge with which Carey and his circle of Baptist friends had to contend. Hyper-Calvinists in this period maintained that, because the unsaved could not respond to the call of Christ in the preaching of the gospel without the enablement of God, then it was not their responsibility to repent and believe, and consequently, pastors had no duty to exhort the lost to come to Christ.

Carey's close friend, Andrew Fuller, had handily refuted this error in his tremendous exegetical study *The Gospel Worthy of All Acceptation* [1785; 1801 (2nd ed.)]. In this work, Fuller demonstrated from the Scriptures that it was the *duty* of sinners to believe the gospel even though the *power* to believe was entirely dependent on God's grace. He also showed that the gospel must be freely offered to sinners far and wide. Carey took Fuller's theology in this regard as his own starting-point. Further, in his written defence of cross-cultural missions, *An Enquiry into the Obligations of Christians, To Use Means for the Conversion of the Heathens* (1792), he noted that some of his contemporaries had argued that the command to make disciples from all the nations was no longer incumbent upon the church. The ancient church, they maintained, had actually fulfilled that command. Moreover, according to Carey, they argued thus: "we have enough to do to attend to the salvation of our own countrymen; and that, if God intends the salvation of the heathen, he will some way or other bring them to the gospel, or the gospel to them."[26]

In his *Enquiry*, Carey was able to refute this entire argument by pointing out that the two other aspects of the text in Matthew 28—baptism and the presence of Christ—had no temporal limitations on them. The command to baptize was still very much in force and the promise of Christ's abiding presence was still a comfort in time of trouble and turmoil.

---

25 See Iain H. Murray, "William Carey: Climbing the Rainbow," *The Banner of Truth*, 349 (October 1992): 20–21; Michael A.G. Haykin, "John Collett Ryland & His Supposed Hyper-Calvinism Revisited" (*Historia ecclesiastica*, October 9, 2007; http://www.andrewfullercenter.org/index.php/2007/10/jonh-collett-ryland-his-supposed-hyper-calvinism-revisited/).

26 *Enquiry*, 8.

CAREY AN ARMINIAN—EH?

Given this theological atmosphere it is not surprising that people could react to Carey in the manner described by the younger John Ryland as follows. This description comes from Ryland's diary entry for July 8, 1788:

> Asked Brother Carey to preach. Some of our people who are wise above what is written, would not hear him, called him an Arminian, and discovered a strange spirit. Lord pity us! I am almost worn out with grief at these foolish cavils against some of the best of my brethren, men of God, who are only hated because of their zeal.[27]

Carey was a Calvinist, but an evangelical one, of the same ilk as John Bunyan, the powerful preacher of the previous century, Jonathan Edwards, the great New England theologian of revival, and George Whitefield, the leading evangelist of the eighteenth century. In his theology, Carey married a deep-seated conviction in God's sovereignty in salvation to an equally profound belief that in converting sinners God uses means.[28]

Now, what is striking with regard to much of the literature about William Carey is that it is decidedly atheological, as if Carey's theology was of little importance to his missionary zeal and achievement. However, as Iain H. Murray, the well-known biographer and historian, has written regarding biographical studies:

> Biographies show that doctrinal belief is not a secondary or theoretical thing; rather, it has vital consequence in the way Christians live. Weak doctrine produces weak lives. Those who "turn the world upside down" are always those "mighty in the Scriptures."[29]

---

27 Cited A. de M. Chesterman, "The Journals of David Brainerd and of William Carey," *The Baptist Quarterly*, 19 (1961–1962): 151–152.
28 David Kingdon, "William Carey and the Origins of the Modern Missionary Movement," in *Fulfilling the Great Commission* (London: The Westminster Conference, 1992), 88.
29 "A Revival of Calvinism," *Tabletalk*, 35, no. 8 (August 2011): 78.

If Murray is right, and I for one believe he is, then, when we ask the question, "What made William Carey?" and we fail to refer to his doctrinal convictions, we fail to read Carey's life aright. To put it plainly: Without understanding Carey's consistent delight in Calvinism throughout his life, we cannot understand the man, his motivation or eventually the shape of his mission. And, one of the best places to see this delight is in what is called "The Leicester Covenant."

THE WITNESS OF THE LEICESTER COVENANT

Carey moved to Leicester in the early summer of 1789 to pastor the Baptist church there, Harvey Lane Baptist Church, which had been founded in 1760. But, by the time Carey came to the town in 1789, this work was weak, dispirited and some of its members were leading openly dissolute lives. One of the latter was the previous pastor, John Blackshaw, who preached his final sermon in June 1788, but was disfellowshipped the following year for being "frequently intoxicated with liquor."[30] The members were divided over what to do to restore the work, so Carey took the radical step of dissolving the church in 1790 and reforming it on the basis of a new covenant.

This new covenant, known as the Leicester Covenant, was drawn up by Carey in 1790 and was based in part on the church's original 1760 covenant.[31] Most of this covenant, as was typical of such documents in Baptist circles, dealt with issues of practice and behaviour. But in the second article, Carey laid out the theological convictions upon which membership in the church was based:

> ...we receive the Bible as the Word of God, and the only Rule of Faith, and Practice, in which we find the following Doctrines taught, namely, that in the Deity are three equal Persons, the Father, the Son, and the Holy Spirit, Who sustain distinct offices in the economy of Human Salvation; We believe that all Things were fully known to God from the foundation of the world, that

---

30 Sheila Mitchell, *Not Disobedient... A history of United Baptist Church, Leicester including Harvey Lane 1760–1845, Belvoir Street 1845–1940 and Charles Street 1831–1940* ([Leicester], 1984), 20.

31 Mitchell, *Not Disobedient*, 25.

he from Eternity chose his People in Christ to Salvation through sanctification of the Spirit and belief of the Truth; that all rational Creatures are under indispensable Obligation to obey the Law of God, which is Holy, just and good, but that all Men have broken it and are liable to eternal Punishment; that in the fullness of Time God sent his Son to redeem his People whose Blood was a sufficient Atonement for sin, and by the imputation of whose righteousness we are accounted righteous before God, and accepted with him; and that being Justified by Faith we have Peace with God through our Lord Jesus Christ. We further believe that Men are totally depraved, and that the carnal Mind is enmity against God, and that we are convicted, and converted only by the sovereign operations of the Holy Spirit upon our Hearts, being made willing in the Day of his Power, and that the life of Grace is maintained by the same Divine Spirit, who is the Finisher as well as the Author of our faith, that those who are received thus shall persevere in the way of Holiness, and at last obtain everlasting Happiness through the mercy of God.[32]

In addition to the standard evangelical convictions about the authority of the Scriptures and the classical doctrine of the Trinity, Carey also affirmed here God's sovereign election of a people whom he saved by his Son's atoning work and justified by the imputation of his Son's righteous, flawless life. This work of grace was needed due to the radical depravity of all humankind, for this pattern of wrongdoing and sin was so deeply embedded in the human heart and made human beings so hostile to God that only the unconquerable work of the Spirit could overcome it. As Carey later said: one "may well expect to see fire and water agree, as persons with sinful hearts and desires cordially approve of the character of God."[33] Again, the Baptist leader later commented that he took great comfort from the fact that "divine

---

[32] From John Appleby, '*I Can Plod… William Carey and the early years of the first Baptist Missionary Society* (London: Grace Publications Trust, 2007), 285. He, in turn, transcribed it from a photocopy of the original church minute book held in The Record Office for Leicestershire, Leicester & Rutland, Wigston Magna, Leicester.

[33] Cited Carey, *Memoir of William Carey*, 418.

power can subdue all things; and without the Holy Spirit, nothing effectual can be done anywhere, or under any circumstances."³⁴ Moreover, this work of the Spirit was rooted in the fact that Christ

> died in the stead of sinners. We deserved the wrath of God; but he endured it. We could make no sufficient atonement for our guilt; but he completely made an end of sin...³⁵

Once people have been converted, Carey went on to affirm in the Leicester Covenant, the all-divine Holy Spirit will keep them loyal to Christ to the end when they shall "obtain everlasting Happiness through the mercy of God." It is noteworthy that Carey himself was certain that those "proofs I have of the evil tendency of my heart... convince me that I need the constant influence of the Holy Spirit; and that, if God did not continue his loving-kindness to me, I should as certainly depart from Him, and become an open profligate, as I exist."³⁶

THE *ENQUIRY*

William Carey wrote one truly seminal work, *An Enquiry into the Obligations of Christians, To Use Means for the Conversion of the Heathens* (1792). With a minimum of emotional colouring and rhetoric, this tract argued that the mandate which Christ laid upon the church in Matthew 28:18–20 to evangelize the nations of the world was binding for all time. It was thus incumbent upon local churches of Carey's day to determine what were the appropriate means for accomplishing the task. While it does not appear to have been a bestseller at the time of its publication, this tract has been aptly described as "the classical presentation of the argument for the World Mission of the Church."³⁷

---

34 Letter to Samuel Pearce, January 29, [1795], *Periodical Accounts Relative to the Baptist Missionary Society* (Clipstone: J.W. Morris, 1800), I, 127.

35 Cited Carey, *Memoir of William Carey*, 418–419.

36 Cited Carey, *Memoir of William Carey*, 19–20. For this quote and the previous one, I am indebted to Andrew Kerr's work on Carey's adherence to the so-called five points of Calvinism, "The Botanist's Tulip: Calvinism in the Writings of William Carey" (Unpublished paper, March 2009).

37 J.B. Middlebrook, *William Carey* (London: The Carey Kingsgate Press, 1961), 19.

When this tract was published in 1792, it contained five sections. In the first, Carey tackled head-on the theological objections raised by hyper-Calvinists to the evangelization of other nations. Some argued that the mandate to evangelize the nations of the world as found in Matthew 28 was required only of the apostles, and they had actually fulfilled it in their lifetime. In fact, this line of argument was not uncommon in various European Protestant circles, where it was supported by reference to proof texts like Romans 10:18, Mark 16:20 and Colossians 1:23. Even an author as astute as the Puritan John Owen asserted that no local church has the authority to "ordain men ministers for the conversion of infidels." Since the cessation of the apostolic office, Owen maintained, only God by an act of "divine providence" could send men overseas to establish churches in those lands where the gospel was not known.[38] A more pragmatic line of reasoning also declared that there was "enough to do to attend to the salvation of our own countrymen" without sailing to the ends of the earth.[39]

Carey's response to the first of these arguments was drawn directly from Matthew 28:18–20. If the commission with regard to evangelism that Christ gave in this passage applied only to the apostles, should not this also be the case for the direction to baptize those who became his disciples? Since Carey's tract had as its principal audience fellow Baptists who obviously took very seriously the command to baptize, this would have been a telling point. Then, what of those individuals who have gone to other nations and planted local churches? If the hyper-Calvinists were correct, they must have gone without God's authorization. Yet, as Carey would show in Section II of the tract, God has been with these men and women, and blessed their efforts. Finally, Christ's promise to be with his church till the end of time made little sense if the command to evangelize the world was to be completed by the end of the first century A.D.

Turning to the argument that there was enough to do at home, Carey readily agreed that there were "thousands in our own land as far from God as possible." This state of affairs ought to spur the Baptists

---

[38] John Owen, *The True Nature of a Gospel Church and Its Government*, in *The Works of John Owen*, ed. William H. Goold (1850–1853 ed.; repr. Edinburgh: The Banner of Truth Trust, 1968), 16:93.

[39] Carey, *Enquiry*, 35–36.

on to yet greater efforts to plant local churches throughout Great Britain from which the gospel could be faithfully proclaimed and these thousands reached. Yet, it still remained a fact that most of the nations of the world of that day had no copies of the Scriptures in their own tongues and no means of hearing the faithful proclamation of the Word.[40] In this section of the tract, Carey showed that missionary work was not reserved for a bygone era, but was the present duty of the church. As one of the keywords of the tract's title stated, Christians had an obligation to engage in mission.

HISTORY, GEOGRAPHY, AND REALITY: SECTIONS II TO IV OF THE *ENQUIRY*

Section II of the tract then traced the history of missions down to Carey's own day, which demonstrated that God had blessed missionary endeavours beyond the apostolic era. Following it was a section primarily composed of a statistical table of all the countries of the then-known world, detailing their length and breadth in miles, the size of their respective populations, and the religious affiliation of the majority of their inhabitants. None of this was guesswork. It was the fruit of many hours spent scouring the latest geographical handbooks and the *Northampton Mercury*, the local newspaper, for facts and notices about the nations of the world.[41] From this spare table of facts and figures, Carey concluded that the vast majority of the world was sunk in "the most deplorable state of heathen darkness, without any means of knowing the true God, except what are afforded them by the works of nature," and "utterly destitute of the knowledge of the gospel of Christ."[42]

The fourth section of the tract demolished the practical obstacles that Carey's contemporaries were wont to raise in response to what he was proposing. Confronting the real problems posed by keeping life going in other nations of the world, their distance from Great Britain, their different languages, their supposed "barbarism" and purported treatment of Europeans, Carey cogently argued that none of these rendered the evangelization of these nations impracticable.

---

40 Carey, *Enquiry*, 40–41.
41 Ernest A. Payne, "Introduction" to Carey, *Enquiry*, 20–21.
42 Carey, *Enquiry*, 88.

PRACTICAL ISSUES

Section V, the final section of the tract, was concentrated on outlining what was entailed in the other keyword of the work's title, means. First in importance among these means was "fervent and united prayer."

> However the influence of the Holy Spirit may be set at nought, and run down by many, it will be found upon trial, that all means which we can use, without it, will be ineffectual. If a temple is raised for God in the heathen world, it will not be by might, nor by power, nor by the authority of the magistrate, or the eloquence of the orator; but by my Spirit, saith the Lord of Hosts. We must therefore be in real earnest in supplicating his blessing upon our labours.[43]

As missiologist Andrew F. Walls has noted, this text cannot be fully appreciated apart from the background of prayer meetings for revival that had been going on since 1784 in the Baptist circles in which Carey was now moving. Carey was thoroughly convinced from the record of Scripture and the history of the church that "the most glorious works of grace that ever took place, have been in answer to prayer."[44] Prayer therefore had to be the first resource or means that the church used to fulfill Christ's mandate.

Prayer was vital, but, Carey argued, there were other means which Christians could employ. Turning to the world of eighteenth-century commerce for an analogy, Carey noted the way in which merchants would form trading companies, outfit ships with care and then, venturing all, "cross the widest and most tempestuous seas," face inhospitable climates, fears and other hardships to successfully secure material wealth. They do such things "because their souls enter into the spirit of the project, and their happiness in a manner depends on its success." The truest interest of Christians, on the other hand, lies in the extension of their Lord's kingdom. Carey thus made the following suggestion:

---

43 Carey, Enquiry, 103.
44 Andrew F. Walls, "Missionary Societies and the Fortunate Subversion of the Church," *The Evangelical Quarterly*, 60 (1988): 144; Carey, Enquiry, 104.

Suppose a company of serious Christians, ministers and private persons, were to form themselves into a society, and make a number of rules respecting the regulation of the plan, and the persons who are to be employed as missionaries, the means of defraying the expense, etc., etc. This society must consist of persons whose hearts are in the work, men of serious religion, and possessing a spirit of perseverance; there must be a determination not to admit any person who is not of this description, or to retain him longer than he answers to it.[45]

Out of the members of this society a small committee could be established which would oversee such things as the gathering of information and the collection of funds, the selection of missionaries and the equipping of them for missions overseas. "All of this sounds so trite today," Walls comments, "because we are used to the paraphernalia of committees and councils of reference and subscriptions and donations." To Baptist churches in the eighteenth century, however, all of this would have been quite new and, in some ways, quite extraordinary. Carey had no desire at all to subvert the primacy of the local church, but he had grasped the simple fact that the way that Baptist congregations were then organized made it next to impossible for them to engage effectively in missions overseas.[46] Here, Carey was drawing upon a tradition in English Protestant circles in which voluntary, religious associations were formed in order to achieve specific goals.

EARLY TRIALS AND BLESSINGS IN INDIA

What Carey formulated here in his *Enquiry* was realized at Kettering later that year. On October 2, 1792, fourteen men, including Carey, Fuller, Ryland and Sutcliff met in the back parlour of the home of a Martha Wallis (d.1812), the widow of a deacon of Kettering Baptist Church, and formed the Baptist Missionary Society (at the time called "The Particular Baptist Society for propagating the Gospel amongst the Heathen"). Carey, then aged thirty-one, became the Society's first appointee, along with John Thomas (1757–1801), a doctor who had

---

45 Carey, *Enquiry*, 108.
46 Walls, "Missionary Societies," 146.

trained at Westminster Hospital, London, and who had gone out to India in the 1780s as a surgeon on one of the ships of the East India Company. He thus knew Bengal and convinced the leaders of the Baptist Missionary Society that this needed to be their first field of missionary endeavour. Carey and Thomas sailed to India with their families in 1793.

Among the numerous challenges that Carey faced prior to his six-month voyage to the orient was the fact that his wife Dorothy Plackett (1756–1807) was utterly unwilling at first to go to India, though she was eventually persuaded to do so. But once in India, Dorothy began to lose her grip on reality when one of their sons, their third boy, Peter (1789–1794), died at Mudnabati, near Dinajpur (now northern Bangladesh), where William had gone to be the manager of an indigo factory after their money soon ran out in Calcutta. None of the neighbouring Hindus or Muslims would initially help the grieving family by acting as gravediggers, coffin-makers or even pallbearers, though eventually four Muslims did dig a grave for their son.[47] Over the next few years Dorothy reached the point where she was completely delusional and believed that her husband was an unrepentant adulterer. She publicly accused him of such in quite vile terms and subsequently also made two attempts to kill him. By June 1800, William Ward simply stated in his diary: "Mrs. Carey is stark mad."[48]

Carey biographers have not been kind to Dorothy, and the way she has been treated in biographies of the Baptist leader are a fascinating study in their own right. Thankfully, James Beck, senior professor of counselling at Denver Seminary and a licensed clinical psychologist, had drawn up a very balanced account of Dorothy's life in his *Dorothy Carey: The Tragic and Untold Story of Mrs. William Carey*.[49] I first read this work in 1992, when its publication coincided with the bicentennial of the formation of the Baptist Missionary Society. Recently re-

---

47 On the help of these Muslims, see William Carey, Letter to Samuel Pearce, January 29, [1795], *Periodical Accounts*, I, 127.

48 Cited James Beck, *Dorothy Carey: The Tragic and Untold Story of Mrs. William Carey* (Eugene: Wipf and Stock, 2000), 152. For a helpful overview of Dorothy's loss of sanity, see Paul Pease, *Travel with William Carey* (Leominster: Day One, 2005), 83–86.

49 See note 48 for bibliographical data.

reading parts of it, I was impressed with the judicious balance of Beck's analysis, especially given the fact that Dorothy, illiterate when William married her, left not one scrap of written text. Attempting to draw a psychological portrait of her through the eyes of others is understandably difficult, and the danger to engage in pure speculation enormous. Beck has avoided this danger while at the same time producing an excellent psychological portrait of a very unhappy woman. Along the way, he raises important questions about areas of Carey's mission that need to be faced if an accurate account of Carey and the Serampore mission is to be given. Beck does not question Carey's greatness, but shows that, like the rest of us, he had clay feet.

Carey spent five years in this remote village of Mudnabati. Four things came out of this time of isolation and great trial. First, given the fact that there were next to no Europeans in the area Carey was forced to acquire a remarkably extensive knowledge of Bengali. He also had time to begin learning Sanskrit, the classical language of the Indian subcontinent. Although Sanskrit was no longer a spoken language at the time when Carey was in India, Carey soon realized that Indians regarded this language as the only language worthy of literary production. It was a classical language that functioned much like Latin did in Europe during the Middle Ages. Carey realized that if the Bible were to be taken seriously by Indian religious leaders, it had to be translated into Sanskrit. Sanskrit was also the basis for many other Indian languages, so Carey hoped that mastery of this language would make the task of translating the Scriptures into other languages easier.

Second, as soon as he had mastered elements of the Bengali language Carey began work on the translation of the New Testament into Bengali—thus creating the dominant mould for his future ministry, namely, the translation of the Word of God. This Bengali New Testament, completed in 1797, would eventually progress through eight editions, each of them incorporating revisions, and sometimes involving a complete re-translation. In time Carey would go on to do translations in five of the great languages of India: Bengali, Sanskrit, Marathi, Hindi and Oriya, as well as several other languages, like Assamese and Telugu.

It was also at Mudnabati that Carey's long-standing interest in botany began to flower (pun intended!). He began a garden and started researching ways to improve the agricultural lot of Bengali farmers, which would eventually result in Carey becoming a leader in agricultural reform.[50] When he moved to Serampore, he would have five acres or so under cultivation and was continually asking his friends and correspondents to send him seeds, roots and bulbs. For instance, in a letter to his close friend John Sutcliff that he wrote in August 1809, Carey asked the English pastor to send him "a few tulips, daffodils, snowdrops, lilies." When Sutcliff dragged his feet about collecting them, Carey chided him:

> Were you to give a penny a day to a boy to gather seeds of cowslips, violets, daisies, crowfoots, etc., and to dig up the roots of bluebells, etc., after they have done flowering, you might fill me a box each quarter of a year; and surely some neighbours would send a few snow-drops, crocuses, etc., and other trifles. All your weeds, even your nettles and thistles, are taken the greatest care of by me here. The American friends are twenty times more communicative than the English in this respect.... Do try to mend a little![51]

In time Carey became an expert in the flora of Bengal, and would be the main editor for William Roxburgh's *Hortus Bengalensis* (1814), which catalogued the plants in the East India Company's garden in Calcutta, as well as *Flora Indica* (1832), also by Roxburgh.[52]

Finally, Dorothy's illness forced him to develop a deeper trust in God. As Carey told his sisters in December 1796, "I am very fruitless and almost useless but the Word and the attributes of God are my hope, and my confidence, and my joy, and I trust that his glorious designs will undoubtedly be answered."[53]

---

50 Franklyn J. Balasundaran, "Carey, William," in Scott W. Sunquist, ed., *A Dictionary of Asian Christianity* (Grand Rapids: Eerdmans, 2001), 119.

51 Letter to John Sutcliff, August 12, 1809 (Carey, *William Carey*, 507).

52 For this area of Carey's life, see especially Keith Farrer, *William Carey: Missionary and Botanist* (Kew: Carey Baptist Grammar School, 2005), 75–110.

53 Letter to Mary Carey and Ann Hobson, December 22, 1796 (*The Journal and Selected Letters of William Carey*, ed. Terry G. Carter [Macon: Smyth & Helwys, 2000], 249).

THE SERAMPORE TRIO

In late 1799 Carey moved with his family to Serampore, a Danish colony situated on the west bank of the River Hooghly, a dozen or so miles from Calcutta. There he linked up with two new missionaries who had just arrived from England. William Ward was a printer whom Carey had met before he left England. He would become the best preacher at Serampore, and prove to be all but indispensable as the mission's "printing press manager, cross-cultural pastoral counselor, and peacemaker."[54] During his younger years he had been involved in radical politics—a leaning and inclination he put forever behind him when he went out to India. Joshua Marshman was a man of tremendous diligence and blessed with an iron constitution. More pugnacious by nature than either Carey or Ward, Marshman easily assumed the role of apologist for the mission. Carey once described Marshman to Ryland as "all eagerness for the work" of making Christ known in India. He had seen him, he told his English correspondent, seek to refute "men of lax conduct or deistical sentiments, and labour the point with them for hours together without fatigue." When it came to zeal, Carey felt he had to conclude, "he is a Luther and I am Erasmus."[55] Such zeal was needed at Serampore, for two Moravian missionaries had previously laboured there from 1777 to 1792, but quit the field with the statement that preaching at Serampore was like plowing up a rock.[56]

So began the Serampore Mission, based around the partnership of these three men, a partnership that has few parallels in Christian history, and a work which, in the words of William Wilberforce, became "one of the chief glories of our country."[57] In all of the extant literature and manuscripts of these three men there is amazingly no trace of mutual jealousy or severe anger. Henry Martyn (1781–1812),

---

54 A. Christopher Smith, "Ward, William," in Gerald H. Anderson, *Biographical Dictionary of Christian Missions* (Grand Rapids: Eerdmans, 1998), 717.

55 Letter to John Ryland, May 24, 1810 (cited A. Christopher Smith, "Echoes of the Protestant Reformation in Baptist Serampore, 1800–1855," *The Baptist Review of Theology*, 6, no. 1 [Spring 1996]: 28–29).

56 Balasundaran, "Carey, William," 120.

57 E. Daniel Potts, *British Baptist Missionaries in India, 1793–1837* (Cambridge: Cambridge University Press, 1967), 17.

an evangelical Anglican and missionary to the Persians, said that never were "such men...so suited to another and to their work."

CAREY THE TRANSLATOR

The principal contribution of Carey to the Serampore Mission was through his remarkable linguistic ability. By the time that Carey moved to Serampore he had acquired an extensive knowledge of both Bengali and Sanskrit. The Bengali New Testament, though translated by 1797, was not completely published until February 1801. Seven years later the New Testament in Sanskrit was being seen through the press. All told, Carey translated or supervised the translation of the Scriptures into thirty-four Asian languages or dialects. In fact, in these early years of the modern missionary movement, forty-three percent of first translations of the Scriptures into new languages anywhere in the world were published at Serampore.

Now, as a grammarian Carey was brilliant. As a translator, though, it must be admitted that he lacked "a keen sensitiveness to the finer shades and nuances of ideas and meaning," a failing which dogged all of his translations.[58] Carey remarked frequently that he knew the translations were not perfect and he hoped that others would build on them. Carey believed that a translation should be geared as much as possible to the grammatical structure and wording of the original Hebrew or Greek. But in doing so he failed to make the Scriptures communicate in the living language of the people of India. It is not fortuitous that the translation which survived the longest was his translation into Sanskrit. It was thirty-three years before it was replaced with a new translation. Perhaps it lasted longer because it was a classical, written language, and not a spoken, vernacular language. Carey's failure to understand at times the subtleties of translation was, it should be noted, a common failing of the day among translators. A good exception is Adoniram Judson's (1788–1850) translation of the Scriptures into Burmese. His Burmese Bible is still in use, and has remained readable, whereas none of Carey's translations are still being used.

---

58 Stephen Neill, *A History of Christianity in India 1707–1858* (Cambridge: Cambridge University Press, 1985), 190.

Driving Carey, though, was the deep conviction that the Word of God had to be available to the people-groups that he was trying to reach. He was rightly convinced that the Word of God is in itself the great instrument for the conversion of unbelievers. Yet, he would have probably achieved more if he had attempted less.

THE CONVERSION OF KRISHNA PAL

Up until the move to Serampore, Carey had not seen any lasting spiritual fruit among the Indian people. Within a year of the start of the mission at Serampore, however, converts began to come in. The first was Krishna Pal (1764–1822), a Hindu carpenter and long-time seeker after truth. Pal had heard the gospel already from one of the Moravian missionaries who had laboured in the vicinity of Serampore up until 1792, but it had made no lasting impression on his mind. On the morning of November 25, 1800, however, while he was washing in the River Hooghly, not far the Serampore mission, he fell on the slippery bank and dislocated his shoulder. He sought help from John Thomas, who came to his home with Marshman and Carey; Thomas set his arm and the three missionaries shared some Scripture with Pal. That evening Thomas and Marshman returned and gave Pal this rhyme to ponder along with a full explanation of its meaning (Pal was used to such forms of wording since mantras played a large role in his Hindu convictions):

> Sin confessing, sin forsaking,
>   Christ's righteousness embracing,
>   The soul is free.[59]

A month or so later, Krishna Pal told Thomas that he believed that "Christ gave his life up for the salvation of sinners," and that he had personally embraced this gospel truth. He subsequently broke caste by eating with the missionaries, and Ward commented rightly: "the door of faith is open to the Gentiles; who shall shut it? The chain of

---

59 See also the anonymous *The First Hindoo Convert: A Memoir of Krishna Pal* (Philadelphia: American Baptist Publication Society, 1852), 9–11.

the caste is broken, who shall mend it?"[60] On Sunday, December 28, 1800, a few days after his profession of faith and in the presence of a huge crowd of Europeans, Hindus and Muslims, Carey baptized Krishna Pal in the Hooghly River.[61]

Pal was the first of hundreds who were converted through the witness of the Serampore Mission over the next three decades. By 1821, over 1,400 believers—half of them Indians—had been baptized and Krishna Pal, who died the following year, had become one of the finest preachers of the Mission. Carey once described an early sermon of this Indian brother as "fluent, perspicuous, and affectionate, in a very high degree."[62] And in 1811, Carey told John Sutcliff in a letter that Krishna was a "zealous, well-informed, and I may add, eloquent minister of the gospel," who was regularly preaching twelve to fourteen times a week in Calcutta or its environs.[63]

Krishna also wrote hymns to express his love, and that of his fellow Bengali believers, for Christ. One of them, translated into English, is still in use in certain evangelical circles. Its first stanza runs thus:

O thou, my soul, forget no more,
  The Friend who all thy misery bore;
Let every idol be forgot,
  But, O my soul, forget him not.[64]

In its cross-centredness and the power of the cross to deliver from idolatry, this verse is quintessentially evangelical and well captures the heart of why Carey and his colleagues were in India. It is very easy today to view the Serampore Trio and their colleagues primarily as

---

60 Cited "Memoir of the Rev. William Ward," *New Evangelical Magazine and Theological Review*, 10 (1824): 3.
61 *First Hindoo Convert*, 14–17.
62 Cited *First Hindoo Convert*, 38.
63 Cited *First Hindoo Convert*, 67.
64 See Hymn 145, stanza 1 in *Grace Hymns* (London: Grace Publications Trust, 1975), For a study of the hymn, see David W. Music, "Krishna Pal's "O Thou, My Soul, Forget No More" and "Global Hymnody" Among Nineteenth-Century Baptists," *American Baptist Quarterly*, 28 (2009): 194–207. Music argues that Joshua Marshman, who translated the hymn into English, has reshaped elements of it to reflect a profounder theology.

social reformers, for they helped abolish such social ills as *sati* (the self-immolation of a widow on the funeral pyre of her husband) and the prostitution of children in the Hindu temples, and educational activists—their founding of Serampore College in 1818 is a remarkable achievement. But this would be to confuse the core of their ministry with its fruit. Sending forth the gospel with its message of the crucified Christ whose death alone delivered from sin and its consequences was the main thing these men and women were about. The social and educational impact of that proclamation was a happy byproduct of their gospel preaching. To view them as primarily social reformers is to do them a grave injustice.

SERAMPORE FORM OF AGREEMENT (1805)

The core principles by which Carey, Marshman and Ward operated can be found in the *Serampore Form of Agreement*, drawn up in 1805, and a brief review of this text is vital to understanding the heart of this Christian mission.

First of all, Carey and his colleagues expressed their conviction that the non-Christian peoples of India had to be valued for what they were—immortal souls but men and women who had no true knowledge of their Maker. As the Serampore missionaries wrote:

> In order to be prepared for our great and solemn work, it is absolutely necessary that we set an infinite value upon immortal souls; that we often endeavour to affect our minds with the dreadful loss sustained by an unconverted soul launched into eternity. It becomes us to fix in our minds the awful doctrine of eternal punishment, and to realise frequently the inconceivably awful condition of this vast country, lying in the arms of the wicked one. If we have not his awful sense of the value of souls, it is impossible that we can feel aright in any other part of our work, and in this case it had been better for us to have been in any other situation rather than in that of a missionary. Oh! may our hearts bleed over these poor idolaters, and may their case lie with continued weight on our minds, that we may resemble that eminent Missionary, who compared the travail of his soul, on

account of the spiritual state of those committed to his charge, to the pains of childbirth.[65]

The "eminent Missionary" in view here is obviously the apostle Paul and the biblical text being alluded to is Galatians 4:19. The Serampore text went on to express the hope that, if God could plant saving truth among "the sottish and brutalised Britons," he could just as easily do the same in India. The British missionaries were thus confident that God would eventually "famish all the gods of India" and cause idolaters in the Indian subcontinent "to cast their idols to the moles and to the bats, and renounce for ever the work of their own hands."[66]

In order to best reach the various people groups of India, each of them had to be approached in their own language. This entailed the missionary learning the local language of the people that he was trying to reach. This was a fundamental of Carey's mission, and was the impetus behind the attempt to make the Scriptures available in as many tongues of India as possible.[67] Linked to this translation project was also a commitment to become deeply familiar with the "modes of thinking,…habits,…propensities,…[and] antipathies" of the Indian people.[68] One of the ways in which Carey sought to do this was by printing various Indian texts that best exemplified the worldview of the Indian people. Not surprisingly, this caused some concern back home in England, but Carey was adamant that this was needed to understand why the Indians thought the way they did.[69]

Then, although Carey and his colleagues were not averse to point outing to their Indian hearers what they judged to be the weaknesses and imperfections of Hinduism and Islam, they did not begin with such a critique. As the *Serampore Form of Agreement* put it: "Nor is it advisable at once to attack their prejudices by exhibiting with acrimony the sins of their gods; neither should we upon any account do violence to their images, nor interrupt their worship: the real con-

---

65 *Serampore Form of Agreement* I.
66 *Serampore Form of Agreement* I.
67 See also *Serampore Form of Agreement* IX.
68 *Serampore Form of Agreement* II.
69 Neill, *History of Christianity in India*, 191–192 and 504, n. 20.

quests of the gospel are those of love: 'And I, if I be lifted up, will draw all men unto me' [see John 12:32]."⁷⁰ As far as possible, they sought to avoid giving offence to non-Christians: "Those parts of English manners which are most offensive to them should be kept out of sight as much as possible. We should also avoid every degree of cruelty to animals."⁷¹ The latter remark was, of course, necessary in a Hindu context where numerous animals were the object of devotion.⁷²

Fourth, Carey and his friends were determined to place Christ crucified at the heart of their preaching. They were convinced that this was Paul's methodology, for the "doctrine of Christ's expiatory death and all-sufficient merits has been, and must ever remain, the grand means of conversion." Proof of the efficacy of this type of preaching was found in the fact that the cross was central to the preaching of the Reformers and that of such eighteenth-century evangelists as George Whitefield. The Serampore missionaries had also found that "the astonishing and all-constraining love exhibited in our Redeemer's propitiatory death" was foremost in the conversion of every Hindu to that point in time through their mission.⁷³

While baptism was not long delayed for new converts, it was to be followed by a period of Christian instruction and nurture.⁷⁴ Nor was it necessary to change the names of Indian converts so as to replace these names by biblical ones. Thus, the first convert, Krishna Pal, had been

---

70 *Serampore Form of Agreement* III. The one striking exception to this principle took place when a booklet deeply critical of Muhammad, known to history as *The Persian Pamphlet*, was printed in 1807 by the Serampore Press after Ward had only given it a cursory reading. See Peter Morden, "Andrew Fuller as an Apologist for Missions," in Michael A.G. Haykin, ed., '*At the Pure Fountain of Thy Word*': *Andrew Fuller as an Apologist* (Carlisle: Paternoster Press, 2004), 247–248.

71 *Serampore Form of Agreement* III.

72 The deep interest Carey had in botany has been noted previously. He was also fascinated by the animal world. Carey saw in the animal world incontestable proof of "the wisdom and goodness of the universal Parent of all creatures." Study of the various animals should ultimately "raise the mind to sublime meditation upon and admiration of their Maker." (William Carey, "On the Study of Nature," *The Friend of India* [Monthly Series], 8 [1825]: 247–250).

73 *Serampore Form of Agreement* V.

74 *Serampore Form of Agreement* VII.

named after a Hindu deity, but retained his name after his conversion.[75] On the other hand, conversion did entail a renunciation of caste and the caste-system. By eating with the missionaries and the other native believers, whatever their social background, new converts demonstrated the reality of their desire to be part of the Christian family.[76]

Fifth, every encouragement was to be given to Indian believers to develop their gifts with the confidence that some of them would become preachers, for, the Serampore missionaries believed, "it is only by means of native preachers that we can hope for the universal spread of the Gospel throughout this immense continent."[77] This in turn would soon lead to Indian churches pastored by Indian brethren, who, in due course, would send out missionaries to the four corners of the subcontinent.[78] As an autodidact, Carey especially knew the value of knowledge and the Serampore covenant emphasized that in "preparing the Hindoos for casting their idols to the moles and the bats" it was essential to have native schools to give future pastors and missionaries an elementary education.[79] Within a few years the missionaries had established a hundred or so of these schools.[80] And in 1818, they started Serampore College as primarily a divinity school for leaders and pastors, though non-Christians could also pursue studies there. By the time of Carey's death sixteen years later, the college had over eighty students.[81]

Finally, the *Serampore Form of Agreement* stressed the need for prayer to undergird the entirety of the mission. It is "secret, fervent, believing prayer"—what Carey also called "a heart given up to God in closet religion"—that is essential to both a holy life and a useful life in God's

---

75 *Serampore Form of Agreement* VIII.
76 See the comments of Neill, *History of Christianity in India*, 198.
77 *Serampore Form of Agreement* VIII.
78 *Serampore Form of Agreement* VIII.
79 *Serampore Form of Agreement* IX. See the detailed argument about this point in William Carey, Joshua Marshman and William Ward, *College for the Instruction of Asiatic Christian and Other Youth, in Eastern Literature and European Science, at Serampore, Bengal* (London: Black, Kingsbury, Parbury, and Allen, 1819), 1–6.
80 Neill, *History of Christianity in India*, 199–200.
81 Neill, *History of Christianity in India*, 200–201.

"great work of human redemption."[82] Surely the fact that the Baptist Missionary Society had been born in prayer and that Carey had seen the beginnings of the impact of corporate prayer meetings for revival in England lay behind this emphasis on prayer.

FINAL YEARS AND LEGACY

In his final years Carey became increasingly vocal in his writings about his only plea for acceptance with God: the shed blood of Jesus Christ for his sins. In a letter that he wrote in 1831 to his son Jabez, he told him:

> I am this day seventy years old—a monument of divine mercy and goodness; though, on a review of my life, I find much, very much, for which I ought to be humbled in the dust. My direct and positive sins are innumerable; my negligence in the Lord's work has been great; I have not promoted his cause nor sought his glory and honour as I ought. Notwithstanding all this, I am spared till now and am still retained in his work. I trust for acceptance with him to the blood of Christ alone; and I hope I am received into the divine favour through him. I wish to be more entirely devoted to his service, more completely sanctified, and more habitually exercising all the Christian graces, and bringing forth the fruits of righteousness to the praise and honour of that Saviour who gave his life a sacrifice for sin.[83]

Here are two theological themes that were foundational to the entirety of Carey's thought and mission that has been sketched above. First, the death of Christ for sinners was the Christian's only plea with regard to salvation when he stood in the presence of a holy God at the final judgement. Second, the ultimate goal of the Christian life was the glory of God. Carey felt that he had not made the latter uppermost throughout his life, hence his comfort in the former.

Similar thoughts fill another letter that Carey wrote in 1831, this one to his sisters in England. John Webster Morris, whom Carey had known many years earlier, was hoping to write something about

---

82 *Serampore Form of Agreement* X.
83 Carey, *Memoir of William Carey*, 566–567.

Carey to satisfy a British public clamoring for details about the life of the Baptist missionary. Carey had clearly become something of a celebrity. Carey wanted nothing to do with such "celebrification." As he told his sisters:

> Dear Morris wrote to me for letters and other documents to assist him in writing memoirs of me after my death, but there was a spirit in his letter which I must disapprove. I therefore told him so in my reply, and absolutely refused to send anything. Indeed I have no wish that anyone should write or say anything about me; let my memorial sleep with my body in the dust and at the last great day all the good or evil which belongs to my character will be fully known. My great concern now is to be found in Christ. His atoning sacrifice is all my hope; and I know that sacrifice to be of such value that God has accepted it as fully vindicating his government in the exercise of mercy to sinners and as that on account of which he will accept the greatest offender who seeks to him for pardon. And the acceptance of that sacrifice of atonement was testified by the resurrection of our Lord from the dead and by the commission to preach the gospel to all nations, with a promise or rather a declaration that whosoever believeth on the Son shall be saved, "shall not come into condemnation but is passed from death unto life" [John 5:24].[84]

Given such sentiments it is not surprising that Carey gave explicit instructions that apart from his date of birth and death, nothing was to be inscribed upon his tombstone but these words from a hymn of Isaac Watts: "A wretched, poor, and helpless worm, On Thy kind arms I fall."[85]

What, then, is Carey's legacy? A number of things could be cited, but two are especially prominent. First, Carey models the vital importance that prayer must occupy in the life of God's children. Is prayer—both private and corporate—as great a priority in our lives as it was in

---

[84] From Ernest A. Payne, "A "Carey" Letter of 1831," *The Baptist Quarterly*, 9 (1938–1939): 240–241.

[85] Carey, *Memoir of William Carey*, 572–573.

Carey's and that of his friends? We gladly confess with Carey that "if a temple is raised for God in the heathen world, it will be by" the Spirit of God. But do we carry our beliefs into action by prayer for his empowering and blessing?

Second, Carey was an activist. Though he often reproached himself for his indolence, his life was focused powerfully on winning the lost for Christ and advancing the kingdom of Christ in this rebellious world. In the words of David Kingdon, Carey and his colleagues knew that they were debtors to grace, and they were thus willing to "hazard health and comfort to bring the gospel to heathen multitudes lost in darkness. They believed in the eternal punishment, not the annihilation, of the impenitent. They entertained no hopeful views of the salvific possibilities of general revelation nor speculated that people could be saved apart from the proclamation of the gospel."[86]

This twofold legacy is well summed up by the two sections of Carey's most famous sermon, which he preached on Wednesday, May 30, 1792, at the annual meeting of the Northamptonshire Association, held that year in Nottingham. Based on Isaiah 54:2–3, the sermon was definitely catalytic in the formation of the Baptist Missionary Society. Although the sermon is not extant, the headings were long remembered and have become something of a motto for Carey's life and thought: "Expect great things [from God]"—"Attempt great things [for God]."[87] The order of these points is important as is the fact that, for an evangelical like Carey, the two points are inseparably yoked together: prayer must precede action but prayer is never alone—it leads to action.

---

[86] "William Carey and the Origins of the Modern Missionary Movement," 89. In light of the recent teaching of universalism by Rob Bell, this is an important aspect of Carey's legacy.

[87] On the circumstances surrounding the sermon and its impact, see Haykin, *One heart and one soul*, 216–218. The original headings did not include "from God" or "for God," though these phrases were obviously implied. For the date of the sermon, see Thomas J. Budge, "Date of 'Deathless Sermon,'" *The Baptist Quarterly*, 33 (1989–1990): 335.

10

The Holy Spirit, the *charismata* and signs and wonders

Some evangelical perspectives from the eighteenth century[1]

> The ordinary influences of the Holy Spirit are of far more importance to the individuals who partake of them, than his extraordinary gifts. —JOHN RYLAND[2]

---

[1] An earlier and shorter version of this article appeared in *The Baptist Review of Theology*, 3, no. 2 (1993): 4–27. It, in turn, had its origin in an address given at a conference sponsored by Central Baptist Seminary, Toronto, in the fall of 1992 as part of a response to the so-called Toronto Blessing. This version appeared in *The Southern Baptist Journal of Theology* 16, no. 4 (Winter 2012): 54–73. Used by permission.

[2] John Ryland, "The Design of Spiritual Gifts," in *Pastoral Memorials: Selected from the Manuscripts of the Late Revd. John Ryland* (London: B.J. Holdsworth, 1828), II, 67.

The emergence of Pentecostalism at the turn of the twentieth century, along with the rise of the Charismatic Movement in the 1960s and the more recent development of the Association of Vineyard Churches have ensured that the work of the Holy Spirit has been keenly debated within the ranks of evangelical Christianity in the last century or so. The way in which this discussion has often been conducted, however, has caused many of its participants to be blind to the fact that this is *not* the first time in the history of the church that the activity of the Spirit has come under such intense and prolonged scrutiny. For instance, eighteenth-century evangelicals on both sides of the Atlantic—heirs to the in-depth analysis of the Spirit's work by the Puritans and with their interest in things pneumatological quickened by their experience of revival—were involved in an extensive debate over such fundamental questions of pneumatology as the indwelling of the Spirit, the doctrine of assurance, the Spirit's work in sanctification and the experience of the Spirit's power.[3] The study of a previous pneumatological debate like that in the eighteenth century is, of course, valuable in its own right. Examination of the eighteenth-century evangelical

---

3   Timothy L. Smith, "Foreword" to Harald Lindström, *Wesley and Sanctification* (Grand Rapids: Zondervan, 1980), n.p. Cf. the remark of Alan C. Clifford, "The Christian Mind of Philip Doddridge (1702–1751): The Gospel According to an Evangelical Congregationalist," *The Evangelical Quarterly*, 56 (1984): 236: "With the advent of the Methodist revival, attention became focused on the doctrine and work of the Holy Spirit." See also Ronald Reeve, "John Wesley, Charles Simeon, and the Evangelical Revival," *Canadian Journal of Theology*, 2 (1956): 203–214, *passim*. For eighteenth-century evangelical thought about (1) the indwelling Spirit, see Thomas Templeton Taylor, "The Spirit of the Awakening: The Pneumatology of New England's Great Awakening in Historical and Theological Context" (PhD Thesis, University of Illinois at Urbana-Champaign, 1988), *passim*; (2) the doctrine of assurance, see Arthur S. Yates, *The Doctrine of Assurance with Special Reference to John Wesley* (London: Epworth, 1952); David Bebbington, *Evangelicalism in Modern Britain: A History from the 1730s to the 1980s* (1989 ed.; repr.; Grand Rapids: Baker, 1992), 42–50; (3) the sanctifying Spirit, see Timothy L. Smith, "George Whitefield and Wesleyan Perfectionism," *The Wesleyan Theological Journal*, 19, no. 1 (1984): 63–85; Timothy L. Smith, "Whitefield and Wesley on Righteousness by Grace," *TSF Bulletin*, 9, no. 4 (1986): 5–8; (4) and for the power of the Spirit, see R. Tudur Jones, "The Evangelical Revival in Wales: A Study in Spirituality," in *An Introduction to Celtic Christianity*, ed. James P. Mackey (Edinburgh: T&T Clark, 1989), 237–267.

experience of and reflection on the work of the Holy Spirit, however, can also generate some fresh perspectives on current debates about the Spirit's activity. For, as William DeArteaga has noted, there are definite parallels between the evangelical revivals of the eighteenth century and renewal movements in the present day.[4]

PHILIP DODDRIDGE AND HIS BIOGRAPHY OF COLONEL JAMES GARDINER

Known to his friends as "the happy rake," James Gardiner (1688–1745), a Scottish military officer and dragoon, was regarded by his friends as one of the most fortunate men alive during the second decade of the eighteenth century.[5] Tall, stately in his bearing, and gifted with a fine constitution, he had distinguished himself a number of times on the field of battle and seemed destined for a brilliant career. Although he had been raised by a mother who had taken great pains to "instruct him with great tenderness and affection in the principles of true Christianity," Gardiner had long since rejected this childhood instruction.[6] Stationed in Paris during the 1710s as an *aide-de-camp* to the British ambassador, John Dalrymple (1673–1747), the second Earl of Stair, Gardiner went from one sexual encounter to another in an unbridled pursuit of pleasure. In the words of Philip Doddridge, the Dissenting minister who was later his close friend and biographer, "if not the whole business, at least the whole happiness of his life" consisted of these sordid affairs.[7] This immersion in a lifestyle of sex, seduction and lust, though, was not without some pangs of conscience. On one occasion, when some of his companions were congratulating him on the

---

4 William DeArteaga, *Quenching the Spirit: Examining Centuries of Opposition to the Moving of the Holy Spirit* (Lake Mary: Creation House, 1992), 29.

5 Philip Doddridge, *Some Remarkable Passages in the Life of the Honourable Col. James Gardiner* 22 (*The Works of the Rev. P. Doddridge* [Leeds, 1803], IV, 19). Further references to this work will cite it as *Life of the Honourable Col. James Gardiner* and further identify these references according to paragraph numbers. The complete story of Gardiner's conversion may be found in *Life of the Honourable Col. James Gardiner* 30–37 (*Works of the Rev. P. Doddridge*, IV, 24–29). A brief account of Gardiner's life and conversion may be found in F.W.B. Bullock, *Evangelical Conversion in Great Britain 1696–1845* (St. Leonards on Sea: Budd & Gillatt, 1959), 16–21.

6 Doddridge, *Life of the Honourable Col. James Gardiner* 9 (*Works*, IV, 11).

7 Doddridge, *Life of the Honourable Col. James Gardiner* 22 (*Works*, IV, 19).

felicity of his way of life, a dog happened to enter the room in which they were seated, and Gardiner could not help but think to himself, "Oh that I were that dog!"[8] A few half-hearted attempts to mend his ways always proved far too weak to resist the force of temptation. But, when he was thirty-one, Gardiner underwent a conversion so striking that Doddridge would later describe it with words such as "astonishing," "remarkable," "extraordinary" and "amazing."[9]

Toward the middle of July 1719, Gardiner had spent an evening in the company of some friends, the party breaking up around eleven o'clock. Gardiner had a rendezvous with a married woman planned for midnight, and, not wanting to arrive early, he decided to kill the intervening hour by reading. Quite unintentionally, it was a religious book that he picked up to read: *The Christian Soldier; or Heaven taken by storm* (1669) by the Puritan divine Thomas Watson (died c.1686). While he was reading, an unusual blaze of light suddenly fell upon the book, which at first he thought might have been caused by a nearby candle. Lifting up his eyes, though, he saw, to his utter astonishment, a vision of Christ. In the words of Doddridge:

> There was before him, as it were, suspended in the air, a visible representation of the Lord Jesus Christ upon the cross, surrounded on all sides with a glory; and [he] was impressed, as if a voice, or something equivalent to a voice had come to him, to this effect (for he was not confident as to the very words): "Oh sinner! did I suffer this for thee, and are these thy returns?"...Struck with so amazing a phenomenon as this, there remained hardly any life in him; so that he sunk down in the arm-chair in which he sat, and continued, he knew not very exactly how long, insensible.[10]

When he opened his eyes, the vision had gone, but not the impression it had forever made upon his heart and life. He completely forgot his midnight rendezvous.

---

8 Doddridge, *Life of the Honourable Col. James Gardiner* 23 (*Works*, IV, 19).
9 Doddridge, *Life of the Honourable Col. James Gardiner* 28, 29, 36 (*Works*, IV, 22, 23, 27).
10 Doddridge, *Life of the Honourable Col. James Gardiner* 32 (*Works*, IV, 25).

He rose in a tumult of passions not to be conceived, and walked to and fro in his chamber, till he was ready to drop down, in unutterable astonishment and agony of heart, appearing to himself the vilest monster in the creation of God, who had all his lifetime been crucifying Christ afresh by his sins, and now saw, as he assuredly believed, by a miraculous vision, the horror of what he had done. With this was connected such a view, both of the majesty and goodness of God, as caused him to loathe and abhor himself, to repent as in dust and ashes. He immediately gave judgment against himself, that he was most justly worthy of eternal damnation.[11]

The rest of the night he spent meditating on God's purity and goodness, his spurning of God's grace and many of the providential escapes from death that he had experienced. His former lifestyle now appeared to him as utterly abhorrent, his sexual addiction was gone and he was determined to spend the remainder of his time on earth in God's service. Indeed, from this extraordinary conversion till he fell at the Battle of Prestonpans on September 21, 1745, fighting against the Jacobite army of Charles Edward Stuart (1720–1788), otherwise known as Bonnie Prince Charlie, his was an "exemplary and truly Christian life."[12]

---

11 Doddridge, *Life of the Honourable Col. James Gardiner* 33 (*Works*, IV, 25).

12 Doddridge, *Life of the Honourable Col. James Gardiner* 35 (*Works*, IV, 27). While Doddridge clearly regarded Gardiner's conversion as most unusual, he did mention that he was aware of at least one other like it. He did not name the individual, who was still living at the time when Doddridge wrote his biography of Gardiner in 1747. He merely stated that the individual of whom he was speaking was "one of the brightest living ornaments" of the Church of England, a man who has both an "exemplary life" and a "zealous ministry" (Doddridge, *Life of the Honourable Col. James Gardiner* 36 [*Works*, IV, 27–28]). The man in question was George Thomson (1698–1782), vicar of St. Gennys, a windswept village in North Cornwall perched atop the cliffs overlooking the Atlantic. For a couple of years after his coming to St. Gennys, Thomson had lived a careless life, characterized by "debaucheries" and similar in many ways to that of Gardiner before the latter's conversion. Yet, in 1733 or 1734, Thomson was awakened from his benighted state by a dream, which was repeated three times in one night with ever-increasing terror. In the first instance of the dream, he was told: "This day month, at six in the afternoon, you must appear before the judgment seat of Christ, to give an account of the dreadful abuse of all your talents, and the injuries

Now, occasionally gracing the evangelical revival, which began in the mid-1730s, were scenes every bit as "extraordinary" as that which had attended the conversion of Gardiner. It is not surprising, therefore, that in Doddridge's biography of Gardiner, which was written in 1747, two sections of the biography were devoted to this revival. Doddridge particularly mentions the Scottish revival at Cambuslang in February 1742 and the preaching of William McCulloch (1691–1771), the minister of Cambuslang—at that time a rural parish a few miles to the southeast of Glasgow—which was instrumental in the inception of this revival. McCulloch was far from being an accomplished speaker. In the jargon of the day, he was a yill- or ale-minister, a term used of ministers whose preaching was so dry that when their turn came to preach at the large outdoor communion gatherings then held once a year by the Scottish churches, many of the audience would leave to quench their thirst from nearby ale barrels provided for refreshment.[13]

---

done the souls committed to your care." Thomson woke in alarm, but soon shrugged off the dream with the thought, "Glad I am it was no more than a dream; I am no old woman to mind dreams," and promptly fell back asleep. The dream was repeated "with greater circumstances of terror," and Thomson awoke again, this time deeply shaken. After much tossing and agitation, he was able to go back to sleep once more, only to be awakened after the dream had been repeated yet a third time. Thomson, now "filled with horror" and convinced that he had but a month to live, called together his friends and the leading individuals in the parish. He recounted his dream to them, told them to find someone to fill his place and to return to conduct his funeral in a month. He then shut himself up in his home and for two weeks was "in the depth of despair," since he was persuaded that it was not consistent with God's honour for him to forgive one who had brought such dishonour upon his holy name. After a fortnight of distress, however, Thomson was led to Romans 3, where he "clearly saw that God could be glorified in his salvation, through the propitiation of Christ's most precious blood." Thomson returned to his pulpit and began to preach those doctrines which would soon be the hallmark of the evangelical revival: the atoning death of Christ and the imputation of his righteousness, the necessity of the new birth and the absolute need of the Holy Spirit's power and presence to begin and carry on a saving change in heart and life. For the full account of Thomson's conversion, see I. Davidson, "Some Account of the Rev. George Thomson," *The Evangelical Magazine*, 9 (1800): 221–225. This account consists of a letter written by Davidson in 1772. For a good study of Thomson's ministry, see G.C.B. Davies, *The Early Cornish Evangelicals 1735–1760: A Study of Walker of Truro and Others* (London: S.P.C.K., 1951), 30–34, 37–52.

13 Michael J. Crawford, *Seasons of Grace: Colonial New England's Revival Tradition in Its British Context* (Oxford: Oxford University Press, 1991), 160.

Yet it was under McCulloch's preaching in mid-February 1742, that, according to Doddridge, around 130 people, most of whom had sat under McCulloch's preaching for a number of years, "were awakened on a sudden to attend to it, as if it had been a new revelation brought down from heaven, and attested by as astonishing miracles as ever were wrought by Peter or Paul."[14] In July of the same year, George Whitefield arrived at Cambuslang, where he was soon preaching to huge, receptive audiences. In August, for instance, some 30,000 attended an outdoor communion service, where Whitefield preached a number of sermons over the course of a three-day weekend. Alexander Webster, a minister from Edinburgh, whose description of this event was read by many, including Doddridge,[15] wrote of some of the happenings of that weekend:

During the time of divine worship, profound reverence overspread every countenance. They hear as for eternity.... Thousands are melted into tears. Many cry out in the bitterness of their soul. Some...from the stoutest man to the tenderest child, shake and tremble and a few fall down as dead. Nor does this happen only when men of warm address alarm them with the terrors of the law, but when the most deliberate preacher speaks of redeeming love.[16]

Doddridge also received an account of the Cambuslang revival from Gardiner, who regarded it as "a matter of eternal praise."[17] Doddridge went on to say that Gardiner was of the same frame of mind when it came to "intelligence of a like kind from England; whether the clergy

---

14 Doddridge, *Life of the Honourable Col. James Gardiner* 135 (*Works*, IV, 88).
15 Doddridge, *Life of the Honourable Col. James Gardiner* 135 (*Works*, IV, 88).
16 Cited in Arnold A. Dallimore, *George Whitefield: The Life and Times of the Great Evangelist of the Eighteenth-Century Revival* (Westchester: Cornerstone, 1980), 2:128. For further details and discussion of this revival, see especially Arthur Fawcett, *The Cambuslang Revival: The Scottish Evangelical Revival of the Eighteenth Century* (London: The Banner of Truth Trust, 1971); Crawford, *Seasons of Grace*, passim.
17 Doddridge, *Life of the Honourable Col. James Gardiner* 135 (*Works*, IV, 88). See also Geoffrey F. Nuttall, *Calendar of the Correspondence of Philip Doddridge (1702–1751)* (London: Her Majesty's Stationery Office, 1979), 147.

of the established church, or dissenting ministers, whether our own countrymen, or foreigners, were the instruments of it."[18] Gardiner, Doddridge wrote, had particularly mentioned to him one minister—in the biography, Doddridge leaves him unnamed—"who had been remarkably successful in his ministry," but who had been ill-treated by some. Gardiner remarked: "I had rather be that despised persecuted man, to be an instrument in the hand of the Spirit, in converting so many souls, and building up so many in their holy faith, than I would be emperor of the whole world."[19] Here Doddridge is actually quoting from a letter, still extant, which he had received from Gardiner in 1742. In this letter, dated November 16 and written to Doddridge from Ghent, Gardiner mentioned that he had recently been the recipient of a letter from George Whitefield. He then proceeded to express the very sentiments with regard to the Anglican evangelist that have just been cited from Gardiner's biography.[20] Presumably Doddridge left Whitefield unnamed in his biography of Gardiner for the basic reason that Whitefield was still living as he wrote.

In detailing Gardiner's views toward the revival, Doddridge was also clearly indicating where his own sympathies lay. Doddridge himself had first written to Whitefield on December 12, 1738, and enquired as to whether he had any intentions of coming near Northampton, where Doddridge lived. Although the two had never met, Doddridge wrote that he would "gladly undertake a day's journey to meet and confer" with Whitefield, so that he might, as he puts it, "light my lamp by yours and gain that assistance in my way heavenward which a knowledge of you will, I hope, give me."[21] It appears that the two men met for the first time on May 23, 1739, when Whitefield preached in the open air to around 3,000 people at Northampton. In his *Journal*, Whitefield mentions that prior to his preaching he had been "most courteously received by Dr. Doddridge."[22] The following month Doddridge thanked God in

---

18 Doddridge, *Life of the Honourable Col. James Gardiner*, 136 (*Works*, IV, 88).
19 Doddridge, *Life of the Honourable Col. James Gardiner*, 136 (*Works*, IV, 89).
20 Nuttall, *Calendar of the Correspondence of Philip Doddridge*, 161.
21 Graham C.G. Thomas, "George Whitefield and Friends: The Correspondence of Some Early Methodists," *The National Library of Wales Journal* 27 (1991–92): 65.
22 *George Whitefield's Journals* (London: The Banner of Truth Trust, 1960), 273. For Doddridge's sympathies with the leaders in the revival, see especially Alan C. Clifford,

his *Diary* for "adding to me the friendship of some excellent persons, among whom I must mention Mr. Whitefield and Colonel Gardiner."[23]

Four years later, Doddridge preached for Whitefield at his Tabernacle in London, which caused quite a stir among his fellow Dissenters. For example, Isaac Watts, Doddridge's mentor and friend, wrote to him and stated that he had been the recipient of "many questions" about Doddridge's preaching or praying at the Tabernacle, and "of sinking the character of a Minister…among the dissenters so low thereby."[24] When Doddridge reciprocated by having Whitefield preach at his church in Northampton in October of that year, Watts and other Dissenters were deeply concerned.[25] Central to their concern was the fear that Doddridge's support of the evangelist was simply aiding and abetting that chief of eighteenth-century phobias, "enthusiasm."[26]

"ENTHUSIASM" AND THE EVANGELICAL REVIVAL

The *mentalité* of the eighteenth century, which gloried in reason, moderation and order, regarded "enthusiasm" in religion as a particularly unsavoury phenomenon. To be charged with enthusiasm in this sphere was to be accused of claiming extraordinary revelations and powers from the Holy Spirit, though the word could be used more loosely to denote any kind of religious excitement.[27] John Locke (1632–1704), in

---

"Philip Doddridge and the Oxford Methodists," *Proceedings of the Wesley Historical Society* 42 (1979): 75–80. As W.R. Ward puts it: by the 1740s Doddridge "was a Methodist in the sense of an adherent of the movement of revival and reform" [*The Protestant Evangelical Awakening* (Cambridge: Cambridge University Press, 1992). 348].

23 *The Correspondence and Diary of Philip Doddridge*, ed. John Doddridge Humphreys (London: Henry Colburn and Richard Bentley, 1831), V, 401.

24 Nuttall, *Calendar of the Correspondence of Philip Doddridge*, 183. On Watts' relationship to Whitefield, see K.L. Parry, "Isaac Watts and 18th Century Dissent," *Transactions of the Congregational Historical Society* 16 (1949–1951): 21–22; David G. Fountain, *Isaac Watts Remembered* (Worthing: Henry E. Walter, 1974), 92–94.

25 See Clifford, "Philip Doddridge and the Oxford Methodists," 77–78; Malcolm Deacon, *Philip Doddridge of Northampton 1702–1751* (Northampton: Northamptonshire Libraries, 1980), 88.

26 See especially the letters of Nathaniel Neal to Doddridge, dated October 11 and 15, 1743 (Doddridge, *Correspondence and Diary*, ed. Humphreys, IV, 241–281).

27 Henry D. Rack, *Reasonable Enthusiast: John Wesley and the Rise of Methodism* (London: Epworth, 1989), 276.

his epoch-making work *An Essay concerning Human Understanding* (1689), used the word to denote the mindset of those who have "an Opinion of a greater familiarity with GOD, and nearer admittance to his Favour than is afforded to others," and have thus persuaded themselves that they have an "immediate intercourse with the Deity, and frequent communications from the divine Spirit."[28] Such a mindset, Locke was convinced, arises from "the Conceits of a warmed or over-weening Brain."[29] Clearly dependent upon Locke, the lexicographer Samuel Johnson (1709–1784) defined enthusiasm as "a vain belief of private revelation; a vain confidence of divine favour or communication."[30] To all intents and purposes, George Whitefield agreed. "The quintessence of enthusiasm," he declared in a sermon first published in 1746, was "to pretend to be guided by the Spirit without the written word." All inner impressions must be tried by "the unerring rule of God's most holy word," and if found incompatible, rejected as "diabolical and delusive."[31] From personal experience Whitefield knew of the dangerous shoals of enthusiasm, for he later realized that in the first few years of his ministry he had been occasionally imprudent in relying on subjective impressions.[32]

However, if Whitefield and other leaders in the revival were wary of falling prey to enthusiasm, their critics were certain that they had succumbed. Two early criticisms can be taken as representative of the

---

28 John Locke, *An Essay concerning Human Understanding* 4.19.5, ed. Peter H. Nidditch (1975 ed.; repr. Oxford: Clarendon Press, 1984), 699.

29 Locke, *An Essay concerning Human Understanding* 4.19.7, ed. Nidditch, 699.

30 Samuel Johnson, *A Dictionary of the English Language* (London, 1755), s.v. "Enthusiasm."

31 George Whitefield, "Walking with God," in *Select Sermons of George Whitefield* (London: The Banner of Truth Trust, 1958), 104. For the position of John Wesley, the other key figure in the evangelical revival, with respect to enthusiasm, see Rack, *Reasonable Enthusiast*, 275–278, 334–342, 539–540; Lowell O. Ferrel, "John Wesley and the Enthusiasts," *Wesleyan Theological Journal*, 23, no. 1 and no. 2 (Spring–Fall 1988): 180–187.

32 Arnold A. Dallimore, *George Whitefield. The Life and Times of the Great Evangelist of the Eighteenth-Century Revival* (1970 ed.; repr. Westchester: Cornerstone Books, 1979), 1:540; Christopher J.L. Bennett, "The Great Awakening of 1740 and the Problem of Phenomena," in *Perfecting the Church Below* (London: Westminster Conference, 1990), 73.

charges levelled against the revival and its participants throughout the eighteenth century. John Barker (1682–1762), an English Presbyterian minister and correspondent of Doddridge, wrote to the latter on May 24, 1739, to tell him that he had heard Whitefield preaching in London in the open air and later also at Bath. Though he thought him sincere, Barker told Doddridge:

> I still fancy that he is but a *weak* man,—much too positive, says rash things, and is bold and enthusiastic. I am most heartily glad to hear of piety, prayer, reformation, and every thing that looks like faith and holiness, in the North or South, the East or the West, and that any *real* good is done anywhere to the souls of men, but whether these Methodists are in a right way, whether they are warrantable in all their conduct, whether poor people should be urged (through different persons, successively) *to pray from four in the morning till eleven at night*, is not clear to me; and I am less satisfied with the high pretences they make to the Divine influence. I think what Mr. Whitefield says and does comes but little short of an assumption of inspiration or infallibility.[33]

Joseph Butler (1692–1752), the bishop of Bristol, also criticized Whitefield and his fellow evangelist John Wesley for what he perceived to be enthusiasm. In an interview with Wesley on August 18, 1739, Butler accused both of the evangelists of "pretending to extraordinary revelations and gifts of the Holy Ghost," which he found "a horrid thing—a very horrid thing." Wesley denied this charge and stated that he sought only "what every Christian may receive and ought to expect and pray for."[34]

If he had been present, Whitefield would also have strongly disputed the accuracy of Butler's accusation, for he was adamant that the extraordinary gifts of the Spirit, such as prophecy, glossolalia, and miraculous powers, had ceased with the passing of the apostles. In his sermon "The Indwelling of the Spirit, the Common Privilege of All

---

33 Doddridge, *Correspondence and Diary*, ed. Humphreys, III, 381.
34 *The Journal of the Rev. John Wesley, A.M.*, ed. Nehemiah Curnock (1911 ed.; repr.; London: Epworth, 1960), II, 256–257, n.1.

Believers," which Wesley helped him edit for publication in the summer of 1739, Whitefield declared that Christ's promise of the Spirit in John 7:37–39 has nothing to do with receiving power "to work miracles, or show outward signs and wonders." Whitefield suggested that such signs and wonders occurred only when "some new revelation was to be established, as at the first settling of the Mosaic or gospel dispensation." Indeed, he continued:

> I cannot but suspect the spirit of those who insist upon a repetition of such miracles at this time. For the world being now become nominally Christian (though God knows, little of its power is left among us) there need not outward miracles, but only an inward cooperation of the Holy Spirit with the word, to prove that Jesus is the Messiah which was to come into the world.[35]

The only major group of individuals in the English-speaking Protestant world at that time who insisted upon the "repetition" of the miracles which occurred in the early church were the "French Prophets." This group had its origins among the Protestants of southern France. Following the revocation of the Edict of Nantes in 1685, these Protestants had been savagely persecuted by the French Roman Catholic state. In this crucible of persecution a movement had arisen replete with visions, prophecies, glossolalia and trances, in which young people were especially prominent. The summer of 1706 saw the appearance of three prophets from this movement in London. Within the space of a couple of years, there were close to 400 French Prophets, as they came to be called, and their charismatic manifestations had caused considerable public interest and consternation among the churches in the English capital. A turning-point for the movement, though, came in the summer of 1708 when it was prophesied that one of their number who had died, Thomas Emes, would be resurrected on May 25 from his grave in Bunhill Fields, the burying-ground for London Nonconformists.

---

35 George Whitefield, *Sermons on Important Subjects* (London: Thomas Tegg, 1833), 432. For the historical circumstances surrounding the publication of this sermon, see Timothy L. Smith, "Whitefield and Wesley on Righteousness by Grace," *TSF Bulletin*, 9, no. 4 (1986): 6–7.

When the predicted resurrection failed to transpire, the French Prophets became increasingly withdrawn and quiescent.³⁶

With the beginning of the evangelical revival in the mid-1730s, however, the voices of the French Prophets once again were heard in Great Britain as they sought to win recruits for their own movement from those involved in the revival.³⁷ It is plain from the text cited above that Whitefield would not have been impressed with the claim of the French Prophets to possess the extraordinary gifts of the Spirit. From his perspective, genuine manifestations of these gifts occurred only to authenticate the giving of fresh revelation. "The world being now become nominally Christian"—that is, the "world" having intellectually accepted the truth of Christianity—the Spirit's work was circumscribed to making this intellectual commitment a reality in heart and life. Even from the vantage-point of the eighteenth century, there seems to be a certain theological *naïveté* in Whitefield's remark that the world which he knew was "nominally Christian."³⁸ Nevertheless, in arguing for a cessationist position with regard to the gifts, Whitefield was simply affirming what had come to be a theological axiom for most eighteenth-century, English-speaking Protestants.³⁹ Doddridge, for

---

36 For studies of the French Prophets, see Hillel Schwartz, *Knaves, Fools, Madmen, and that Subtle Effluvium: A Study of the Opposition to the French Prophets in England, 1706-1710* (Gainesville: The University Presses of Florida, 1978); Hillel Schwartz, *The French Prophets: The History of a Millenarian Group in Eighteenth-Century England* (Berkeley: University of California Press, 1980); Clarke Garrett, *Spirit Possession and Popular Religion: From the Camisards to the Shakers* (Baltimore: The Johns Hopkins University Press, 1987), *passim*.

37 For contacts between the French Prophets and those involved in the evangelical revival, see Schwartz, *French Prophets*, 202-208; Garrett, *Spirit Possession*, 79-85.

38 For brief discussions of Whitefield's perspective on the gifts of the Spirit, see Victor Budgen, *The Charismatics and the Word of God: A biblical and historical perspective on the charismatic movement* (Welwyn: Evangelical Press, 1985), 162-163; Taylor, "Spirit of the Awakening," 299, 317-318.

39 Robert Bruce Mullin, "Horace Bushnell and the Question of Miracles," *Church History*, 58 (1989): 461. In the previous century, the Puritans—except for such left-wing groups as the Quakers—had maintained a similar position. See Garth B. Wilson, "The Puritan Doctrine of the Holy Spirit: A Critical Investigation of a Crucial Chapter in the History of Protestant Theology" (ThD thesis, Knox College, The Toronto School of Theology, 1978), 296-300; J.I. Packer, "John Owen on Spiritual Gifts," in his *A*

instance, in his response to a deistic attack on Christianity by Henry Dodwell (d.1784), plainly stated:

> It is of great importance...to recollect...that many things in Scripture, which relate to the operations of the Spirit of God on the mind, have a reference to those extraordinary gifts, which were peculiar to the apostles, and in which we of these later ages have no further concern, than as the general knowledge of them may establish our regard to the writings of those eminent servants of Christ, who were wisely and graciously distinguished by their divine Master, by such extraordinary endowments, to fit them for the extraordinary office they sustained.[40]

It should be noted, however, that John Wesley questioned this axiom, for he was thoroughly convinced that the miraculous gifts of the Spirit definitely continued beyond the close of the New Testament era. Christian literature from the second and third centuries, Wesley maintained, contains clear evidence for the existence of these gifts. It was only when Constantine came to imperial power in the first quarter of the fourth century and began to favour the church that these gifts started to disappear. In a sermon on 1 Corinthians 12:31, which first appeared in the July and August 1787 issues of *The Arminian Magazine*, Wesley declared:

> It does not appear that these extraordinary gifts of the Holy Ghost were common in the church for more than two or three centuries. We seldom hear of them after that fatal period when the Emperor Constantine called himself a Christian, and from a vain imagination of promoting the Christian cause thereby heaped riches, and power, and honour, upon the Christians in general; but in particular upon the Christian clergy. From this time they almost

---

Quest for Godliness: The Puritan Vision of the Christian Life (Wheaton: Crossway, 1990), 219–230.

40 Philip Doddridge, *Three Letters to the Author of a late Pamphlet, entitled Christianity not founded on Argument* (*The Miscellaneous Works of Philip Doddridge* [London: William Ball, 1839], 1161). See also Doddridge's *A Course of Lectures on the Principal Subjects in Pneumatology, Ethics, and Divinity* (*Miscellaneous Works*, 397).

ceased; very few instances of the kind were found. The cause of this was not (as has been vulgarly supposed) "because there was no more occasion for them," because all the world was become Christian. This is a miserable mistake: not a twentieth part of it was then nominally Christian. The real cause was: "the love of many"—almost of all Christians, so called—was "waxed cold." The Christians had no more of the Spirit of Christ than the other heathens.... This was the real cause why the extraordinary gifts of the Holy Ghost were no longer to be found in the Christian church—because the Christians were turned heathens again, and had only a dead form left.[41]

These reflections on the history of the gifts in the early church are not necessarily the best source for actually discovering what happened in these early centuries.[42] Notwithstanding, this is an important text, for Wesley succinctly rejects the reason posited by Whitefield for the cessation of the gifts. In no uncertain terms he labels it a "miserable" misconception. Wesley grants that there did occur a cessation of the gifts, but he located it in the middle of the fourth century and not, as Whitefield and most other eighteenth-century, English-speaking Protestants were wont to do, at the end of the first. Wesley finds the reason for the cessation of these gifts in the words of Matthew 24:12: the love of the church "waxed cold," that is, her love for God and the

---

41 John Wesley, "The More Excellent Way," in *The Works of John Wesley*, ed. Albert C. Outler (Nashville: Abingdon, 1986), 3:263–264. For the following discussion of Wesley's position on the gifts of the Spirit, I am indebted to Lycurgus M. Starkey, Jr., *The Work of the Holy Spirit: A Study in Wesleyan Theology* (Nashville: Abingdon, 1962), 73–77; Ted A. Campbell, "John Wesley's Conceptions and Uses of Christian Antiquity" (PhD thesis, Southern Methodist University, 1984), 194–204; Ted A. Campbell, "John Wesley and Conyers Middleton on Divine Intervention in History," *Church History* 55 (1986): 39–49. Popular Pentecostal historiography has frequently misrepresented Wesley's "open" position on the gifts by depicting him as a forerunner of Pentecostalism. Undoubtedly, Pentecostalism emerged from a theological matrix that owed its shape and structure to the theology of Wesley. But it is one thing to admit this indebtedness of Pentecostalism to Wesley's theology; it is quite another thing to argue that Wesley was a proto-Pentecostal.

42 Campbell, "Divine Intervention in History," 48.

charismatic presence of his Spirit decreased in proportion as her material wealth and temporal influence increased. Moreover, Wesley tempers his assertion with regard to the cessation of the gifts with the adverb "almost." The Methodist leader is not prepared to dogmatically assert that genuine occurrences of the extraordinary gifts of the Spirit cannot be found in the history of the church after the fourth century. In fact, the reason which he gives for their disappearance leaves open, in principle, the possibility of their being found in any age of the church. Where God is loved and the charismatic presence of his Spirit relished as in the pre-Constantinian church, there the gifts *might* be found.[43]

A similar allowance for the occurrence of extraordinary charismatic phenomena in the history of the church appears in another of Wesley's sermons, "The Nature of Enthusiasm," first published in 1750. Speaking of those who expect to be directed by God through "visions or dreams," the Methodist leader did not "deny that God has, of old times, manifested His will in this manner; or, that He can do so now: Nay, I believe He does, in some very rare instances."[44] Yet, he went on to emphasize, pride and "warm imagination" frequently mislead people into ascribing visions, dreams and mental impressions to God's authorship, which, when closely examined, are found to bear no divine imprint. Wesley knows of only one fitting description for such behaviour: it is "pure enthusiasm."[45] Earlier in the sermon Wesley had specified other types of individuals whom he also considered to be guilty of this eighteenth-century bugbear. For instance, those who imagine "themselves to be endued with a power of working miracles, of healing the sick by a word or a touch, of restoring sight to the blind" are all clear-cut enthusiasts, as are those who think they have the power to raise the dead, "a

---

43 See also his statement in his response to an anti-Methodist tract written by William Warburton (1698–1779), the Bishop of Gloucester: *A Letter to the Right Reverend The Lord Bishop of Gloucester* II.16, in *The Works of John Wesley*, vol. 11: *The Appeals to Men of Reason and Religion and Certain Related Open Letters*, ed. Gerald R. Cragg (Oxford: Clarendon, 1975), 514–515.

44 John Wesley, "The Nature of Enthusiasm" 21, in *Wesley's Standard Sermons*, ed. Edward H. Sugden (4th ed.; London: Epworth, 1956), II, 95–96.

45 Wesley, "The Nature of Enthusiasm" 21, in *Wesley's Standard Sermons*, ed. Sugden, II, 96.

notorious instance of which," Wesley adds, "is still fresh in our own history."[46] This "notorious instance" is probably the failed prediction of the resurrection of the French Prophet Thomas Emes.

Thus, both Whitefield and Wesley insisted that it was completely inappropriate to view Methodism as a species of enthusiasm. Public opinion, though, thought otherwise, and the charge of enthusiasm was regularly hurled at those committed to the revival. One reason for this was the fact that there were some in the leadership of the revival who did lay claim to miraculous powers of the Spirit. For instance, George Bell (d.1807), a former corporal in the Life Guards, who was converted in 1758. In 1761, he was involved in the healing of a woman with painful lumps in one of her breasts, a healing that Wesley continued to endorse as genuine many years later.[47] Soon Bell claimed that he and a coterie of London Methodists possessed the power to regularly heal the sick, and they proceeded to attempt to give sight to the blind and to raise the dead. Bell himself also believed that he possessed broad prophetic powers, including the gift of the discernment of spirits. These he sought to exercise in 1762 when he predicted the end of the world on February 28, 1763. At this point Wesley stepped in, disowned Bell as a Methodist, and denounced his prediction as fraudulent. He defended his actions with regard to Bell: "The reproach of Christ I am willing bear; but not the reproach of Enthusiasm if I can help it."[48] Indeed, for many years afterward, the memory of the Bell affair continued to confirm people's suspicions that the Methodists were bona fide enthusiasts.[49]

Nor were matters helped by the fact that eighteenth-century evangelicals opposed deistic trends of thinking by emphasizing that the

---

46 Wesley, "The Nature of Enthusiasm" 18, in *Wesley's Standard Sermons*, ed. Sugden, II, 93.

47 Rack, *Reasonable Enthusiast*, 338; see also Rack, "Doctors, Demons and Early Methodist Healing," in *The Church and Healing*, ed. W.J. Sheils (Oxford: Basil Blackwell, 1982), 149.

48 Cited in Susie I. Tucker, *Enthusiasm: A Study in Semantic Change* (Cambridge: Cambridge University Press, 1972), 34.

49 For the details of the Bell affair, see L. Tyerman, *The Life and Times of the Rev. John Wesley, Founder of the Methodists* (5th ed.; London: Hodder and Stoughton, 1880), II, 433–444, 460–462; Rack, *Reasonable Enthusiast*, 338–441.

indwelling of the believer by the Holy Spirit was an affective experience. As Whitefield declared: to "say we may have God's Spirit without feeling it...is, in reality, to deny the thing itself."[50] When the Spirit of God takes up residence in a person's life, his presence has an impact on the entire personality; the mind, the will, the emotions—and even on occasion the body—are touched and affected. For instance, in a description not atypical of certain periods of the revival, Howel Harris informed Whitefield in March 1743 of what God the Holy Spirit was doing through the preaching of his fellow evangelist and countryman, Daniel Rowland:

> I was last Sunday at the Ordinance with Brother Rowlands where I saw, felt and heard such things as I cant sent on Paper any Idea of. The Power that continues with Him is uncommon. Such crying out and Heart breaking groans, Silent Weeping and Holy Joy, and shouts of Rejoicing I never saw.... Tis very common when He preaches for Scores to fall down by the Power of the Lord, pierced and wounded or overcom'd by the Love of God and Sights of the Beauty and Excellency of Jesus, and lie on the Ground ... Some lye there for Hours. Some praising and admiring Jesus, free Grace, Distinguishing Grace, others wanting the words to utter.[51]

In 1759 similar scenes took place in Cambridgeshire under the preaching of John Berridge, the eccentric, evangelical vicar of the village of Everton. An account of these scenes has been preserved in the pages of John Wesley's *Journal*. Four, possibly five eyewitnesses, including Berridge and a certain John Walsh,[52] sent Wesley reports of the revival at Everton, which Wesley then brought together into a single account. For instance, Walsh wrote to Wesley that on the afternoon of Sunday, July 14, Berridge was compelled to preach in the open air due to the large number of people who had come to hear him. As

---

50 Whitefield, "Indwelling of the Spirit" in *Sermons*, 433.
51 Cited Jones, "Evangelical Revival in Wales," 251–252.
52 John Walsh was a converted Deist. For a few details regarding his life, see *The Works of John Wesley*, vol. 26: *Letters*, II: 1740–1755, ed. Frank Baker (Oxford: Clarendon, 1982), 616, n.1.

Berridge preached—and Walsh says nothing about the content of the sermon—a number of people who "were...pricked to the heart were affected in an astonishing manner." One man, he reported to Wesley,

> would have dropped [to the ground], but others, catching him in their arms, did, indeed prop him up, but were so far from keeping him still that he caused all of them to totter and tremble. His own shaking exceeded that of a cloth in the wind. It seemed as if the Lord came upon him like a giant, taking him by the neck and shaking all his bones in pieces.... Another roared and screamed in a more dreadful agony than ever I heard before.... I saw one who lay two or three hours in the open air, and, being then carried into the house continued insensible another hour, as if actually dead. The first sign of life she showed was a rapture of praise intermixed with a small, joyous laughter.[53]

Given the mindset of the eighteenth century, it is not surprising that such emotional and physical manifestations were regarded as sheer madness by many contemporary observers. Thomas Morgan (1729–1799), a Welsh Calvinistic minister who in 1763 became the pastor of the Congregationalist church in Morley, West Yorkshire, was scandalized by similar displays of emotion he witnessed in North Wales in 1762. "To all true and serious Christians," he wrote to a friend, the Welsh Methodists "are stark mad, and given up to a spirit of delusion, to the great disgrace and scandal of Christianity."[54]

Wesley's life-long approval of such displays of emotion also contributed to the charge of enthusiasm. While he was well aware of the possibility of over-valuing such manifestations, he felt that it was just as dangerous "to regard them too little, to condemn them altogether; to imagine they had nothing of God in them, and were a hindrance to

---

53 *The Journal of the Rev. John Wesley*, ed. Nehemiah Curnock (London: Epworth, 1913), IV, 336. For a good discussion of these events at Everton, see Nigel R. Pibworth, *The Gospel Pedlar: The Story of John Berridge and the Eighteenth-Century Revival* (Welwyn: Evangelical Press, 1987), 49–70.

54 Jones, "Evangelical Revival in Wales," 251.

his work."[55] On the other hand, as early as 1739, Whitefield had come to a somewhat different perspective. It was

> tempting God to require such signs. That there is something of God in it I doubt not; but the devil, I believe, does interpose. I think it will encourage the French Prophets, take people from the written word, and make them depend on visions, convulsions, etc., more than on the promises and precepts of the Gospel.[56]

Whitefield does not deny that some of these manifestations could issue from God. Yet, he is rightly convinced that such manifestations can easily become the focus of attention and interest rather than the Scriptures, the unalloyed revelation of God.

JONATHAN EDWARDS, THE "THEOLOGIAN OF REVIVAL"

The most incisive eighteenth-century perspective on these unusual displays of physical and emotional behaviour comes from the pen of Jonathan Edwards, whom Martyn Lloyd-Jones has identified as the "theologian of revival."[57] Between the years 1736 and 1748 Edwards wrote a series of works defending the fact that the revivals that took place in New England during the 1730s and 1740s were indeed the work of the Holy Spirit.[58] Edwards, however, was not uncritical of the extremism and excesses which had accompanied these revivals. His criticism is most trenchant in *A Treatise concerning Religious Affections* (1746), in which the American theologian wrestles with such fundamental questions as: What is the nature of true Christian experience? What place do the "affections" have in the Christian life? What are the marks that distinguish a genuine work of the Spirit from religious "enthusiasm"?

---

55 Wesley, *Journal* (November 25, 1759), IV, 359. See also the comments on Wesley's position in this regard by Garrett, *Spirit Possession*, 83, 87–89.

56 Cited Dallimore, *George Whitefield*, 1:328.

57 D. Martyn Lloyd-Jones, "Jonathan Edwards and the Crucial Importance of Revival," in his *The Puritans: Their Origins and Successors* (Edinburgh: The Banner of Truth Trust, 1987), 361.

58 For fuller discussion of these works, see Michael A.G. Haykin, *Jonathan Edwards: The Holy Spirit in Revival* (Darlington: Evangelical Press, 2005).

Jonathan Edwards
(1703–1758)

The extremism at which Edwards is taking aim in this work is evident in some of the assertions of James Davenport (1716–1757), a Congregationalist minister from Southhold, Long Island, and Davenport's friend, Andrew Croswell (1709–1785), the pastor of a Congregationalist church in Groton, Connecticut. At the height of the revival in New England in the early 1740s, both of these men assured individuals who either fell to the ground, or experienced bodily tremors, or saw visions during the preaching of God's Word that such experiences were a sure sign of the Spirit's converting work. In Croswell's words, only those who have had such "divine Manifestations...know what true Holiness means."[59] He asserted that "God never works powerfully, but men cry out of disorder; for God's order differs vastly from their nice and delicate apprehensions" of it.[60] Davenport, for his part, claimed to have the ability to distinguish who was among the elect of God, a "gift" that he especially sought to exercise when he called into question the spiritual state of certain ministers who had refused to allow him to preach from their pulpits. Prominent also in Davenport's ministry was a devotion to loud, boisterous singing. While vibrant singing has regularly been a mark of movements of revival in the history of the church, some of the lyrics written by Davenport were cause for deep concern. For instance, in *A Song of Praise for Joy in the Holy Ghost* (1742), Davenport wrote the following of the Holy Spirit's work in the believer's life:

> This makes me Abba Father cry,
>   With confidence of soul.
> It makes me cry, My Lord, My God,
>   And that without control.[61]

To profess the loss of self-control as the work of the Spirit of God was worrisome to both advocates and critics of the revival.[62]

---

59 Garrett, *Spirit Possession*, 115.
60 Garrett, *Spirit Possession*, 115.
61 Cited Taylor, "Spirit of the Awakening," 325.
62 For a discussion of the role of Davenport and Croswell in the evangelical revival, see Garrett, *Spirit Possession*, 114–115, 119–126; Iain H. Murray, *Jonathan Edwards: A*

Although Davenport later confessed that he had been wrong in much of what he had said and done, he and Crosswell had helped to spark a "wild-fire" spirit, which in many places made havoc of the revival. Moreover, they had furnished anti-revival forces with ammunition for their attacks. These forces were captained by Charles Chauncy (1705–1787), co-pastor of the most prestigious Congregationalist church in Boston, who could say of Davenport in particular: "he is the *wildest Enthusiast* I ever saw."[63] Edwards himself was convinced that Davenport did more "towards giving Satan and those opposers [of the revival] an advantage against the work than any other person."[64]

Now, among other things, *A Treatise concerning Religious Affections* tackles head-on the assertion by both Davenport and Crosswell that the experience of unusual bodily phenomena is unmistakable evidence of conversion. "Great effects on the body," Edwards maintains, "certainly are no sure evidences" that "the affections" which give rise to them come from the Spirit of God, "for we see that such effects oftentimes arise from great affections about temporal things, and when religion is in no way concerned."[65] Moreover, as Edwards observed on another occasion:

> The Spirit of God may act upon a creature, and yet not in acting communicate himself. The Spirit of God may act upon inanimate creatures; as, *the Spirit moved upon the face of the waters*, in the beginning of the creation; so the Spirit of God may act upon the minds of men in many ways, and communicate himself no more than when he acts upon an inanimate creature.[66]

New Biography (Edinburgh: Banner of Truth, 1987), 223–229; Taylor, "Spirit of the Awakening," 322–331; Robert E. Cray, Jr., "More Light on a New Light: James Davenport's Religious Legacy, Eastern Long Island, 1740–1840," *New York History*, 73 (1992): 5–27.

63 Charles Chauncy, *A Letter from a Gentleman in Boston, to Mr. George Wishart, One of the Ministers of Edinburgh, Concerning the State of Religion in New-England*, in *The Great Awakening. Documents on the Revival of Religion, 1740–1745*, ed. Richard L. Bushman (New York: Atheneum, 1970), 121.

64 Murray, *Jonathan Edwards*, 225.

65 Jonathan Edwards, *The Religious Affections* (Edinburgh: The Banner of Truth Trust, 1986), 59.

66 Jonathan Edwards, *A Divine and Supernatural Light, Immediately Imparted to the*

The Holy Spirit can produce effects in many things, both animate and inanimate, to which he does not communicate or impart his nature. Thus, in Genesis 1:2, it is stated that the Spirit of God moved upon the face of waters, but in doing so he did not impart his nature to the waters. In other words, a person may well be the subject of powerful spiritual experiences and not actually be indwelt by the Spirit. On the other hand, Edwards knows of no reason why "a view of God's glory should not cause the body to faint."[67] Indeed, there are a number of Scriptural texts which indicate that "true divine discoveries, or ideas of God's glory, when given in a great degree have a tendency, by affecting the mind, to overbear the body."[68] Edwards refers his readers at this point to passages like Psalm 119:120, where the psalmist expressly states that his "flesh trembleth for fear" of God, or Revelation 1:17, where, at the vision of the risen Christ, the apostle John "fell at his feet as dead."[69] Those who say that God cannot or will not "give the like clear and affecting ideas and apprehensions of the same real glory and majesty of his nature" in his day, Edwards considers "very bold and daring."[70]

Not only could Edwards quote Scripture in support of his appreciation of such phenomena, but he could also turn to the experience of his wife Sarah (1710–1758). In *Some Thoughts concerning the Present Revival of Religion in New-England* (1743), Edwards had devoted a section of this book to detailing, without naming her, his wife's experiences.[71] From 1736 on Sarah had frequently had "extraordinary views of divine things," which had deprived her body of "all ability to stand or speak." For instance, on one occasion Sarah was given an "extraordinary sense of the awful majesty, greatness, and holiness of God," which, her husband tells us, took away her bodily strength. Another time, it was "an overwhelming sense of the glory of the work of redemption, and the way of salvation by Jesus Christ" that caused her

---

Soul by the Spirit of God, in *The Works of Jonathan Edwards* (1834 ed.; repr. Edinburgh: The Banner of Truth Trust, 1974), 2:13.
  67 Edwards, *Religious Affections*, 60.
  68 Edwards, *Religious Affections*, 60.
  69 Edwards, *Religious Affections*, 61.
  70 Edwards, *Religious Affections*, 62.
  71 *Works of Jonathan Edwards*, 1:376–378.

body to faint. On yet another occasion, "a sense of the glory of the Holy Spirit, as the great Comforter, was such as to overwhelm both soul and body."[72] Her husband was at pains to point out that Sarah's experiences were never "attended with any enthusiastic disposition to follow impulses, or any supposed prophetical revelations." Edwards is ever insistent that the Spirit of God always leads those whom he indwells to view the Scriptures as "the great and standing rule for the direction of his church in all religious matters, and all concerns of their soul, in all ages."[73] Enthusiasts, on the other hand, "depreciate this written rule, and set up the light within or some other rule above it."[74] Sarah's experiences were also accompanied by "an increase of humility and meekness," "a gentleness, and benevolence of spirit" and "a great alteration" for the better with regard to her former weaknesses and failings.[75] Without the presence of these God-centred affections, the physical manifestations would have been of no spiritual value. Little wonder that Edwards can burst out at the conclusion of his account of Sarah's experience:

> Now if such things are enthusiasm, and the fruits of a distempered brain, let my brain be evermore possessed of that happy distemper! If this be distraction, I pray God that the world of mankind may be all seized with this benign, meek, and beneficent, beatifical, glorious distraction![76]

One of Edwards' final works devoted to the subject of revival was *An Humble Attempt to Promote Explicit Agreement and visible Union of God's People in Extraordinary Prayer for the Revival of Religion and the Advancement of Christ's Kingdom on Earth, pursuant to Scripture-Promises and Prophecies concerning the Last Time* (henceforth referred to as the *Humble Attempt*). This treatise was inspired by information that Edwards received in 1745 about prayer meetings for revival which had been started by a number of Scottish evangelical ministers, including

---

72 *Works of Jonathan Edwards*, 1:376, 377.
73 Jonathan Edwards, *The Distinguishing Marks of a Work of the Spirit of God* in *Jonathan Edwards on Revival* (Edinburgh: The Banner of Truth Trust, 1965), 113–114.
74 Edwards, *Distinguishing Marks* in *Jonathan Edwards on Revival*, 114.
75 *Works of Jonathan Edwards*, 1:376, 378.
76 *Works of Jonathan Edwards*, 1:378.

William McCulloch of Cambuslang. In order to implement a similar "concert of prayer" in New England, Edwards gave a sermon in February 1747, on Zechariah 8:20–22, in which he sought to demonstrate how the text supported a call for believers to meet together to pray for revival. Within the year a revised and greatly expanded version of this sermon was published as the *Humble Attempt*.

The treatise opens with a number of observations on Zechariah 8:20–22. Edwards argues that this passage predicts a time when

> there shall be given much of a spirit of prayer to God's people, in many places, disposing them to come into an express agreement, unitedly to pray to God in an extraordinary manner, that he would appear for the help of his church, and in mercy to mankind, and pour out his Spirit, revive his work, and advance his spiritual kingdom in the world, as he has promised.[77]

In order to hasten this glorious time, Edwards infers that God's people in the American colonies should gather together and, with "extraordinary, speedy, fervent and constant prayer," pray for those "great effusions of the Holy Spirit" which will dramatically advance the kingdom of Christ.[78] In the second part of the treatise Edwards provides a number of reasons why Christians should participate in this concert of prayer. Our Lord Jesus, for example, shed his blood and his tears, and poured out his prayers in order to secure the presence and power of his blessed Spirit for his people.

> The sum of the blessings Christ sought, by what he did and suffered in the work of redemption, was the Holy Spirit.... The Holy Spirit, in his indwelling, his influences and fruits, is the sum of all grace, holiness, comfort and joy, or in one word, of all the spiritual good Christ purchased for men in this world: and is also the sum of all perfection, glory and eternal joy, that he purchased for them in another world.[79]

---

77 Jonathan Edwards, *An Humble Attempt*, ed. Stephen J. Stein, in *The Works of Jonathan Edwards* (New Haven: Yale University Press, 1977), 5:317.

78 Edwards, *Humble Attempt*, ed. Stein, in *Works of Jonathan Edwards*, 5:320.

79 Edwards, *Humble Attempt*, ed. Stein, in *Works of Jonathan Edwards*, 5:341.

Edwards rightly concludes:

> If...this is what Jesus Christ, our great Redeemer and the head of the church, did so much desire, and set his heart upon, from all eternity, and which he did and suffered so much for, offering up "strong crying and tears" [Heb 5:7], and his precious blood to obtain it; surely his disciples and members should also earnestly seek it, and be much and earnest in prayer for it.[80]

Furthermore, the Scriptures are full of commands, incentives and illustrations regarding prayer for the Holy Spirit. For instance, there is the encouragement given to believers in Luke 11:13: "If ye then, being evil, know how to give good gifts unto your children, how much more shall your heavenly Father give the Holy Spirit to them that ask him?" As Edwards read these words of Christ, prayer for the Holy Spirit is one request that God the Father is especially delighted to answer in the affirmative.[81] Or one might consider the example of the early disciples who devoted themselves to "united fervent prayer and supplication... till the Spirit came down in a wonderful manner upon them," as it is related in Acts 1–2.[82] In essence, the *Humble Attempt*, like Edwards' various other works which relate to the revival, seeks to develop and recommend a "fullblown theology of radical dependence on the Spirit."[83]

THE CALVINISTIC BAPTISTS OF ENGLAND

The *Humble Attempt* bore its greatest fruit more than twenty-five years after the death of Edwards. In the spring of 1784, the English Calvinistic Baptist pastor John Ryland, Jr. received a copy of the *Humble Attempt*, which had been sent to him by John Erskine (1721–1803), a Scottish Presbyterian minister.[84] When Erskine was in his twenties he had been present at the revival at Cambuslang. Later he had entered

---

80 Edwards, *Humble Attempt*, ed. Stein, in *Works of Jonathan Edwards*, 5:344.
81 Edwards, *Humble Attempt*, ed. Stein, in *Works of Jonathan Edwards*, 5:347–348.
82 Edwards, *Humble Attempt*, ed. Stein, in *Works of Jonathan Edwards*, 5:356.
83 Richard Lovelace, "Pneumatological Issues in American Presbyterianism," *Greek Orthodox Theological Review*, 31 (1986): 345–346.
84 See Jonathan Yeager, *Enlightened Evangelicalism: The Life and Thought of John Erskine* (Oxford: Oxford University Press, 2011).

into correspondence with Edwards, and had imbibed many of the theological perspectives of the American divine. Erskine's correspondence with Ryland appears to have begun in 1780 and lasted till the former's death in 1803. Erskine sent the Baptist pastor not only letters, but also on occasion bundles of fascinating books and tracts which he was seeking to promote. So it was in April, 1784 that Erskine mailed to Ryland a copy of Edward's *Humble Attempt*.

Ryland and his pastoral colleagues—notably Andrew Fuller and John Sutcliff—were so deeply impacted by the force of Edwards' argumentation in the *Humble Attempt* that a concert of prayer was begun that very year in the English Midlands by the association of churches to which they belonged, the Northamptonshire Association.[85] This prayer movement had profound consequences for the Calvinistic Baptists in England. Many of their congregations were revitalized after decades of stagnation or even decline, and numerous new works were begun. Moreover, as we have seen in chapters 7 and 8, it was among these Northamptonshire Baptists that the modern missionary movement was born, as the Baptist Missionary Society was founded in 1792 and William Carey sent to India as the Society's first missionary.

In the early years of the evangelical revival Howel Harris had once compared the Nonconformist denominations, which would have included the Calvinistic Baptists, and his friend Whitefield: "whilst they are in their warm rooms, he ventures his life for God."[86] As Geoffrey F. Nuttall has pointed out, this telling contrast can be given both a spatial and a spiritual interpretation. By and large eighteenth-century Nonconformist ministers stayed within their meeting-houses to proclaim the Word of God, while the early Methodists who had been

---

85 For further discussion of the circumstances surrounding this prayer movement, see Ernest A. Payne, *The Prayer Call of 1784* (London: Baptist Laymen's Missionary Movement, 1941); Michael A.G. Haykin, "John Sutcliff and the Concert of Prayer," *Reformation and Revival Journal* 1, no. 3 (1992): 65–88; Michael A.G. Haykin, "'A Habitation of God, Through the Spirit': John Sutcliff (1752–1814) and the Revitalization of the Calvinistic Baptists in the Late Eighteenth Century," *The Baptist Quarterly*, 34 (1991–1992): 309–311; Michael A.G. Haykin, *One heart and one soul: John Sutcliff of Olney, his friends, and his times* (Darlington: Evangelical Press, 1994), 153–171.

86 Geoffrey F. Nuttall, *Howel Harris 1714–1773: The Last Enthusiast* (Cardiff: University of Wales Press, 1965), 46.

impacted by the revival took the gospel into the open air, into the highways and byways. To be sure, there were legal restrictions that sought to confine Nonconformist preaching to the meeting-houses. For many Nonconformist pastors, however, obedience to these laws was as much grounded in a spiritual "settledness" as in a desire to be law-abiding citizens. All too many of the Nonconformist pastors whom Harris knew well were content to live on past experience and displayed little hunger for the presence and power of God in their lives.[87]

By the 1780s and 1790s, as we have noted in chapter 8, the situation was markedly different. There was now a growing openness to the revival among the Nonconformists, including the Calvinistic Baptists. And Edwards' works on revival had played a vital role in the change of perspective. The revival that came to the Calvinistic Baptist denomination between the 1780s and the 1820s did so with remarkably few of the unusual manifestations which occurred in the early years of the evangelical revival. And in continuity with most other eighteenth-century evangelicals, there was no seeking the so-called extraordinary gifts of the Spirit. For example, in a sermon that John Ryland, Jr. preached on 1 Corinthians 14:8 in 1813, he unequivocally declared regarding the abuse of glossolalia in the first-century church of Corinth that "no one is now in danger of falling into precisely the same mistake, because the gift of tongues has long ceased."[88] Like George Whitefield, Ryland believed that the extraordinary gifts of the Spirit were given to the church in the apostolic age in order to validate the initial preaching of the gospel. Such gifts were bestowed "for the purpose of attesting the truth, at its first publication."[89] Ryland regularly drew a contrast between the extraordinary gifts of the Spirit and his "ordinary influences." As he stated in a sermon entitled "The Love of the Spirit", which was based on Romans 15:30:

> The ordinary influences of the Holy Spirit are of far more importance to the individuals who partake of them, than his extraordinary gifts; that is, it is better to be a saint than a prophet; better

---

87 Nuttall, *Howel Harris*, 46.
88 John Ryland, *The Necessity of the Trumpet's giving a certain Sound* (Bristol, 1813), 4.
89 Ryland, "The Design of Spiritual Gifts," in *Pastoral Memorials*, II, 67.

to be made holy, than to be inspired; better to be directed into the love of God, than into the knowledge of futurity. Herein the blessed Spirit communicates himself in his own proper nature, as the Spirit of holiness.[90]

Why did Ryland believe that the "ordinary influences of the Holy Spirit" are of greater import than "his extraordinary gifts"? The former impart personal holiness, and it is only those who have experience of these "sanctifying influences" of the Spirit who can have any legitimate assurance of eternal life. Those who are indwelt by the sanctifying Spirit are "sealed to the day of redemption" and stamped for an eternity in heaven. The "extraordinary gifts" of the Spirit, on the other hand, give no such assurance, for there is no inseparable connection between the gifts and holiness. In other words, the presence of the fruit of the Spirit is evidence of salvation, whereas that of his gifts is not.

As for the unusual manifestations witnessed during the early years of the evangelical revival, Baptists like Ryland were quite willing to acknowledge their genuineness. However, they were not at all convinced that they were necessary for the advance of God's kingdom. Ryland's close friend, William Carey, wrote a marvellous letter to his sister Mary in 1789 that discussed these manifestations. Evidently she was wrestling with assurance of salvation, and he asked her:

> Do you doubt because you have not seen visions, heard voices, or felt impulses? This I know is what many Christians place dependence upon. But suppose that you have felt nothing of all this, there is no reason for you to despair; and if you have been favoured with repeated instances of this nature this is no proof

---

90 Ryland, "The Love of the Spirit", in *Pastoral Memorials*, II, 42. See also Ryland's remarks in a sermon that he delivered in 1802 at the ordination of Thomas Morgan (1776–1857): *The Difficulties of the Christian Ministry, and the Means of surmournting* (sic) *them: with the Obedience of Churches to their Pastors explained and enforced* (Birmingham, 1802), 18–19. Also see his "The Desirableness of a Spiritual Taste," in *Pastoral Memorials: Selected from the Manuscripts of the Late Revd. John Ryland* (London: B.J. Holdsworth, 1826], I, 118); John Ryland, "Remarks on the Quarterly Review," in *Pastoral Memorials*, II, 348; "Remarks upon the Notion of Extraordinary Impulses and Impressions on the Imagination," in *Pastoral Memorials*, II, 417–419.

John Ryland, Jr.
(1753–1825)

of your Christianity. I apprehend that too many place too much confidence in things of this nature and make a shining light, an audible voice, or the sudden application of a passage of Scripture an evidence of their being the children of God. But where is the part of God's Word that informs us of any such evidence of religion as these are? Or if a person had no other evidence than such, would you, could you encourage him to depend or take comfort from this? That these are extraordinary interpositions of Divine Power upon extraordinary occasions I don't deny but 'tis God and not us that must judge of the emergency of our case; and even if he does interpose in a singular way, 'tis the matter and not the manner of his interposition that we ought to depend upon, and that not as an evidence of grace but as a Divine support in the path of duty. No doubt but the tempter is aware of the taste of the age and therefore endeavours to seduce us by things miraculous to which the mind of man is much prone, and while we thus listen to his devices and limit the Holy One of Israel we distress ourselves and dishonour him. But we have a more sure word of Prophecy whereunto we do well that we take heed.[91]

Carey did not deny that such unusual phenomena as "a shining light"—may well be an allusion to Gardiner's conversion, an account that Carey knew well—or "an audible voice" could be from God. But such occurrences were given according to God's sovereignty, and not man's desire. Moreover, these experiences were no proof that the subject of them genuinely knew God. "Real religion," Carey went on to emphasize in the letter, consisted of things quite different: "repentance, faith, obedience, submission, zeal and consolation."

Yet it bears remembering that late eighteenth-century Calvinistic Baptists like Ryland and Carey, nurtured on the writings of Jonathan Edwards, had a great hunger and desire for the Spirit's presence and power, as the following text bears witness. It was written by Ryland in 1792, at the height of the French Revolution, as part of a circular

---

91 William Carey, Letter to Mary Carey, December 14, 1789 (Baptist Missionary Society Archives, Angus Library, Regent's Park College, Oxford). Some of the punctuation has been added to make this section of the letter read better.

letter sent out by the Northamptonshire Baptist Association to its member churches.

> Surely the state both of the world, and of church, calls loudly upon us all to persist in wrestling instantly with God, for greater effusions of his Holy Spirit.... Let us not cease crying mightily unto the Lord, "until the Spirit be poured upon us from on high" [Isaiah 32:15]; then the wilderness shall become as a fruitful field, and the desert like the garden of God. Yes, beloved, the Scriptures cannot be broken. Jesus must reign universally. All nations shall own him. All people shall serve him. His kingdom shall be extended, not by human might, or power, but by the effusion of His Holy Spirit [cf. Zechariah 4:6].[92]

This text is redolent with the pneumatological thought of Edwards, especially in its emphasis on patient but diligent prayer for the outpouring of the Holy Spirit, and its optimism regarding the irresistible advance of Jesus' kingdom throughout the world by the power of the outpoured Spirit. Such are the signs and wonders that Ryland and Carey, genuine heirs of Edwards and the evangelical revival that he promoted, longed to see.

THREE LESSONS

What then do we learn from our evangelical forebears in the eighteenth-century with regard to this issue of "signs and wonders"? First, eighteenth-century evangelicals by and large limited what they described as the "extraordinary" gifts of the Spirit—gifts such as speaking in tongues, miraculous healings, prophecy—to the apostolic era. Yet, they longed for, and *were granted*, the experience of the Spirit's power in revival, and this to such a depth that the evangelical revival of the eighteenth century has acquired an almost paradigmatic quality. The

---

92 John Ryland, *Godly Zeal, Described and Recommended* (Nottingham, 1792), 1–2, 15. See also Richard Lovelace, "Baptism in the Holy Spirit and the Evangelical Tradition," *Pneuma*, 7 (1985): 115. On Ryland's pneumatology, see Michael A.G. Haykin, "'The Sum of All Good': John Ryland, Jr. and the Doctrine of the Holy Spirit," *Churchman* 103 (1989): 332–353.

only Protestant group in the Anglophone world at that time that did press for a full restoration of all the apostolic gifts were the French Prophets, a rather insignificant sect whose major role in the revivals was to act as an object-lesson of fanaticism.

Second, there did occur a variety of unusual physical and emotional manifestations in many areas touched by this revival, such as uncontrollable trembling and weeping, jumping, falling to the ground, striking dreams and visions. Evangelicals displayed a range of responses to these manifestations, but never rejected them *in toto*. In fact, these manifestations were instrumental in prompting the New England divine Jonathan Edwards to write an entire series of works defending the revival, in which he sought to elucidate the Spirit's work in such a way that the unique aspects of the Spirit's activity in the apostolic era were safeguarded "without unnecessarily limiting the Spirit's mysterious work in regeneration and sanctification."[93]

Third, it was the writings of Jonathan Edwards that God used to revitalize the Calvinistic Baptists and in the process initiate the modern missionary movement, by means of which evangelical Christianity was spread to the four corners of the earth. This dissemination of the gospel was certainly not achieved by mere human might or determination. It was nothing less than a wondrous work of the Spirit. As William Carey had once remarked: "If a temple is raised for God in the heathen world, it will not be "by might, nor by power," nor by the authority of the magistrate, or the eloquence of the orator; "but by my Spirit, saith the Lord of Hosts" (Zechariah 4:6).[94] In other words, we must recognize the Spirit's power in the full range of his activities throughout the history of the church, and not confine him within the limits of what some today call "signs and wonders."

---

93 Taylor, "Spirit of the Awakening," 290.
94 William Carey, *An Enquiry into the Obligations of Christians to use Means for the Conversion of the Heathens* (1792 ed.; repr.; Didcot: Baptist Missionary Society, 1991), 103.

Index

Act of Toleration, 101–102
Anderson, Christopher, 146
Antinomianism, 29–30, 95–96, 146
Arminianism, 7, 32, 74, 88 n23, 149, 184

Baker, Frank, 50, 74, 76
Balleine, G.R., 86
Baptist Missionary Society (BMS), 79, 132, 145, 156–157, 168, 170, 198
Barker, John, 181
Baxter, Richard, 78
Beck, James, 157–158
Beddome, Benjamin, 114–115, 121–122
Bell, George, 187

Bennet, George, 138
Bergen, Ole, 47–48
Berridge, John, 84, 188–189
Blackshaw, John, 150
Brainerd, David, 133
Brevint, Cosme, 43
Brevint, Daniel, 43
Bunyan, John, 59, 78, 149
Burkitt, William, 15
Butler, Joseph, 181

Calvin, John, 42–43, 133
Carey, Ann, 145, 168–169
Carey, Dorothy, 157–159
Carey, Edmund, 139
Carey, Eustace, 139
Carey, Jabez, 168
Carey, Jonathan, 140

Carey, Mary, 145, 168–169, 200, 202
Carey, Peter (son), 157
Carey, Peter (uncle), 140
Carey, William, 8, 79, 88–90, 93, 98, 124, 137–170, 198, 200–203, 204
Cattell, Thomas, 106
Charles, Thomas, 55, 63
Chater, Thomas, 143
Chauncy, Charles, 193
Clive, Robert, 137
Clunie, Alexander, 83–84
Colman, Benjamin, 11
Cook James, 138, 144–145
Cooper, William, 11
Cowper, William, 84–87, 139
Cox, Francis Alexander, 10–11
Crabtree, William, 66–67, 77
Crosley, David, 106
Croswell, Andrew, 192–193
Cudworth, William 30

Dalrymple, John, 173
Davenport, James, 192–193
DeArteaga, William, 173
Deism, 67, 69, 83, 103, 110, 122
Doddridge, Philip, 82, 88 n23, 173–179, 181, 183–184
Dodwell, Henry, 184
Dixon, Philip, 102–103
Dutton, Anne, 8, 33, 101–117
Dutton, Benjamin, 107–108

Edwards, Jonathan, 7, 82, 88 n23, 133–134, 144, 149, 190–199, 202–204

Edwards, Sarah, 194–195
Eliot, John, 133
Emes, Thomas, 182, 187
Enlightenment, 103
Erskine, Ebenezer, 21–22
Erskine, John, 197–198
Erskine, Ralph, 21–22
Evans, Caleb, 96, 103

Fawcett, John, 78–79
Fawcett, Stephen, 78
Fawkner, Robert, 125–128
Fielding, Henry, 3
Flavel, John, 78
Fletcher, John, 35
Foster, John, 11–12
Francis, Benjamin, 134–135
French Prophets, 182–183, 187
Fuller, Andrew, 8, 103, 119–135, 145, 146, 148, 156, 198

Gardiner, James, 173–179, 202
Gee, Joshua, 22
George I, 2, 23
Gill, John, 56, 103, 115, 131
Goodwin, Thomas, 56, 104
Griffiths, Vavasor, 56
Grimshaw, Sarah Sutcliffe, 69
Grimshaw, William, 8, 35, 65–79
Guyse, John, 6, 8
Gwynne, Marmaduke, 51

Hall, Mr., 92
Hall, Robert, Jr., 132
Hall, Robert, Sr., 146–147
Harris, Howel, 7, 30, 32 n81, 51, 54, 56, 109, 188, 198–199

Hartley, James, 77
Hastings, Selina (author), 1, 3
Hastings, Selina, Countess of Huntingdon, 23, 30, 58, 60, 69, 109
Henry, Matthew, 15
Hervey, James, 92, 116
Hoby, Hames, 10–11
Holy Club, 14, 92
Howe, John, 38
Huguenot, 43
Huntingdon, William, 95–96
Hussey, Joseph, 107
hyper-Calvinism, 56, 77, 107, 124, 146, 147–148, 153

Ingham, Benjamin, 69–70
Ivimey, Joseph, 108

Jay, William, 92, 94
Jennings, David, 82
Johnson, Samuel, 180
Judson, Adoniram, 161

Keach, Benjamin, 1–2, 121–122
Kingdon, David, 170
Kingswood, 17
Knollys, Hanserd, 106

Lee, Thomas, 75
Leicester Covenant, 150–152
Lloyd-Jones, D. Martyn, vi, 8, 55, 190
Locke, John, 179–180
Lovelace, Richard, 121
Luther, Martin, 14, 41, 133, 160

Marshman, John C., 93
Marshman, Joshua, 93, 146, 160, 162–163, 164
Martyn, Henry, 160–161
McCulloch, William, 176–177, 196
Milton, John, 66
Montcalm, Louis Joseph, 138
Moore, John, 106
Moravians, 43, 160, 162
Morgan, Thomas, 189
Morris, John Webster, 93, 147, 168–169
Mortimer, Sarah, 102
Murray, Iain H., 144, 149–150

Newman, A.H., 122
Newton, Elizabeth, 82–83
Newton, John, 8, 68, 72, 76–77, 81–99, 138–139
Newton, John (father), 83
Niceno-Constantinopolitan Creed, 102, 113
Nichols, Clarke, 140, 142
Northamptonshire Baptist Association, 93, 130, 146–147, 170, 198, 203
Nuttall, Geoffrey F., 198

O'Brien, Susan, 82
Owen, John, 56, 70, 86, 153

Packer, J.I., 32
Pal, Krishna, 162–164, 166–167
Parker, John, 77
Parsons, Jonathan, 10
Pearce, Samuel, 97–99

Pearce, Sarah, 97–99
Phillips, David, 122
Plumb, J.H., 2, 4
Prince, Joseph, 10
Puritans, 5, 6. 14, 15. 38, 41, 56, 67, 70, 78, 88 n23, 104, 120, 153, 172, 174, 183 n39,

Rattenbury, J. Ernest, 43
Reformation, 8, 14, 16, 41, 102
revival,
   eighteenth-century, 6–8, 11, 14, 18–19, 21, 31–32. 41, 43, 49, 63, 81, 124, 130, 144, 149, 155, 168, 172–173, 176 n12, 179–204
   Haworth, 72–78
   Scottish (Cambuslang), 176–178, 196, 197–198
   Welsh, 54–55
Ridgley, Thomas, 116–117
Roberts, Philip, 124
Robinson, Thomas, 89
Romaine, William, 70, 79, 103, 110–117
Rowland, Daniel, 7, 84, 188
Ryland, John, Jr., 86, 91–97, 98, 132, 134, 143–144, 145, 146, 149, 156, 160, 171, 197–200, 202–203
Ryland, John Collett, Sr., 91, 92–93, 95, 96, 143–144, 147–148

Sandemanianism, 56, 122
Scougal, Henry, 14–15
Servetus, Michael, 102

Seward, William, 109
Skepp, John, 106, 107
Skerrett, Maria, 2
Smith, Joseph, 16
Smith Richard, 77, 78
Socinianism, 102–103, 110, 122
Sozzini, Lelio Francesco, 102
Sozzini, Fausto, 102
Spurgeon, Charles Haddon, 122
St. John, Henry, Viscount Bolingbroke, 11
Stillness Controversy, 43–44
Stout, Harry, 20
Stuart, Charles Edward, 175
Sutcliff, John, 120–121, 130, 146, 156, 159, 163, 198

Thomson, George, 175–176 n12
Thornton, Henry, 89
Thomas, John, 89, 156–157
Toplady, Augustus Montague, 11
Trelawny, Jonathan, 4
Trinitarianism, 101–117
Turner, Thomas, 5
Tyerman, Daniel, 138

Unitarianism, 102, 122

Vetö, Miklós, 133
von der Schulenburg, Louise Sophie, Countess of Delitz, 23–24
von der Schulenburg, Melusina, Countess of Kendal, 23

Walpole, Robert, 2
Walker, Austin, 146

Wallis, Martha, 156
Walls, Andrew F., 155, 156
Walsh, John, 188–189
Ward, William, 79, 146, 157, 160, 162, 164
Warfied, B.B., 120
Warr, John, 140–143
Watson, Thomas, 174
Watts, Isaac, 6, 8, 55, 82, 169, 179
Webster, Alexander, 177
Wesley, Charles, vi, 7, 8, 14, 31, 37–51, 55, 69, 74, 92
Wesley, John, 7, 14, 17 n23, 18 n25, 31, 32–35, 38, 43, 47, 67, 69, 74, 87, 92, 116, 180 n31, 181–182, 184–190
Wesley, Sarah Gwynne, 51

West, John, 129
White, George, 75
Whitefield, Elizabeth, 12
Whitefield, George, 7–8, 9–35, 54, 58, 60, 63, 74, 78, 82, 84, 92, 106–107, 109, 116, 133, 149, 166, 177–190, 198–199
Whitefield, Thomas, 12
Wilberforce, William, 86–91, 160
Williams, Anne, 103
Williams, Joseph, 11, 40
Wiiliams, Mary Francis, 56
Williams, Peter, 60
Williams, William, 8, 53–63
Wolfe, James, 137–138, 140
Wycliffe, John, 133

Zwingli, Huldrych, 41–42

BOOKS & PUBLICATIONS

A Call to the Unconverted to Turn and Live, 78
A Discourse upon the Self-Existence of Jesus Christ (1755), 110–117
A Letter on the Divine Eternal Sonship of Jesus Christ: As the Second Person in the Ever-blessed Three-one God (1757), 103–117
A Letter To such of the Servants of Christ, who May have any Scruples about the Lawfulness of Printing any Thing written by a Woman (1743), 109
A Treatise concerning Religious Affections (1746), 190–194
Aleluia: Collection of hymns on various themes, 58
An Enquiry into the Obligations of Christians, To Use Means for the Conversion of the Heathens (1792), 148, 152–156
An Essay concerning Human Understanding (1689), 180
An Humble Attempt to Promote Explicit Agreement and visible Union of God's People in Extraordinary Prayer for the Revival of Religion and the Advancement of Christ's Kingdom on Earth, pursuant to Scripture-Promises and Prophecies concerning the Last Time, 195–198

Christ, the Believer's Wisdom, Righteousness, Sanctification and Redemption (1742), 26, 29
Divine Energy: or The Efficacious Operations of the Spirit of God upon the Soul of Man (1722), 107
Dorothy Carey: The Tragic and Untold Story of Mrs. William Carey, 157–158
Flora Indica (1832), 159
Gloria in Exclesis: or, Hymns of Praise to God and the Lamb (1772), 58
God's Operations of Grace but no Offers of Grace (1707), 107
Help to Zion's Travellers (1781), 146
Hortus Bengalensis (1814), 159
Hosannah to the Son of David: or, Hymns of Praise to God for our glorious redemption by Christ (1759), 58
Hymns on the Lord's Supper, 43–51
Pilgrim's Progress, 59, 78
Serampore Form of Agreement (1805), 164–168
Some Thoughts concerning the Present Revival of Religion in New-England (1743), 194–195
The Arminian Magazine, 184–185
The Character, Preaching, etc. of the Rev. George Whitefield, 16
The Christian Sacrament and Sacrifice (1673), 43
The Christian Soldier; or Heaven taken by storm (1669), 174
The Crocodile of Egypt's River Seen on Mount Zion (1767), 56
The Doctrine of Justification by Faith Through the Imputation of the Righteousness of Christ, Explained, Confirmed, & Vindicated (1677), 70
The Gospel Worthy of All Acceptation, 126, 148
The Life of God in the Soul of Man, 14–15
The Nature and Necessity of our Regeneration or New Birth in Christ Jesus (1737), 25

Also available from Joshua Press

| THE CHRISTIAN MENTOR | Volume 1

THE CHURCH FATHERS AS SPIRITUAL MENTORS: "FAITH IS ILLUMINED"

Historian Michael Haykin examines the lives of such church fathers as Irenaeus of Lyons, Cyprian of Carthage, Basil of Caesarea, Gregory of Nyssa, Macarius and Augustine, as he uncovers the theological debates, councils, creeds and preaching of the ancient church (A.D. 100—600). After the foundational ministry of the apostles, these early church leaders were pivotal to the formation of theological creeds, the defence of the faith against error and heresy and the development of early church ecclesiastical structure.

Defending the authority of the Scriptures, the doctrine of the Trinity, the godhead of the Holy Spirit and the deity of Christ, these church leaders provide a great example of the apologetic work of the ministry and the need for pastors to be astute to the theological challenges of the day. Dr. Haykin also considers the influence of the emperor Constantine and the development of the papacy and addresses such "modern" issues as abortion and the millennium. We owe the church fathers a great debt for their example of a committed, living faith.

ISBN 978-1-894400-81-7; 224 pages

| **THE CHRISTIAN MENTOR** | Volume 2

THE REFORMERS AND PURITANS AS SPIRITUAL MENTORS: "HOPE IS KINDLED"

Historian Michael Haykin examines the lives of such Reformers as William Tyndale, Thomas Cranmer and John Calvin to see how their display of the light of the gospel in their day provides us with a "usable past"—models of Christian conviction and living who can speak into our lives today. Born in a time of spiritual darkness, they model what reformation involves for church and culture: a deep commitment to God's Word as the vehicle of renewal, a willingness to die for the gospel and a rock-solid commitment to the triune God. As a reminder that at the heart of the Reformation was a confessional Christianity, an essay on two Reformation confessions is also included.

The Puritan figures who are studied are Richard Greenham, Oliver Cromwell, John Owen, Richard Baxter and his wife Margaret, and John Bunyan. In addition, a study of the translation of the King James Bible (KJB) reminds us that the Puritans, like the Reformers, were Word-saturated men and women—may we be as well.

ISBN 978-1-894400-39-8; 196 pages

www.joshuapress.com

Deo Optimo et Maximo Gloria
To God, best and greatest, be glory

www.joshuapress.com

www.ingramcontent.com/pod-product-compliance
Lightning Source LLC
Chambersburg PA
CBHW020230170426
43201CB00007B/381